This book explores how Horace's poems construct the literary and social authority of their author. Bridging the traditional distinction between "persona" and "author," Ellen Oliensis considers Horace's poetry as one dimension of his "face" – the public, projected self-image that is the basic currency of social interactions. She reads Horace's poems not only as works of art but also as social acts of face-saving, face-making, and self-effacement. These acts are responsive, she suggests, to the pressure of several audiences, explicit and implied: Horace shapes his poetry to promote his authority and to pay deference to his patrons while taking account of the envy of contemporaries and the judgment of posterity. Drawing on the insights of sociolinguistics, deconstruction, and the new historicism, the author teases out the social implications of Horace's successive generic choices, charting the poet's shifting strategies of authority and deference across his entire literary career.

HORACE
AND THE RHETORIC
OF AUTHORITY

HORACE
AND THE RHETORIC
OF AUTHORITY

Ellen Oliensis

Assistant Professor of Classics
Yale University

CAMBRIDGE
UNIVERSITY PRESS

PUBLISHED BY THE PRESS SYNDICATE OF THE UNIVERSITY OF CAMBRIDGE
The Pitt Building, Trumpington Street, Cambridge CB2 IRP, United Kingdom

CAMBRIDGE UNIVERSITY PRESS
The Edinburgh Building, Cambridge CB2 2RU, United Kingdom
40 West 20th Street, New York, NY 10011-4211, USA
10 Stamford Road, Oakleigh, Melbourne 3166, Australia

First published 1998

Printed in the United Kingdom at the University Press, Cambridge

Typeset in Bembo 11/13   [SE]

A catalogue record for this book is available from the British Library

Library of Congress Cataloging in Publication data

Oliensis, Ellen.
Horace and the rhetoric of authority / Ellen Oliensis.
p.   cm.
Includes bibliographical references and index.
ISBN 0 521 57315 7 hardback
1. Horace – Technique. 2. Literature and society – Rome – History.
3. Authors and patrons – Rome – History. 4. Authors and readers –
Rome – History. 5. Latin language – Social aspects. 6. Authority in
literature. 7. Persona (Literature) 8. Rhetoric, Ancient.
1. Title.
PA6436.O45   1998
874'.01–dc21   97-33353   CIP

ISBN 0 521 57315 7 hardback

12204680

RCO

For my parents

CONTENTS

ACKNOWLEDGMENTS

I would like to thank Wendell Clausen for his genial encouragement of my earliest thoughts on Horace; Alessandro Barchiesi, Gregory Nagy, Michael Putnam, Richard Tarrant, and audiences at Brown University, Haverford College, Princeton University, Smith College, and SUNY/Buffalo, for their helpful responses to various sections of this book; Niall Rudd, for pages of detailed criticisms of Chapters 1 and 5 (although he will still find much to disagree with here, I have benefited greatly from his generosity); and Charles Martindale and Gordon Williams, for reading and improving the whole. At Cambridge University Press, Pauline Hire shepherded the book through with patience and good humor, and Susan Moore copy-edited it with imagination and care. As will be obvious to anyone familiar with his work, my greatest debt is to my husband, John Shoptaw. His theory and practice of reading have left their mark on every page of this book.

I began work on this book during my three years at the Harvard Society of Fellows and completed it with the help of a Morse Fellowship from Yale University; I am indebted to those institutions for their support. Chapters 2 and 4 incorporate, in a revised form, material that has previously appeared in *Arethusa* 24 (1991) and 28 (1995), and an early version of my discussion of *Satires* 2 will have appeared in T. N. Habinek and Alessandro Schiesaro (eds.) *The Roman Cultural Revolution* (Cambridge, 1997); I am grateful to the publishers for permission to reprint.

With a few exceptions (noted as they arise), where I follow the Teubner text of Friedrich Klinger (Leipzig, 1959), all citations of Horace are culled from the text of E. C. Wickham and H. W. Garrod (Oxford, 1912). Unless otherwise noted, all translations are my own.

ABBREVIATIONS

In addition to standard abbreviations for ancient authors and works
and for journals, the following are used for Horace's works:

Ars	*Ars poetica*
C.	*Odes* (*Carmina*)
E.	*Epistles*
I.	*Epodes* (*Iambi*)
S.	*Satires*

INTRODUCTION

Every member of society has not only a face but "face" – the public, projected self-image that is the basic currency of social interactions.[1] In any given encounter, this "face" can be saved or lost, enhanced or maintained, effaced or even defaced. Behind the scenes, and sometimes (more or less discreetly) in mid-scene, faces are changed. We are constantly moving between spheres (social, spatial, and temporal) that put different valuations and demands on our social faces. A face can be put on in the morning and taken off in the evening. It can be "made up," as we say, or cosmetically altered. One face (for example, blushing or bold) can be applied on top of another; such faces acquire the character of false fronts or masks concealing the purportedly true self – the special face we show to ourselves and to those "other selves" who form our most intimate society. Let us say, then, that everyone has not only "face" but also a potentially infinite set of "faces." Although these senses of "face" are in principle distinguishable ("face" suggesting "reputation" or "honor," "faces" a plurality of selves or personae), they are also inextricably linked – one's face depends on the cumulative and shifting reception of one's faces.

Like the rest of us, Horace will have presented different faces to different people in different situations. He wore one face, we may presume, in the presence of Augustus, and a quite different face when he was giving orders to his slaves. Most of these faces are unavailable to us. We cannot know, for example, how Horace behaved when he was at dinner with Maecenas – what manner he adopted, how he dressed, how he held himself, how much or how little he spoke. But we do know how Horace behaves in his poetry. It is because Horace's poetry is itself a performance venue that I make no clear, hard-and-fast distinction between

---

[1] Cf. Goffman (1967) 5; Brown and Levinson (1987) 61.

I

the author and the character "Horace." Horace is present in his personae, that is, not because these personae are authentic and accurate impressions of his true self, but because they effectively construct that self – for Horace's contemporary readers, for us, and also for Horace himself.[2] The reason I prefer the concept of face (a concept native to Latin as well as English, as the semantics of Latin os, "face" and frons, "brow" indicate) to the new-critical concept of the persona is that it registers this de facto fusion of mask and self. I will sometimes call this face the "authorial persona," by which I mean the first-person speaker who gradually accumulates characteristics associated with the figure known as "Horace" – friend of Maecenas, friend of Virgil and Varius, son of a freedman, owner of a Sabine villa, author of Satires 1 (in Satires 2), author of the Epodes (in the Odes), author of the Carmen saeculare (in Odes 4), and so on. This is a character in whose doings Horace has a particular stake: Horace may be held accountable for what "Horace" says and (thereby) does.

Horace's poetic "face" is not identical to Horace, but it will be identified with him. When Horace calls upon the services of a persona in the strict sense – a differentiated character usually distinguished by a distinctive proper name (Alfius in Epode 2, Ofellus in Satires 2.2) – it is precisely in order to disavow his authorial responsibility: "this is not Horace speaking." Critics do the same when they attempt to save Horace's face by attributing behavior they find offensive (for example, the misogynous obscenities of his epodes) to a conventional persona (the inherited mask of Archilochean invective). The author, in this view, is situated far above or behind the characters – including the first-person speaker – of his poetry, whom he views, perhaps, with the same critical eye as the modern critic. This may be a fair description of Horace's relation to certain of his personae. But the theatrical metaphor is misleading insofar as it obscures Horace's interest in the doings of his faces – obscures, that is, the extent to which Horace is in fact doing things with his faces, whether they bear the name "Alfius" or the name of the author.[3] It may not always be Horace speaking, but it is always Horace acting.

The division between "art" and "life" that is an unquestioned tenet of much classical scholarship does not take account of the fact that works of art are themselves pieces of reality – "Part of the res itself, and not about it," as Wallace Stevens puts it. One premise of this study is that Horace's poems are not detached representations of society but consequential acts

---

[2] Cf. Martindale (1993) 16–18.   [3] On the Alfius epode, see further below, 84–7.

within society. This is so, moreover, not only when Horace performs the potentially risky act of addressing Augustus, but also when he addresses the slave who works as bailiff on his Sabine farm, the god Faunus, and even (for example, in *Satires* 1.5) no one at all. Horace's poems are very much words that do things; they are, in J. L. Austin's terminology, "speech acts."[4] They save face, deface, and make faces; they praise, insult, excuse, stake claims, and warn off trespassers. Sometimes they do the opposite of what they say; in *Satires* 2.6, for example, Horace demonstrates his trustworthiness by announcing that he does not enjoy Maecenas' trust.[5] And sometimes the conflicting impulses of self-promotion and self-effacement twist Horace's poems in unexpected ways; it is this conflict, as we will see, that produces the evasions of *Epistles* 1.7 and the dramatic swerve of the "Cleopatra" ode.

My concern, then, is with the way Horace conducts his life in and by means of his poetry. My approach is thus "biographical" in a particular sense: I am interested not in the light Horace's poetry can shed on his extrapoetic life but in the life that happens in his poetry. I read Horace's poems, accordingly, as complex gestures performed before and for a variety of audiences. I single out authority and deference as the characteristic and complementary strategies of what we might call (following Erving Goffman) Horace's "face-work."[6] Gestures of authority are potentially rude; they set the poet on a podium some height above his audience, thereby inviting admiration but also envy. Gestures of deference, by contrast, are typically polite; they are the linguistic equivalent of an envy-deflecting bow. While either kind of gesture readily converts into the other – an exaggerated claim of authority can function as a self-parodying self-deflation, an excessive show of deference as an insulting irony – their basic orientation remains constant. Authority makes a claim for the poet's face; deference pays tribute to the face of the audience(s). These poetic postures correspond to the social extremes of which Horace advises his young friend Lollius to steer clear in *Epistles* 1.18: self-assertive arrogance on one side, self-abasing servility on the other. This is advice Horace lives by throughout his poetry, and not only as regards his patron Maecenas. As we will see, gestures of pure deference and pure authority are much rarer in Horace's work than mixtures of the two. When he is addressing an unproblematically subordinated "other" such

---

[4] Austin (1975).   [5] See Griffin (1984) 198–9.
[6] Goffman (1967) 5–45 (on face-work), (1967) 56–76 (on deference).

as a slave, Horace regularly cedes some of his authority, making a display – for the reader's if not the addressee's benefit (the servile addressee is not positioned as a reader of Horatian poetry) – of his gracious affability. And when he is addressing an undeniably superior "other," most notably Augustus, he always takes care to safeguard his own authority, even if that means indulging in a certain calculated ungraciousness.

Social and sociolinguistic approaches to Horace have been made in recent years by John Henderson, P. H. Schrijvers, and R. O. A. M. Lyne.[7] I follow these scholars in reading Horace's poems as preeminently "polite" acts, in the broad sense of acts oriented toward face needs; this book is, among other things, a study of Horatian politeness. To this end, I draw on the insights of the sociolinguists Penelope Brown and Stephen Levinson.[8] Brown and Levinson distinguish between "negative face" (the desire to be unencumbered and unimpeded) and "positive face" (the desire for recognition and approval) and between their corresponding forms of politeness. "Negative politeness" conveys respect and maintains distance ("Excuse me, sir"); "positive politeness" presumes familiarity and promotes intimacy ("Hey, pal"). These techniques include not only conventional forms of politeness (respectful and familiar forms of address such as "sir" and "pal") but also the basic elements of grammar and rhetoric (contrast the relatively formal "excuse me" with the casual expletive "hey"). As we will see, Horace often avoids a face-threatening face-off by switching from the authoritative first person singular to the communal first person plural and/or from the confrontational second person to the oblique third person. And he uses rhetorical figures (hyperbole, simile, fable, etc.) not only to delight or to persuade but also to lend his poetic actions a measure of "plausible deniability." In sociolinguistic terms, Horace tends to hedge his speech-acts so as to render them nonactionable.

Horace's strategies change over time. Where Brown and Levinson emphasize the synchronic and the universal, my focus is on the diachronic and the particular – the evolution of Horace's distinctive face.

---

[7] Henderson (1993) offers a sociolinguistic analysis of S. 1.9; Schrijvers (1993) 75–89 surveys Horace's politeness strategies; Lyne (1995) reads Horace's public poems as face-saving acts.

[8] The work of Brown and Levinson is also cited by Henderson and Schrijvers; the three of us – in three different countries! – seem to have come upon this suggestive study independently. The summary overview that follows derives from Brown and Levinson (1987) 61–71. Their taxonomy of polite strategies involves numerous other analytic distinctions that I will be taking up only informally; for a systematic overview of Horatian strategies of politeness, I refer the reader to Schrijvers.

For Horace's face changes not only from situation to situation and from poem to poem (sometimes from one line to the next) but from collection to collection. In the course of his career, and as a consequence of it, Horace's face gains value – what Pierre Bourdieu would term "symbolic capital."[9] Horace cannot assert as much or the same kind of authority at the beginning of his career as he can at its end. The Horace of *Satires* 1 has less face to save or to spend than the Horace of *Satires* 2; and neither of these Horaces has sufficient face to author the late masterwork of deferential authority known as the *Ars poetica*. The more face Horace accumulates, the less effort he needs to devote to maintaining it, especially against threats from inferiors. Indeed, as his face becomes better known and more widely recognized, Horace spends more time defending his negative than promoting his positive face – such is the price of celebrity. As Horace gains authority, moreover, he defers differently – paying more deference to Augustus and less to Maecenas, for example.

On the other hand, a Horatian poem can never function simply as the written equivalent of a gesture such as a bow or a sneer. A compliment or insult delivered in the medium of literature differs significantly from one delivered in everyday social intercourse. For J. L. Austin, this difference was fundamental; Austin excluded literary speech acts from his account on the grounds that "a performative utterance will . . . be *in a peculiar way* hollow or void if said by an actor on the stage, or if introduced in a poem."[10] I agree with Austin that literary speech acts undergo a "sea-change" (Austin's phrase). But the change is such as to render them not "hollow or void" but – to follow Austin's allusion – "rich and strange." Literary performatives are enriched and estranged performatives. Everyday acts of politeness target a limited audience – the immediate addressee(s) and (sometimes) assorted onlookers and eavesdroppers. Horace's poetic acts of politeness, by contrast, outlast their (invented or reconstructed) occasions; they address more audiences and perform more functions. It is true that face-to-face interactions are often similarly overdetermined. A subordinate may bark orders at his underlings with renewed emphasis when his superior is on the scene – the message being less "Do your job!" than "Look how well I am doing mine!"; or he may perform his authority for the sake of his own onlooking self, thereby

---

[9] See Bourdieu (1977) 179 (defining "symbolic capital" as "the prestige and renown attached to a family and a name").

[10] Austin (1975) 22. For an overview of responses to Austin, see Petrey (1990) 70–85.

reassuring himself of his own mastery. But Horace's poetry is not just occasionally but always and inevitably triangulated in this way. Horace's favorite game is the game of "three-cornered catch" (*lusum . . . trigonem*, S. 1.6.126) – a game he plays not only on the grassy Campus Martius but also across the pages of his books.

The game has at least three corners. Horace has several audiences, some or all of whom may be in attendance for any one poem or book of poems: the addressee, what I term the "overreader" (an unnamed but otherwise specified other who may be imagined as reading over the addressee's shoulder),[11] the reading public, and posterity.[12] These audiences (which may coalesce within any given poem – the addressee with posterity, the overreader with the reading public, and so on) are all potentially present, whether or not they are explicitly and directly invoked, in the rhetorical economy of the poem. The addressee is the figure Horace explicitly addresses, usually but not always by name. Horace's addressees include the (still) famous and readily identifiable (Maecenas, Agrippa, Augustus); the little known or unknown (Lollius, Septimius, Scaeva); named and nameless types (Tyndaris in *Odes* 1.17, the ex-slave of Epode 4, the greedy landowner of *Odes* 2.18); and the overtly fictional or mythical (Faunus, Melpomene). In Horace's carefully constructed poetic "situations," this addressee sometimes functions as a conduit for another conversation with an overreader; it is this kind of relation, whereby one person stands in for or in front of another, that makes up what I am calling the rhetorical economy.

I mean the term "overreader" as a response to John Stuart Mill's famous assertion that poetry is not heard but overheard. In Mill's romantic definition, the poet speaks first of all, sincerely and privately, to himself or herself, and secondarily to those overhearing these meditations. Horace, by contrast, tends to speak or write directly to someone and obliquely to someone else. This dynamic is especially pronounced in Horace's epistles, "open letters" which bear one address but are designed to be intercepted by numerous others. But it is at work, to some degree,

---

[11] While my overreader is differently positioned from Barchiesi's paranoid imperial addressee, my interest in "overreading" owes much to his (over)readings of Hor. *E.* 2.1 and Ov. *Tr.* 2; see Barchiesi (1993).

[12] On the Horatian addressee, cf. Johnson (1982) 4–5, 127. For related articulations of Horace's multiple audiences, see Gold (1992); Citroni (1995) 290 and in general 271–375. Citroni's emphasis on the dual orientation of Horace's poetry (always having in view both a smaller circle of friends and a larger, anonymous reading public) provides a useful corrective to Lefèvre (1993), who tends to treat Horace as a coterie poet.

throughout Horace's poetry. When Horace goes on the attack in the *Epodes*, he is performing before and for Maecenas and the young Caesar; he may address a wealthy ex-slave (for example), but his words are not primarily meant for his ears. Contrariwise, when he tells Maecenas that he is disinclined to comply with his latest demands, the declaration targets not only Maecenas but also and perhaps especially the over-reading public, which may be prone to view Horace's relation to Maecenas in an unflattering light. In examples such as these, indirection enables Horace to make an effective demonstration of (instead of merely protesting) his values and his value. Elsewhere, it acts like a discursive extension of the polite grammar that substitutes the third person for the second, enabling Horace to say something to the overreader that he could not say to his face without injuring his own face and/or that of the overreader.[13] It is not by chance that it is within a letter to Lollius (*E.* 1.18) that Horace vents most freely his mixed feelings about friendship with the great. In such cases, whatever is said is said "off the record"; Horace can always claim that he was merely addressing his addressee, not his overreader (here Maecenas), and that his overreader was, in a word, "overreading" – not taking Horace's words at face value.

The less significant Horace's addressee, the more likely s/he is to sub-serve an overreader; a slave, for example, is readily converted to the instrumental function of medial addressee. But even when Maecenas or Augustus is the addressee, Horace always has an eye out for the impres-sion he is making on other overreaders. These overreaders typically include Horace himself (Horace is always situated as an accomplished and interested overreader of his own poems), the reading public (includ-ing especially Horace's invidious critics, whether fictitious or actual), and, more and more, the audience of posterity. In the course of his career, Horace displays a growing awareness that his poetic faces will continue to circulate long after he himself has passed from view. It is this awareness that enables Horace to assert his authority even in (if not exactly to) the face of readers such as Maecenas and Augustus. It is the power of Horace's poems, finally, and not the power of Maecenas or Augustus, that will perpetuate Horace's name.

To clarify the issues I will be raising and the kind of reading I will be pursuing in this study, I turn, by way of example, to *Epistles* 2.2. Horace's

---

[13] On these forms of polite mediation, cf. Schrijvers (1993) 82–6; Seeck (1991) 539–40 (on Horace's "satiric grammar").

second book of epistles comprises two lengthy letters, the first directed
to Augustus himself, the second to a relatively low-profile friend named
Florus, a lawyer and poet in the entourage of Tiberius Nero to whom
Horace has already introduced us in *Epistles* 1.3.[14] It is the initial gesture
of *Epistles* 2.2 that will preoccupy me here.

After saluting Florus in one dignified line, Horace abruptly launches
into an elaborate account of a hypothetical business proposition. Say
someone offered to sell you a slave (*si quis forte velit puerum tibi vendere, E.*
2.2.2); say he quoted you a very reasonable price; say he drew attention to
the boy's good looks (*talos a vertice pulcher ad imos*, 4); say he advertised his
smattering of culture – the boy knows a little Greek (*litterulis Graecis
imbutus*, 7), and he can even sing a bit, nothing polished, but pleasant to
listen to when you're drinking (*quin etiam canet indoctum sed dulce bibenti*,
9). Say, finally, that he added a warning: the boy has been known to shirk
his work and hide under the stairs. If you bought this piece of goods, you
wouldn't have the right to bring a complaint against the seller later on,
would you? After eighteen lines in this vein, Horace finally comes to the
point (20–4):

> dixi me pigrum proficiscenti tibi, dixi
> talibus officiis prope mancum, ne mea saevus
> iurgares ad te quod epistula nulla rediret.
> quid tum profeci, mecum facientia iura
> si tamen attemptas?

> I told you when you were leaving I was slow, I told you I was almost
> crippled when it came to such duties – just so you wouldn't fly into
> a rage at me for not writing you back. What good did it do me, if
> you attack me even though the law is on my side?

Caveat emptor. Horace warned Florus in advance of his failings, and
Florus has no right to complain if he gets, so to speak, just what he paid
for. But it is not only a letter of which Florus claims to have been
cheated. Horace appends a second accusation in what the narratologists
term "free indirect discourse":[15] "And then you complain about this too,
about my not sending you the odes you've been waiting for, liar that I
am" (*quereris super hoc etiam, quod | exspectata tibi non mittam carmina*

---

[14] The date and composition of *E.* 2 remain controversial; it will be evident that I believe that
E. 2.1 and 2.2 were designed as complementary counterparts (whether or not they were
accompanied by a third poem, the *Ars poetica*).

[15] See, e.g., Rimmon-Kenan (1983) 110–13.

mendax, 24–5). In Chapter 4, we will meet two Horatian slaves who bear a certain resemblance to this good-looking, musically-inclined *puer*: the personified slave-book of *Epistles* 1.20 and the cupbearer of *Odes* 1.38. The slave of *Epistles* 2.2 is thus an apt figure for both the letter and the lyrics that are the objects of Florus' frustrated desire – a desire that this epistle itself goes a long way toward satisfying.

But what I want to underscore here is the character of the gesture enacted by these opening lines. Let me note, to begin with, that Horace is offering a defensive excuse and not an apology (for example, the familiar "I'm sorry to have taken so unconscionably long to answer your letter"). Why not? Apologies are inherently deferential speech acts; the apologizer effectively injures his own face by acknowledging that he has done a wrong to the other's. And Horace is not ready to humble himself to this extent before his young friend. On the other hand, it is clear that Horace's tone of mock-huffiness functions here less as a rebuke than as a compliment to Florus. It would have been easy enough for Horace to "pull rank" on Florus. He might have claimed to have more important things, or more important people, on his mind; he might have reminded Florus that he has already done him the honor of addressing him one epistle (*Epistles* 1.3). By laying the blame on his own imperfect head, Horace implicitly concedes Florus' right to expect more.

Horace is making a claim for his own negative face. But he does so in a way that flatters Florus' positive face. The confidential rhetoric of the "sales pitch" is itself an ingratiating piece of positive politeness. By identifying his poetic face with a young and minimally talented *puer*, moreover, Horace temporarily abdicates the social and poetic authority he has acquired over the years. He can afford to, of course; no one could mistake this hilariously self-depreciating image for a straightforward self-portrait. The image saves Horace's face because it so obviously fails to fit it: Horace can jokingly identify the freely tendered *officia* of a friend with the command performances of a slave – a figure who has no negative face at all – only because it is quite clear that he has, in relation to Florus, nothing of the slave about him. But the image saves Florus' face as well. After all, it is the junior poet, not the master poet, whom we might expect to find in the role of the musically-inclined young slave; Horace might have compared Florus to a slave who has (say) performed a song for his master and who is now eagerly awaiting his reward. The problem is that such an apportionment of roles would in this case be too close to the discursive situation of the letter in which it appears – the hyperbole would be insulting to Florus rather than amusing. By casting himself in the junior and subordinate role, Horace graciously keeps Florus out of it.

Neither the friendship between Horace and Florus nor the epistle that helps confirm it exists in isolation. There is, first, an implicit contrast between this friendship and Florus' "friendship" with Tiberius Nero, the emperor's stepson. The contrast is underscored by Horace's opening salutation, where the vocative "friend," which would normally refer to the relation between the speaker and the man thus addressed, refers instead to Florus' relation to Tiberius: "Florus, faithful friend to good and glorious Nero" (*Flore, bono claroque fidelis amice Neroni, E.* 2.2.1).[16] The line gives praise where praise is due, assigning to Florus the cardinal virtue of the subordinate (fidelity), to Tiberius the shining character of a leader. As he announces Florus' fidelity to Tiberius, Horace indirectly evidences his own, offering Tiberius the deferential tribute of a compliment. But the relation between this decorous salute and the hypothetical sales pitch that follows it is not readily apparent. Horace may seem to be drawing a contrast between faithful Florus and his own unreliable self. And yet it is not Horace but Florus, "faithful friend" of Tiberius, who serves an imperial "master" and forfeits some measure of his freedom in that service. It is not that Horace is venting his hostility to Tiberius or actively competing with him for Florus' affections. Rather, he is supplementing formality with informality and work with play. In Horace's company – in his epistle – Florus can play the master, if he likes, to his heart's content.

But there is another relation to which this relatively relaxed epistolary friendship forms an implicit and designed contrast. Whereas *Epistles* 2.2 opens by acknowledging Florus' allegiance to Tiberius, its companion piece in *Epistles* 2 pays homage to Horace's and all Italy's imperial patron – Augustus himself. Horace opens, accordingly, with an apology for his presumption in addressing the greatest man, incorporating a series of compliments into an exemplary gesture of negative politeness (*E.* 2.1.1–4):

> Cum tot sustineas et tanta negotia solus,
> res Italas armis tuteris, moribus ornes,
> legibus emendes, in publica commoda peccem,
> si longo sermone morer tua tempora, Caesar.

---

[16] This is in fact the sole exception to the Horatian norm, which is illustrated by *S.* 2.6.90, *I.* 1.2, *I.* 13.3, *C.* 2.9.5, *C.* 2.14.6, *E.* 1.7.12, *E.* 1.18.106, *E.* 2.2.138, and *Ars* 4.

> Since so many and such great concerns fall upon your shoulders
> alone – since you protect our Italian state with arms, adorn it with
> virtuous habits, correct it with laws – I would sin against the public
> good if I were to take up your time with a lengthy conversation,
> Caesar.

The contrast with the epistle to Florus is instructive. There, Horace protects his own negative face – his right to be free of Florus' demands; here,
it is the emperor's negative face that is at issue. There, Florus is seeking a
token of his friend's esteem as balm for his positive face; here, it is Horace
who is initiating what he represents as a possibly unwelcome contact.
The difference comes into focus when we consider what the effect
would be if Horace's addressees exchanged places. An equivalent apology
to Florus ("Please forgive my trespassing on your valuable time, Florus")
would sound ironic; an equivalent excuse to Augustus ("Don't scold me
for not writing sooner, Augustus, I warned you I wasn't much of a corre-
spondent") would sound presumptuously familiar or even dangerously
self-assertive.

As it happens, another representation of the underlying situation of
the epistle to Augustus has survived. Suetonius preserves part of a letter
to Horace in which Augustus complains, in a tone of flattering familiarity, "I'll have you know I'm angry at you because in all your writings of
this kind you don't talk with me in particular" (*irasci me tibi scito, quod non
in plerisque eiusmodi scriptis mecum potissimum loquaris*); it was in response to
this letter, according to Suetonius, that Horace composed the letter we
know as *Epistles* 2.1. I will have occasion to return to Augustus' letter
later in this book. What interests me here is that this very situation – a
friend writes in mock-anger at not having received the expected tribute
of a letter – furnishes the premise not of Horace's epistle to Augustus but
of Horace's epistle to Florus (*ne mea saevus | iurgares, ad te quod epistula
nulla rediret, E.* 2.2.21–2). The situation decorously suppressed from the
one epistle thus resurfaces in the other. Given that *Epistles* 2.2 is designed
to be overread by Augustus, the de facto dedicatee of the collection, we
could say that the epistle to Florus functions as an oblique and nonactionable rebuke of Horace's imperial complainant. Or at least it enables
Horace to play at, and to play out, a combination of compliant servility
and self-assertive disobedience that he could not perform to the
emperor's face without risking his own face. Let me add that while the
evidence of Suetonius gives added point to the juxtaposition of these
two letters within *Epistles* 2, we do not need his evidence to establish

their overarching complementarity within the rhetorical economy of the collection. The letters compose in effect the positive and negative faces of a single coin.

But *Epistles* 2.2 also circulates in another rhetorical economy, formed by Horace's two epistolary collections. It is often remarked that the letter to Florus recalls the three letters Horace addressed to Maecenas in *Epistles* 1. The epistle to Florus functions, indeed, as a kind of grand composite of the earlier three. Here again, Horace offers his excuses for not composing lyric poems as requested; here again, he adduces his advancing age and the prior claims of philosophy; here again, he heaps mockery on the "gladiatorial combats" in which poets at Rome are forever engaged.[17] These parallels furnish evidence for the formal and topical resemblance of the letters in question. But they also serve to draw our attention to the fact that the letter is not addressed to Maecenas. That is, while it is true that Horace is not addressing (say) Lollius or Aristius Fuscus here, these absent names are simply absent. Maecenas' name, by contrast, is not so much absent as erased. It is because the epistle repeats so precisely the gesture of *Epistles* 1.1 (the rejection of the lyric *ludus* in favor of philosophy) that we can read the scratched-out name of the original addressee. The revision reminds us that if the young Florus doubles for the young Horace, Horace now shares with Tiberius the role of patron – Maecenas' role. Within *Epistles* 2, Horace's only "patron" is Augustus.

What difference would it make if *Epistles* 2.2 were addressed to Maecenas? The story of the shirking slave and the irate master would constitute not a face-saving reversal but a degrading replica of the discursive situation. Even in jest, Horace cannot represent himself as having "sold" himself or his poetry to Maecenas. So too with the oft-cited capsule autobiography that furnishes one of Horace's subsequent excuses to Florus (*E.* 2.2.49–52):

> unde simul primum me dimisere Philippi,
> decisis humilem pennis inopemque paterni
> et laris et fundi, paupertas impulit audax
> ut versus facerem.

---

[17] The epistle draws chiefly on *E.* 1.1 but adds in significant touches from *E.* 1.7 and *E.* 1.19. Horace's "mendacity": *E.* 1.7.2, *E.* 2.2.25. Not composing lyric: *E.* 1.1.1–4, *E.* 2.2.24–5. Advancing age: *E.* 1.1.4–9, *E.* 1.7.25–8, *E.* 2.2.55–7. Claims of philosophy: *E.* 1.1.10–12, *E.* 2.2.141–2. Gladiator-poets: *E.* 1.1.2–6, *E.* 1.19.45–7, *E.* 2.2.97–101.

After Philippi discharged me, leaving me earth-bound, my wings clipped, stripped of ancestral house and lands, bold poverty spurred me to compose verse.

Horace can only purport to expose the mercenary motive of his verse when he is writing to a man to whom he is in no way indebted.[18] Addressed to Maecenas, the joke would turn sour. It would be not only impossibly ungracious to Maecenas ("now that I've gotten what I wanted out of our transaction, you may consider our contract terminated") but excessively self-defacing – Horace's invidious overreaders are all too ready as it is to mistake such self-depreciations for the literal truth. If Horace makes these jokes in a public letter to Florus, where his senior status soothes and yet does not entirely remove their sting, he does so in part to inoculate himself against envy's corrosive bite. Horace's best defense often consists of such self-wounding gestures, gestures that can be neither taken at face value nor entirely discounted.

As this sample reading will have indicated, my focus in this study is on Horace's poems, not on his life or his times or his culture. When I bring up Horace's senior status in this epistle, I do so not because I am interested in plotting the trajectory of Horace's career with poetic "points" such as this but because this self-representation has important implications for our reading of the poem – it matters that Horace is older and further along in his career than his young addressee. Again, when I claim that Augustus is Horace's only "patron" in *Epistles* 2, I am not trying to prove that Augustus took over the patronage of poets from Maecenas; what concerns me here is the way Horace uses Augustus to avoid deferring to Maecenas – just as elsewhere he uses Melpomene to avoid deferring to either Maecenas or Augustus. On the other hand, I do not mean to downplay the (highly complex) relation between Horace's poetry and the actual power wielded by men such as Maecenas and Augustus. My work is in this regard deeply indebted to Stephen Greenblatt's work on "self-fashioning"; Horace is, in effect, a self-made man, the first great

---

[18] Griffin (1993) 2–3 plausibly suggests that Horace means primarily that poverty made him reckless, i.e. a fearlessly outspoken satirist; but the preceding anecdote (E. 2.2.26–40: a soldier, his savings stolen, boldly stormed a king's garrison and earned a handsome reward; his fortunes repaired, he refused to repeat the performance), while consonant with Griffin's interpretation, lends more weight to the traditional interpretation (the two are of course not mutually exclusive). The "king's garrison" (*praesidium regale*, E. 2.2.30) stormed by the impoverished poet has more in common with Maecenas (fated to be Horace's *praesidium* and *rex* – cf. C. 1.1.2, E. 1.7.37) than with the targets of Horace's satiric attacks.

model of Greenblatt's upwardly mobile Renaissance self-fashioners.[19] But whereas Greenblatt's ultimate goal is the "poetics of culture,"[20] mine remains the social and cultural action of Horace's poems.

Let me stress that I do not intend thereby to assert my authority over Horace's or to expose him as the calculating careerist he has sometimes been accused of being. Purity of motive is after all a virtue to which most social actors (including poets and critics) have only the weakest of claims; some degree of interestedness is an unavoidable condition of living and writing in the world. One of Horace's distinguishing features as a poet, and one of the qualities that attracts me to his poetry, is the degree to which he confronts his own implicated and compromised position within society while maintaining the independence of his poems. The final sum of Horace's calculations, in any event, is the making of good poetry, by which I mean poetry that is not exhausted in or fundamentally compromised by the social exchanges in which it participates. That is the kind of poetry, so far as we can tell, that would be likely to please Maecenas. And it is the poet's best means of making his face.

I have arranged this book around the major genres in which Horace worked and in (roughly) chronological order. This arrangement enables me to take into account the changing value of Horace's face – to register the difference between (say) the author of *Satires* 1 and the author of *Epistles* 1. It also suits my focus on the rhetorical economy of Horace's collections. I suggested above that the meaning of *Epistles* 2.2 derives in part from its relation both to *Epistles* 2.1 and to Horace's earlier epistles to Maecenas; this is, as we will see, one way meaning accumulates in all of Horace's collections. Focusing on the collections also enables me to read the recurrent master narrative – the narrative, that is, of acquired social and poetic mastery – of Horace's career. Others have shown how this drama plays out across *Odes* 1–3;[21] one of the aims of this study (although not the primary aim) is to show that the same drama inflects every Horatian genre. If I have chosen to treat Horace's poetry genre by genre (rather than in strict chronological order), one reason, again, is that different books in the same genre circulate in a single rhetorical economy. Another reason is that this organization lets me explore the

---

[19] Greenblatt (1980). On Horace's uses in the Renaissance, see Burrow (1993).
[20] Greenblatt (1980) 5, Greenblatt (1990) 146–60 and *passim*.
[21] Zetzel (1982); Santirocco (1986) 153–68.

social uses and dangers of different generic postures. Throughout this book, I will be preoccupied with the social implications of Horace's aesthetic choices.

In Chapter 1, I look at how Horace both dramatizes and palliates the audacity of his ascent in *Satires* 1 and 2. Horace fashions his satiric face with both elite insiders (in particular Maecenas) and lower-status onlookers in view. Horace's first essay in autobiography is essentially defensive, a sustained apology.[22] Horace puts on a good face – he shows his positive face – to shield himself from accusations of opportunism and servility. By the time he writes *Satires* 2, Horace has made his name as the author of *Satires* 1. As a result, the satirist's mask no longer fits, and Horace hands it down to his social inferiors, moving from center stage to join the (onstage) audience.

In Chapter 2, I read the *Epodes* as uncivil acts of war in which Horace aggressively targets the enemies of what he represents as good order. Horace implicitly justifies the sometimes obscenely rude faces he makes in his epodes by anchoring them to the defense of Rome, figuring himself as a protective gargoyle or Priapus. But the more he makes repulsive faces at his enemy, the more difficulty readers may have telling the two apart. Horace's predicament is epitomized by the witch Canidia, the arch-enemy who functions, in different aspects, as the defaced alter ego of both Horace and Maecenas.

In Chapter 3, I turn to Horace's *Odes*, focusing on the complex blend of authority and deference that characterizes Horace's lyric project. As *Satires* 2 corrects *Satires* 1, so the *Odes* recompose the contorted face of the *Epodes*. With the end of the civil war, Horace consolidates his authority. This new authority is expressed formally in the success with which Horace constructs and governs his lyric domain. While the poet of the odes sometimes mimes the loss of control that is a central feature of his epodes, these performances, which find less of an amplifying echo in the society at large, can register not as synecdoches of civil disorder but as one of the luxuries of social stability. The greatest challenge to Horace's face is now less the danger of indistinguishability than the concentration of distinction in the person of Augustus.

In Chapter 4, I consider Horace's epistles, the poems in which Horace most directly addresses the issues of face-making and face-saving. Horace commences *Epistles* 1 by claiming to have averted his face from the world

---

[22] On autobiography as defense, see Sturrock (1993) 49–50.

but in so doing displays it polished to a new shine. Here my emphasis is on Horace's negotiations with Maecenas on the one hand, the emperor on the other. I close with a discussion of how Horace manages to preserve his own authority when he comes face to face with the emperor in *Epistles* 2.1.

My final chapter takes up the *Ars poetica,* which may not be Horace's last work chronologically but is certainly the work of an established author who has a good deal of face to show and to spend. As I read it, the *Ars* is the manifesto of a self-made poet who champions achievement over birth and innate resources over inherited wealth. Although Horace begins by posing as a deferentially authoritative teacher of social and poetic decorum, he ends the poem by making one of his most extraordinary faces. The monstrous image at the close of the *Ars* is in effect a muscle-flexing self-portrait and a caveat to would-be imitators.

By way of conclusion, I look at the face-work of one of Horace's late lyrics, the ode to Melpomene, a poem that recapitulates many of the issues and strategies I discuss in the course of this study. What Horace offers us here is a kind of death mask – the generic, generalized face of the master poet in repose.

1

Face-saving and self-defacement in the Satires

Horatian satire is conditioned by two contrary messages. On one side, the poet ridicules the foibles of men caught up in the pursuit of wealth or status and extols a traditional ethics of contentment; on the other, the poetry publishes and promotes the poet's own progress from the obscure margins to the shining center of Roman society.[1] The dissonance between the preaching and the practice is audible from the outset (*S.* 1.1–3):

> Qui fit, Maecenas, ut nemo, quam sibi sortem
> seu ratio dederit seu fors obiecerit, illa
> contentus vivat, laudet diversa sequentis?

> Why is it, Maecenas, that no one lives content with his lot, whether
> his by design or thrown in his way by chance, but instead praises
> those who follow other paths?

Horace introduces the theme of man's discontent with his lot (the lot of women is not at issue here) while waving the banner of Maecenas' name – Maecenas, whose favor changed the "lot" of this former Republican considerably, as contemporary readers would have known.

Some readers would have been quick (some still are quick) to put the worst possible construction upon this change.[2] In his biography of Horace, Suetonius describes the poet as having "wound his way into the favor first of Maecenas, of Caesar soon after" (*primo Maecenati, mox Augusto insinuatus*), and Horace's reiterated denials suggest that many of

---

[1] On *S.* 1 as a depiction of the poet's progress from outside the circle of Maecenas to within it, see Zetzel (1980).

[2] For the image of Horace as a time-serving courtier, see Martindale (1993) 19 (citing Dryden, Dr. Johnson, and Wicksted); not too dissimilarly Henderson (1993) 81, characterizing Horatian satire as a "quest to accredit a chaotic and destabilising tyranny."

his contemporaries viewed his ascent in a similarly unflattering light.[3] Hostile readers might convict Horace not only of unscrupulous ambition but of hypocrisy. After all, it was presumably by means of poems such as *Satires* 1.1 that Horace courted and won the favor of Maecenas. The satirist climbs the social ladder by poking fun at social climbers; he enhances his own face by stripping off other men's masks.

I happen to believe that this view of Horace's ascent is reductive and distorted. It derives its plausibility from a cynical tendency to equate the worst available interpretation of a person's motives and actions with "the truth." But while there is no reason to believe that the depths are "really" as dark as they are typically imagined to be, there is also no way to prove that they are not. It is impossible either to convict or to acquit Horace of the charges — unscrupulous ambition, opportunism, materialism, parasitism — to which his autobiography made him vulnerable. Let me stress, then, that my aim in this chapter is not to retry the case against Horace but to explore how the pressure of those charges motivates and shapes his satire.

Horace was acutely aware of the kinds of things that could and would be said about him.[4] His satiric response takes two forms. In *Satires* 1, he labors energetically to defend his integrity as a man and a poet, repeatedly differentiating himself from the targets of his satire.[5] If Horace stands accused of (ab)using his satire to make his face, the defense he mounts in *Satires* 1 rests on the premise that faces are less "made" than born. The stance of *Satires* 2 is equally but differently defensive. Secure in his new Sabine villa and his new authority, the poet of *Satires* 2 mounts a brilliantly entertaining but nonetheless devastating satirical attack on the poet of *Satires* 1. The posture of retrospective self-consciousness distances Horace from his former self ("I am no longer he"). But this division, as Horace himself recognizes, is a fiction that cannot finally be sustained. This case will never be closed.

The discriminating satirist of Satires 1

I begin with *Satires* 1.4 because this is the first poem in which Horace represents himself as having a publicly recognized face (the face of the

---

[3] According to Shackleton Bailey (1982) 15 (correcting Fraenkel [1957] 15–16), Suetonius' *insinuatus* is neutral in tone; contrast, e.g., Lyne (1995) 13–14, who takes it to be derogatory. Whatever Suetonius' meaning, the very ascription of active intent to Horace (*insinuatus* has a reflexive sense) runs counter to the self-image Horace projects in *S.* 1; see further below.

[4] See Rudd (1966) 37–48, 89–90 on the main defensive lines of *S.* 1.4 and 1.6; Lyne (1995) 12–20 on "image-management" in the satires.

[5] This labor goes hand in hand with an implicit defense of the young Caesar's character and intentions, on which see DuQuesnay (1984).

author of *Satires* 1.1, 2, and 3) to save. Recognition entails envy, and the fourth satire both anticipates and attempts to forestall the disfiguration of its author's new face. Horace's defense is a manifold discrimination that aims to distinguish the poet from his undistinguished and indiscriminate detractors. This defense is already under way in the first three satires, where Horace poses as the champion of moderation, contentment, and affability, thereby aggressively preempting accusations of greed, ambition, and malice (key traits of the amoral social climber).[6] But it is only in the fourth satire that Horace directly confronts his readers' (imagined or actual) negative constructions.

The poem centers on the question of discrimination: moral, social, and aesthetic. At the outset, Horace seems to be responding to the charge that he abuses his satiric license by attacking the virtuous along with the vicious. In his opening salvo, accordingly, he fashions a satiric genealogy that combines outspokenness or *libertas* with moral discrimination: the Greek comic poets Eupolis, Cratinus, and Aristophanes made their names by freely censuring all those – and by implication only those – who deserved it (*si quis erat dignus describi . . . multa cum libertate notabant*, *S.* 1.4.3, 5). So too Horace's selective satire targets only those who "merit blame" (*culpari dignos*, 25). Which is to say, Horace adds, practically everybody: "Pick a man, any man, from the midst of the crowd" (*quemvis media elige turba*, 25), and you'll discover he suffers from one of the standard vices. This blanket critique elicits the first explicit formulation of the charge against the satirist: Horace is a mad bull, warns his accuser, who will attack anything that moves; "so long as he can raise a laugh, he won't spare himself or any of his friends" (*dummodo risum | excutiat, sibi non, non cuiquam parcet amico*, 34–5). If laughter typically helps construct the difference between insiders (those who share the joke) and outsiders (those who are targeted by it), for this indiscriminate jokester there is no fixed difference between inside and outside; all faces are up for satiric defacement. Forever creating communities that exist only for the duration of the joke, he avails himself of whatever comic material is at hand, including not only himself (a traditional and always acceptable butt) but his purported "friends" (and the reader is likely to think here of

---

[6] Here I differ with Lyne (1995) 142–3, 149–50, who argues that Horace's critique of avarice in *S.* 1.1 and elsewhere is aimed at the famously rich Maecenas. Surely it is Horace more than Maecenas who is peculiarly vulnerable to the charge of money-grubbing. Moreover, as a beneficiary of Maecenas' generosity, Horace is in no position (either ethically or rhetorically) to accuse his rich friend of being excessively devoted to wealth. For a more nuanced version of Lyne's argument, see Seeck (1991) 541–2.

Maecenas in particular, the only friend Horace has as yet named within his satire), to further his standing with the general public.

At issue, it emerges, is the satirist's ability to make not only generically moral but also particular social discriminations. One burden of the satire, and indeed of the entire collection, is to demonstrate that Horace's satiric eye, so sharp to see the failings of the man in the crowd, succumbs to a respectful blindness when confronted with the great man who picked Horace out of it. *Satires* 1.4 thus complements the preceding satire, where Horace makes a case for what might be called social euphemistics: thinking and speaking the best (rather than the worst) of one's friends. There Horace has in view in particular the treatment of social inferiors (for example Horace) by social superiors (for example Maecenas). In *Satires* 1.4, it is Horace's treatment of his great friend that is implicitly in question.[7] Perhaps Maecenas was a little nervous about having invited a satirist to join the company of his intimate friends. If Horace focuses attention on the proper selection of satiric targets, one reason is his desire to reassure Maecenas that he will not level his satire against him.

This reassurance takes several forms. First, far from slandering his friends, Horace actually rests his defense on their probity. In response to the accusation that he takes a malicious pleasure in causing pain, Horace challenges his accuser to identify his source and substantiate his charge: "who among those with whom I've kept company stands behind that?" (*est auctor quis denique eorum | vixi cum quibus? S.* 1.4.80–1). The implication of this rhetorical question, which takes for granted the answer "no one," is that Horace's friends are not promulgators of malicious gossip, any more than Horace himself is.[8] Having provided this token of his amicable fidelity, Horace proceeds to confirm his own innocence by redirecting the charges (81–9):

---

[7] Taken together, *S.* 1.3 and 1.4 risk suggesting that Horace has touched up his poetic portraits of Maecenas. Horace comes close to flaunting his powers of redescription at *S.* 1.3 (73–5): if you want a friend to overlook your warts, you should forgive him his; "a man who demands pardon for his own faults ought in justice to return the favor" (*aequum est | peccatis veniam poscentem reddere rursus, S.* 1.3.74–5). This passage, which occurs shortly after Horace's description of his unfortunate habit of barging in on Maecenas (63–5), is clearly directed to Maecenas; but the threat, such as it is, remains implicit, and Maecenas' "warts" remain undescribed.

[8] Taking Horace's question at face value, Lefèvre (1993) 56–7 infers that Horace believes himself to have been slandered by a fellow member of Maecenas' circle; but if Horace harbored such a belief, he cannot afford to express it here (that would be to commit the very sin he is deploring).

> absentem qui rodit amicum,
> qui non defendit alio culpante, solutos
> qui captat risus hominum famamque dicacis,
> fingere qui non visa potest, commissa tacere
> qui nequit, hic niger est, hunc tu, Romane, caveto.
> saepe tribus lectis videas cenare quaternos,
> e quibus unus amet quavis aspergere cunctos
> praeter eum qui praebet aquam; post hunc quoque potus.

The man who maligns a friend behind his back and fails to defend him when another attacks him, who fishes for laughs and the reputation of a wit, who invents revelations and spills secrets – *he's* the villain, *he's* one to beware, my fellow Roman. When men are dining four to a couch, you'll often find one who enjoys spattering the company with whatever [mud] he has on hand, sparing only the host – and [he'll smear] the host too, once he's drunk enough.

Maecenas presumably knows from personal experience that Horace does not behave this way at dinner, and this satire itself shows Horace behaving with equal decency and discretion in Maecenas' virtual absence. It is significant that the failure of this dinner party is the fault not only of the wit who flings his indiscriminate mud at all and sundry but also of the host who allowed this undeserving guest to join the company in the first place. The dinner is overcrowded – the couches, designed for three men, are forced to hold four; it is evident that this host does not know how to draw the moral and social line. Hosts get, it seems, the guests they deserve. The contrastive and reciprocal argument, which is not articulated here (it will surface in *Satires* 1.6), is that Maecenas has just as little in common with the injudicious host as Horace has with the malicious guest. Horace's desire to assuage Maecenas' lingering fears also helps generate the satire's climactic speech act: "That vice [treacherous backbiting] will be far from my pages and far from my heart – if I can promise anything sincerely on my part, I promise that" (*quod vitium procul afore chartis | atque animo, prius ut, si quid promittere de me | possum aliud vere, promitto*, 101–3). Underscored by the repetition of its key verb and by the felicitous adverb "sincerely," the speech act seems meant primarily for the anxious eyes of an overreading Maecenas. Subsequent satires will give Horace many opportunities to demonstrate how well he can keep his word.

It is within Horace's overarching argument for moral and social distinctions that the issue of aesthetic discrimination finds its place. In the satire's opening lines, Horace's genealogy of satire proceeds from the Greek comic poets to the Roman satirist Lucilius, whom Horace ide..tifies not as his satiric "father" (as we might have expected) but as an inadequately discriminating practitioner of the satiric art. Lucilius may have taken care, like his Greek models, to choose appropriate targets for his satire, but he was horribly sloppy when it came to choosing his words; he wrote too much too fast, producing a torrential but muddy flow of verse, in need of filtration (*cum flueret lutulentus, erat quod tollere velles, S.* 1.4.11). In short, he was "too lazy to put up with the labor of writing – of writing properly, that is; that he wrote a lot doesn't matter to me" (*piger scribendi ferre laborem, | scribendi recte; nam ut multum, nil moror,* 12–13). The figure of the muddy river derives from the end of Callimachus' Hymn to Apollo (105–12), where Envy reserves his praise for the poet who produces an ocean of verse and Apollo responds by drawing his famous contrast between the vast but muddy river and the thin but pure (καθαρή) spring. Like Callimachus, Horace sides with Apollo, championing quality over quantity, *recte* over *multum*, exclusivity over abundance.

Instead of pitting his aesthetics of discrimination directly against Lucilian excess, Horace proceeds to represent himself as the object of a challenge issued by a certain Crispinus, one of Lucilius' exuberantly overflowing heirs: "Come, take up your writing-tablet; let us determine the place, the time, and our seconds, and see which of us can write more!" (*accipe iam tabulas; detur nobis locus, hora, | custodes; videamus uter plus scribere possit, S.* 1.4.15–16). To issue a challenge is to concede the fact (but not the justice) of one's inferior status. By casting himself not as Lucilius' challenger but as Crispinus' challengee, Horace preserves his authority intact. And instead of encountering Crispinus on the level (to accept a challenge is to grant the challenger a provisional parity), Horace pretends to concede victory, depreciating his talents in language that Crispinus would approve: "The gods did well to fashion me with a poor and puny spirit, one that speaks seldom and then very little" (*di bene fecerunt inopis me quodque pusilli | finxerunt animi, raro et perpauca loquentis,* 17–18). The same strategy produces the mock-modest disavowal of the exalted title of "poet" with which Horace purports to deflect the barbs of his critics a little later in the satire: "Reserve the distinction of that name for the man of genius, the man whose mind is tinged with divinity and whose mouth promises sublime sounds" (*ingenium cui sit, cui mens divinior atque os | magna sonaturum, des nominis huius honorem,* 43–4). Verse composed entirely of "plain language" (*puris . . . verbis,* 54; the adjective derives from Apollo's pure spring) isn't poetry at all.

22

This ironic argument, which sounds one way to Crispinus and another to Horace's Callimachean confreres, reaches its climax in one of the most memorable passages of the *Satires*, a serpentine sentence that at once flaunts and disavows poetic *ingenium* (S. 1.4.56–62):

> his, ego quae nunc,
> olim quae scripsit Lucilius, eripias si
> tempora certa modosque, et quod prius ordine verbum est
> posterius facias, praeponens ultima primis,
> non, ut si solvas "postquam Discordia taetra
> Belli ferratos postis portasque refregit,"
> invenias etiam disiecti membra poetae.

> If you ripped out the fixed meter and measures from what I'm writing now, and from what Lucilius wrote in years past, and put a word that was in front in back, placing the last before the first, you wouldn't still find, as you would if you broke up "after foul Discord broke open the ironwrought posts and gates of War," the limbs of a poet, though in pieces.

A man coming across the phrase "foul Discord" would know he was dealing with a fragment of poetry; not so with the plain language of satire, which is distinguished from prose "merely" by meter and word order. Destroy these (the skeptical argument runs), and there's no trace of poetry left. The irony is heightened by the seeming casualness of that invitation – as if the metrical reordering of words were not itself an essential business of poetry. Horace's self-depreciation here is precisely as serious as his earlier characterization of his refined Callimachean spirit as "poor and puny." As Kirk Freudenburg has pointed out, Horace is parroting the views of those who value expensive verbal materials over painstaking labor, failing to recognize the superior poetic power of Horatian *compositio*. That power is, of course, very much on display in this brilliant passage.[9] Horace may use "plain words" (contrary to what we might expect, the discriminating poet does not espouse an elite or "high-class" poetic diction), but he uses them to dazzling effect. Indeed, his sustained metaphor of the dismembered Orphean text far outdoes the obviously "poetic" but relatively tame personification of Discord to which these lines purport to pay homage.

In Horace's fantasy of textual dismemberment, the disruption of the versified word order offers a kind of microcosm of civic upheaval, with

---

[9] See Freudenburg (1993) 147–8.

the inversion of words representing, in miniature hyperbole, the confusion of social *ordines*. It is no accident that the Ennian verse Horace cites for its exemplary poetic value represents the outbreak of discordant war as a rupture of constructed boundaries. The man who accepts the invitation of Horace's subjunctives implicates his imagination in an analogous act of violence. Horace and Maecenas, by contrast, side with the preservation of distinctions, whether aesthetic or social. For Horace's style of poetry is, it turns out, a good match for Maecenas' style of patronage as Horace characterizes it elsewhere in the collection. As the discriminating poet singles out for satire only those who deserve it (*si quis erat dignus describi*, S. 1.4.3), so his discriminating patron takes care to befriend only worthy men (*cautum dignos adsumere*, S. 1.6.51). Horace selects not only his satiric targets but also his very words with the same care that his patron devotes to the fashioning of his circle: Horace is a poet of few words (*perpauca loquentis*, S. 1.4.18), Maecenas a patron of few men (*paucorum hominum*, S. 1.9.44). Neither makes his selection on the basis of pedigree: Horace prefers common words to fancy poeticisms, and Maecenas does not disdain men (such as Horace) without ancestors. And both know what to do with their select materials. Horace's praise of Maecenas' well-ordered circle, in which "each man has his place" (*est locus uni | cuique suus*, S. 1.9.51–2), also suits his own verbal art: the poet's words, like the patron's friends, are carefully and hierarchically "placed." The analogy suggests not only the friends' like-mindedness but also the authority that poetic mastery confers on Horace. Poetry will always be the place where the "freedman's son" exercises his most untrammeled power.

In the final movement of the satire, however, Horace links his poetry directly to his socially undistinguished roots. Instead of representing himself as "adopted" into the noble clan of comic and satiric poets, Horace identifies his natural father as his original satiric source (S. 1.4.103–6):

> liberius si
> dixero quid, si forte iocosius, hoc mihi iuris
> cum venia dabis: insuevit pater optimus hoc me,
> ut fugerem exemplis vitiorum quaeque notando.

> If my talk happens sometimes to be a bit free, a bit risqué, I hope you'll grant me this much as a right, and pardon me: it was my excellent father who gave me this habit; he used examples to brand each of the vices so I would shun them.

The words that bracket this passage, *liberius* and *notando*, recall the phrase that punctuated the satire's first sentence, *libertate notabant*, "they freely branded" – "they" being the Greek comic poets, now supplanted by Horace's father. The repetition marks a new beginning, and the revision underscores a new satiric affiliation, as the poetic genealogy of the satire's opening lines is displaced by Horace's own family tree. It is significant that Horace's first and longest sample of his father's satire concerns the virtue of contentment (107–11):

> cum me hortaretur, parce, frugaliter, atque
> viverem uti contentus eo quod mi ipse parasset,
> "nonne vides Albi ut male vivat filius, utque
> Baius inops? magnum documentum, ne patriam rem
> perdere quis velit."

> Exhorting me to live simply and within my means, content with what he himself had amassed for me, [he would say] "You see, don't you, how badly Albius' son is living, and how Baius is broke? There's a powerful lesson for anyone thinking of squandering his inheritance."

Horace opened *Satires* I.1 with implicit praise of the rare soul who "lives content with his lot" (*contentus vivat*, S. 1.1.3) – a sentiment authorized, it now appears, by the father who labored to enable his son to "live content" (*viverem uti contentus*, S. 1.4.108). What the son inherits from his father is thus not only a modest material sufficiency but also the moral equipment he needs to rest happily in that sufficiency. Far from enabling Horace to scale the social heights, satire figures here as a leash binding him to and reminding him of his lowly beginnings.

The disavowal of ambition also helps motivate the inward turn that characterizes the satire's final movement. No longer something that amuses or insults a more or less extended public, Horatian satire is now reconfigured as an essentially private and self-reflexive moral activity. Horace's father used his satiric *mots* to shape the character of his young son (*sic me | formabat puerum dictis*, S. 1.4.120–1). As a grown man, the son dutifully internalizes his satiric father, becoming his own ever-present moral instructor (133–7):

> neque enim, cum lectulus aut me
> porticus excepit, desum mihi: "rectius hoc est;
> hoc faciens vivam melius; sic dulcis amicis
> occurram; hoc quidam non belle: numquid ego illi
> imprudens olim faciam simile?"

Nor, when I'm resting or strolling, do I fail myself: "This is the right
way; if I do that, I'll improve my life; this way my friends will be
happy to see me; now that isn't nice: I didn't ever act like that fellow,
did I, in some moment of folly?"

As the father fashioned the son with *dicta*, so the son, taking up the good
work, labors to improve himself. The appropriate object of laborious
care is thus no longer the poetry (compare *scribendi recte*, 13) but the
person; satire is now not an artifact to be polished by the artist's file, but
the file itself. Horace may be a self-made man, then, but he is no self-
promoter. His energy is devoted to, and exhausted in, the labor of a
perfectly irreproachable self-improvement program. It is this self-
improvement program, Horace claims, that makes him *dulcis amicis*, "dear
to his friends" – a fine candidate for the friendship of the judicious
Maecenas, among others. Only in this indirect and laudable fashion can
Horace's satiric art be said to have won him his new position in society.
There is no suggestion here, moreover, that others may find Horace's
satiric file equally useful. This poetry is designed for the consumption of
its producer, and if Horace carelessly jots down his satiric *mots*, it is as the
merest afterthought: "these are my private meditations, behind sealed
lips; when I have a bit of spare time, I scribble them down" (*haec ego
mecum | compressis agito labris; ubi quid datur oti, | illudo chartis*, 137–9).

Situated as it is within a published collection of carefully-wrought
satires, and at the conclusion of a poem that aggressively champions the
value of literary labor, this closing assertion of dilettantism is designed to
be taken with several grains of salt. But it has its part to play, all the same,
in the satire's overarching deferential strategy. Looking back, we can see
that the satire has traveled quite a distance from the publicity of the
comic stage advertised in its opening lines. The distance is covered by a
series of disarming disclaimers which limit the range of Horace's satiric
outspokenness: no one reads his writings (22); he avoids public recitations
(22–3); no dealer offers his book for sale (71–2); he recites his work only
to his friends, and only when compelled (73). The culmination of this
defensive self-effacement is the circumscription of satiric *libertas* within
the arena of Horace's closed mouth (*compressis . . . labris*, 138), an oxy-
moronic portrait of satiric silence that constitutes the satire's final variation on the theme of satiric discrimination.

In *Satires* 1.5, Horace backs up the claims of *Satires* 1.4 by putting its
preaching into practice. Unlike its predecessors, significantly, the poem is
not a conversational *sermo*. Horace does not speak here to Maecenas or to
any other representative friend or enemy about the foibles of their fellow

men. The poem, which commemorates a journey Horace made to Brundisium in the company of Virgil, Varius, and Maecenas, among others (for my purposes, it makes no difference whether or not Horace actually went on such a journey, although the naming of so many potential witnesses suggests that he did), is cast as a private record, a kind of diary entry, the essential fiction of which is that it has no addressees, only overreaders. Designed as it is (or purports to be) primarily for Horace's own eyes, it cannot but tell the truth – this is the implicit claim of its discursive form – about Horace's relations with his eminent traveling companions and about the events of the journey.

The journey, moreover, is one in which Roman readers might be expected to take a particular interest. As Horace reveals in passing, this is not a pleasure-trip but a diplomatic mission assigned to Maecenas and Cocceius, "men accustomed to reconciling friends at variance" (*aversos soliti componere amicos*, S. 1.5.29) – the "friends at variance" being Octavian and Antony, as contemporary readers would have known. But the truth Horace entrusts to his satiric page is designed to frustrate the curious. The diary entry gives us access only to the information the diarist considers worth recording. And for this diarist, it emerges, that means the domestic details of the journey (the weather, the food, the ups and downs of the road, the arrivals and departures of the various travelers) – anything and everything, in other words, but the politics of the moment. Packed with the detritus of daily life, fully preoccupied with "events" that are profoundly uneventful, the satire omits the very history it might be expected to detail.

This resolutely "apolitical" and domestic stance turns the poem into a veritable manifesto of Horatian discretion.[10] The satire that journeys toward the restoration of *amicitia* itself exemplifies the virtue of *amicitia* preserved. Unlike the false friend of *Satires* 1.4, who is so addicted to gossiping that he invents revelations when he has no real secrets to spill (*fingere qui non visa potest, commissa tacere | qui nequit*, S. 1.4.84–5), Horace knows how to keep both his mouth and his eyes shut. At Anxur, while awaiting the arrival of the ambassadors, Horace experiences some opportune eye trouble (S. 1.5.27–32):

> huc venturus erat Maecenas optimus atque
> Cocceius, missi magnis de rebus uterque
> legati, aversos soliti componere amicos,

---

[10] Griffin (1984) 197–8. I put "apolitical" in quotes because Horace's depoliticization of the journey is itself a political gesture; see Kennedy (1992) 32–3.

hic oculis ego nigra meis collyria lippus
illinere. interea Maecenas advenit atque
Cocceius . . .

Hither my dear Maecenas and Cocceius were to come, both dispatched on important business as ambassadors, men accustomed to reconciling friends at variance. Here I smeared black collyria on my irritated eyes. Meanwhile Maecenas and Cocceius arrived . . .

Framed between perfectly symmetrical and redundant namings of the ambassadors, Horace's gesture acquires an emblematic value: history's witness has sealed his eyes shut.[11] Rather than expose his friend's secrets, the satirist literally defaces himself.

Warfare, enmity, and imminent catastrophe do indeed pervade this satire, but only in reassuringly transposed and unthreatening guises. At Forum Appi, early in his journey, Horace tells us, "I declare war on my belly, on account of the absolutely dreadful water" (*propter aquam, quod erat deterrima, ventri | indico bellum, S.* 1.5.7–8). That evening, while night "made ready to spread its constellations" (or "battle standards") "across the sky" (*caelo diffundere signa parabat*, 10), the sailors in charge of the barge and the slaves attending the passengers join in an exchange of insults of almost ritual symmetry (*tum pueri nautis, pueris convicia nautae | ingerere*, 11–12). After nightfall, a wine-soaked sailor and a traveler vie (*certatim*, 17) in singing about the girls they left behind (*absentem ut cantat amicam*, 15; contrast the man who maligns his absent friend, *absentem qui rodit amicum, S.* 1.4.81). The climax of these defanged civil wars is the mock-epic contest of the two buffoons who entertain the united company at dinner at the country house of Cocceius. In Beneventum the next day, their host almost sets the house on fire while busying himself about his eminent guests' supper; but the flame that slips out of the stove and almost licks the roof is easily extinguished. The elements of water and fire, troublesome individually, unite to make mischief in Horace's own Apulia, where a stove burning wet branches produces "teary smoke" (*lacrimoso non sine fumo*, 80). Here the poet waits up late into the night for the visit of a girl who breaks her promise and never shows up (*mendacem . . . puellam*, 82); but this projection of infidelity from the sphere of *amicitia* into the sphere of *amor* defuses its danger, and Horace ends up spattered not with blood but with semen, product of a wet dream (84–5).

It is not only the civil war that is thus erased and displaced. If some of

---

[11] Cf. the willful "self-blinding" derided at *S.* 1.3.25 (*cum tua pervideas oculis mala lippus inunctis*).

Horace's overreaders were hoping for an intimate portrait of Horace's important friends, they are in for a disappointment. Horace's diary entry tells us next to nothing about the society in which he circulates. At no point in this satire does Horace show himself interacting with the great Maecenas. And although he describes his happy reunion with Plotius, Varius, and Virgil with recollective enthusiasm – "how we embraced, how we rejoiced!" (*o qui complexus et gaudia quanta fuerunt! S. 1.5.43*) – he does not record the content of their affectionate exchanges.[12] Nor does Horace regale us with the dinner conversation of this select collection of poets, rhetoricians, and statesmen. Instead, we have to make do with the less than brilliant mud-slinging match of "the wit Sarmentus and Messius Cicirrus" (*Sarmenti scurrae . . . Messique Cicirri, 52*).

The dinner party which is the setting for this contest is designed to provide a pointed contrast to the unamiable affair Horace described in *Satires* 1.4. There, a satirical wit spattered the guests and, when sufficiently drunk, the host himself with his indiscriminate scurrilities (*S.* 1.4.86–9). Here, Sarmentus and Messius hurl insults only at each other. And their attacks are relatively mild. Unlike the dangerously horned "mad bull" satirist of *Satires* 1.4 (cf. *faenum habet in cornu, S.* 1.4.34), Messius is compared to a "wild horse" or unicorn whose horn has been cut out of his forehead (*cornu* | *. . . exsecto frons, S.* 1.5.58–9); he tosses his head threateningly enough, but everyone knows that his satiric thrusts will not draw blood. In contrast with the scurrilous guest of *Satires* 1.4, moreover, these insult-mongers do not disturb but confirm the good fellowship of the diners, as Horace underscores by punctuating his account of their performance with the assertion "we stretched that dinner out in a thoroughly delightful fashion" (*prorsus iucunde cenam producimus illam, 70*).

The other point about this satiric entertainment is that it is not Horace who provides it. For the benefit of those detractors who imagine him to play the buffoon for the amusement of his social superiors, Horace takes care to locate himself very definitely in the audience, far above the satiric boxing ring. The men who take his place in the ring are men without face. This is literally true in the case of Messius, whose brow not only lacks a horn but is disfigured by a hideous scar (*foeda cicatrix* | *. . . frontem turpaverat, S.* 1.5.60–1). But Sarmentus too is symbol-

---

[12] Insofar as these three men are situated as privileged overreaders of this satire, Horace's affectionate exclamation cannot be meant to ring false, as maintained by Freudenburg (1993) 205.

ically defaced and unhorned. He may be a scribe, Messius concedes, but he is still less than a whole man – he remains under the jurisdiction of his mistress; and he is such a puny little thing in any case that he might as well have remained a slave and continued to subsist comfortably on his slave rations (65–9). From the security of his balcony seat, we are to imagine, Horace joins his friends in laughing at these ludicrous creatures. Within *Satires* 1, Horace identifies less with the dehorned Messius than with the figwood statue of the phallic god Priapus who is the speaker of *Satires* 1.8 (a poem to which I will have occasion to return in my next chapter). It is only in his second collection of satires that Horace will publicly disclose just how well the defaced satiric masks of *Satires* 1.5 fit his face.[13] For the duration of *Satires* 1.5, Horace keeps himself out of view of the embedded fun-house mirror.

The defensive work of *Satires* 1.4 and 1.5 is reinforced by *Satires* 1.6, where Horace recounts the origins of his friendship with Maecenas. Although the poem is addressed to Maecenas, it is designed to be over-read by Horace's detractors. It is their accusations (whether actual or imagined) of unscrupulous ambition and parasitism that call forth the reiterated proclamations of passivity and independence that contour Horace's apologetic self-portrait.

Horace begins with the issue of social mobility. Despite his own illustrious ancestry, his broadminded patron is not prejudiced against those less nobly born – for example Horace, the so-called "son of a freedman father" (*S.* 1.6.1–6). When Maecenas claims that a man's parentage makes no difference as long as his father is freeborn, he makes the case to himself, and to Horace too (*persuades hoc tibi vere*, 8), by pointing out that men without notable ancestors have been distinguished by high honors, whereas men of the best families have been rejected as worthless (7–14). By attributing this judgment to Maecenas, Horace avoids making the self-promoting argument himself (for example, "History shows many examples of lowborn men who achieved honors – why should not I?") and also lends the argument his patron's prestige.

Instead of drawing the expected self-enhancing analogy, however ("So

---

[13] Especially Sarmentus: *S.* 2.3 (308–11) will belabor the theme of Horace's small size; *S.* 2.6 (36–7) will reveal that he bears the title of "scribe"; and if Messius can accuse Sarmentus of having fled his mistress' service in the hopes of improving his diet, Davus (*S.* 2.7.29–42) will accuse Horace of having entered the service of a master in the hopes of improving his. While Horace's *amici* may recognize the resemblance, these associations are not yet in place for those readers who meet Horace for the first time when they read *S.* 1. On the mutilated figures of *S.* 1.5, see Gowers (1993b) 61, 65 n. 61.

too with me, the worthy 'freedman's son'"), Horace slides from a defense of social mobility to a defense of the status quo. "The censor would remove me from the senate," Horace remarks, "if I were not the son of a freeborn father" (*censorque moveret | Appius, ingenuo si non essem patre natus*, S. 1.6.20–1). And Horace comments, to our surprise, not "what a foolish prejudice!" but "and that would have been what I deserved for not resting easy in my own skin" (*vel merito, quoniam in propria non pelle quiessem*, 22).[14] The implication of Horace's counterfactual "if I were not the son of a freeborn father" (sc. "but I am") is that Horace is indeed entitled to seek senatorial status; as Gordon Williams has recently argued, there are reasons to believe that Horace came of good Italian stock and that he made his own use of the inaccurate and invidious label "freedman's son."[15] Still, the Aesopian moral holds for the free man's as for the freedman's son: only fools think they can disguise their true nature by donning the costume of a mightier creature. The context, let us note, is not social but (in the narrow sense) political ambition. It is easy enough for Horace to rail against the latter, since he has none. (Nor, for that matter, strictly speaking, does Maecenas, who was notorious for never seeking political office – not that he thereby sacrificed political power. The opposition between political and social ambition is less and less clear in a society evolving rapidly toward the courtly.) But this was not the problem the poem set out to address. Horace has brought in this readily disavowable form of ambition to divert attention from the leap in status that he is in the process of taking.

Horace initiates the next stage of his defense by reiterating the defacing taunt leveled against the upstart – the taunt that tethers the over-achiever to his purportedly base birth: "Now I come back to myself, 'son of a freedman father,' whom everybody carps at for being the 'son of a freedman father'" (*nunc ad me redeo libertino patre natum, | quem rodunt omnes libertino patre natum*, S. 1.6.45–6). This "universal" resentment, which currently targets Horace's intimacy with Maecenas, was formerly aroused by his service as military tribune (47–8). But as Horace hastens to insist, these two promotions should not be lumped together (49–52):

> non, ut forsit honorem
> iure mihi invideat quivis, ita te quoque amicum,
> praesertim cautum dignos adsumere, prava
> ambitione procul.

---

[14] On this slide, see Rudd (1966) 38.   [15] Williams (1995).

> Someone might perhaps justly envy me that military distinction,
> but not your friendship, since you are so careful to take up only the
> worthy, far removed from crooked ambition.

Horace here defends himself by shielding his face with Maecenas'. As the
quasi-parenthetical praise of Maecenas' judiciousness reminds us, the
man who accuses Horace of unworthiness thereby also accuses his patron
of moral laxity; and Maecenas may be a more formidable opponent than
Horace's accuser is ready to take on. There may also be an implied contrast between Horace's former and current sponsors. By conceding that
his military tribuneship might be viewed as an undeserved honor
awarded by an undiscriminating general (Brutus, here discreetly
unnamed), Horace succeeds in representing his Republican past as a
deviation, measured against which his present exudes all the more recti-
tude.

What was it that won Horace the favor of Maecenas? Certainly not
mere enviable good luck. As Horace goes on to stress, his social ascent
was no more Fortune's doing than his own: "I couldn't say I was 'lucky'
in this matter or that 'the lottery of chance' won me your friendship; it
was no accident that put you in my way" (*felicem dicere non hoc | me
possim, casu quod te sortitus amicum; | nulla etenim mihi te fors obtulit, S.*
1.6.52–4). No, it was Virgil and Varius who first brought Horace to
Maecenas' notice – perhaps, as scholars tend to assume, by showing him
some of Horace's early poems.[16] This would mean that it was Horace's
promise as a poet that won Maecenas' favor. Still, let us note that Horace
nowhere in his first book of satires indicates that his poetry had anything
to do with his promotion. Even Virgil and Varius are identified here not
as poets but simply as the individuals who "told you what I was," *dixere
quid essem* (55) – no mention, in this highly condensed version of the
story, of Horace's poetry. The first interview between Maecenas and
Horace is likewise tantalizingly uninformative: Horace gulped out a few
unpretentious words, telling Maecenas "what I was" (*quod eram narro,*
60),[17] and Maecenas answered, "true to form – with just a few words" (*ut
tuus est mos, | pauca,* 60–1; the teasing enjambment reveals that Maecenas
is as addicted to brevity as his Callimachean protégé). Nine months later,
Maecenas called Horace back and enrolled him among his *amici*. The

---

[16] See Fraenkel (1957) 16; Shackleton Bailey (1982) 16.

[17] Suetonius reports the existence of a spurious Horatian letter of self-recommendation
(*epistula prosa oratione quasi commendantis se Maecenati*), which perhaps represents someone's
attempt to capitalize on the desire left unsated by this minimalist account.

criterion for Horace's selection? Not literary but moral excellence: "I think it a great thing that I found favor with you – you, who distinguish the honorable man from the villain not by the eminence of his father but by the purity of his life and character" (*qui turpi secernis honestum,* | *non patre praeclaro sed vita et pectore puro,* 63–4). I am not trying to prove that Horace's poetic talents had nothing to do with his social success. What interests me here is rather the care with which Horace obscures this connection. In this regard, the satire nicely complements *Satires* 1.4: as the defense of Horace's poetic conduct in *Satires* 1.4 excludes any reference to Maecenas, so the defense of Horace's social conduct in *Satires* 1.6 excludes any reference to his poetry. The point is that Horace does not represent himself as using his poetry, or even allowing surrogates to use it on his behalf, to improve his social standing.

The father who enabled Horace to recast his satire as the inaudible musings of a moralist in *Satires* 1.4 performs an equally important service in *Satires* 1.6. If this father was not *praeclarus*, that matters little, since he took pains to ensure that his son would be *honestus*, the kind of man with whom Maecenas would be pleased to associate: if Horace's faults are not too serious, if no one can accuse him of "greed or filth or debauchery" (*S.* 1.6.68), if he is "treasured by his friends" (*carus amicis,* 70), it is his father's work (*causa fuit pater his,* 71). Horace does not follow this ringing tribute with a description, as in *Satires* 1.4, of the satiric remarks with which his father labored to make his son vice-free or at least virtue-prone. In *Satires* 1.6, the educational mantle passes from the father to the schoolmaster. Horace's father's contribution was to ensure that his son got a proper schooling, not in backwoods Venusia but at Rome: "he ventured to take me to Rome when I was a boy to learn the arts that any knight or senator would teach his offspring" (*puerum est ausus Romam portare, docendum* | *artis quas doceat quivis eques atque senator* | *semet prognatos,* 76–8). But he also took care to protect his son from urban corruption, accompanying him on his visits to his various teachers and thereby "preserving my chastity, the chief ornament of a good character, not only from actual harm but also from the foul reproach of it" (*pudicum,* | *qui primus virtutis honos, servavit ab omni* | *non solum facto, verum opprobrio quoque turpi,* 82–4). While we may draw the obvious inference – the father was eager to see his son advance in society; the *artes* Horace studied at school in Rome provided essential equipment for this advancement[18]

---

[18] On the ambitions of Horace's father, see Armstrong (1989) 12–13; Anderson (1995) 158–60.

– this is not the story Horace tells. Instead, he hastens to assure us that his father was not concerned that he might be faulted if this well-groomed son went on to make a relatively humble living as an auctioneer or, following in his father's footsteps, as a banker (*praeco . . . aut, ut fuit ipse, coactor*, 86); "nor," Horace adds, "would I have complained" (*neque ego essem questus*, 87). "But as things are," as Horace decorously phrases it, "he deserves all the more praise, and I owe him all the more thanks" (*at hoc nunc | laus illi debetur et a me gratia maior*, 87–8).

The father safeguards the son's reputation in the textual present as well as the biographical past. In the rhetorical economy of this passage, he provides cover for his son, shielding him from the foul reproaches of the invidious. First, if there is presumption at work here, it is not the son's but the father's (*est ausus*, S. 1.6.76). This is, moreover, an admirable audacity, exercised not on his own but on his son's behalf, and for the most moral of reasons: the father takes his son to Rome because he believes in the intrinsic moral value of a good education – a belief confirmed by his son, who attributes to his education the good character he claimed in the immediately preceding lines. And second, Horace here reserves his gratitude for his father, sparing none, contrary to what we might have expected, for the patron to whom his satire is addressed. Instead of deriving his social value from his association with Maecenas ("thank you for making me what I am today"), Horace ascribes his success to Maecenas' recognition of his worth ("I thank my father for making me worthy of your favor"). The underlying message is that Horace both merits Maecenas' friendship and has done nothing specifically to gain it. Rather, it was the very essence of his character (*quid essem*, 55; *quod eram*, 60) – an essence protected and polished by his (bold but nonetheless unambitious) father – that won him his well-deserved place in Maecenas' circle.

It is a remarkable feat that the poem commemorating the beginnings of Horace's friendship with Caesar's right-hand man leaves us feeling that Horace is one of the most unassuming men in the world. The effect is enhanced by the beguiling description of a typical day in the poet's life with which the poem concludes. The description is framed as if it were proof positive of the advantages attending a life free from political ambitions: "In this way my life is more agreeable than yours, eminent senator" (*hoc ego commodius quam tu, praeclare senator, | . . . vivo*, S. 1.6.110–11); "This is the way men live who are free of the wretched weight of ambition" (*haec est | vita solutorum misera ambitione gravique*, 128–9). But the real burden of the intervening description is to distinguish Horace not from the political aspirant but from the parasitic social climber.[19] It is this contrastive argument that controls the details of the description.

Horace's day begins in the late afternoon, with a ramble through the city: "Wherever my fancy directs, I take my solitary stroll" (*quacumque libido est,* | *incedo solus,* S. 1.6.111–12). In stark contrast to the single-minded determination of men bent on "going places" (Horace will encounter one such man in *Satires* 1.9), Horace's leisurely stroll has no master plot. Ruled only by his own desires, the solitary *flâneur* is evidently neither inclined nor compelled to dance attendance on a great friend. Unlike the ambitious, moreover, Horace is not hoping to "see and be seen." His fancy directs him toward unofficial spaces crowded with unimportant people – the marketplace, the "sharper-haunted circus," and the forum after hours (112–14) – where he can melt unrecognized into the throng, playing the part of a nobody among nobodies. Returning home, he enjoys a meal of suitably common ingredients ("leeks, chickpeas, and biscuits," 115) served by three slaves on plain Campanian ware. It is characteristic of Horace's defensive irony that the satire documenting his acceptance as Maecenas' *convictor* represents him as dining not at Maecenas' but at his own table, a table that is, moreover, a very study in sumptuary simplicity.[20] No one can accuse Horace of parasitism on this purportedly typical occasion.

The same autonomous leisure suffuses Horace's sleeping hours. Having eaten, he tells us, he goes to bed in the happy knowledge that he will not have to get up early and head off for a business appointment (*non sollicitus mihi quod cras* | *surgendum sit mane, obeundus Marsya,* 119–20) – or, for that matter, for an early-morning call upon his patron, a signal duty of the dependent *amicus.* No, our independent Horace sleeps in, and then enjoys another bout of recreations: "after this I wander about or, after reading or writing something for my silent pleasure, I get a rub-down with olive oil" (*post hanc vagor, aut ego lecto* | *aut scripto quod me tacitum iuvet unguor olivo,* 122–3). The inconspicuous place accorded to Horace's writing erases any suggestion that the *officia* of Maecenas' friend might include the production of poems; if Horace slips a little writing (what kind remains unspecified) into his day, it is for his own "silent pleasure." After his rub-down, Horace gets some exercise in the Campus Martius,

---

[19] Cf. Armstrong (1986) 279.
[20] Cf. Shackleton Bailey (1982) 20; as remarked by Hudson (1989) 82, this is the only example in Roman satire of a Roman dining alone (slaves don't count as company).

playing at "three-cornered catch" (*lusum . . . trigonem*, 126); takes a bath; eats lunch; and then "relax[es] at home," *domesticus otior* (128) – a resonant conclusion, compactly contrasting Horace's life to that of men pre-occupied by *negotium*, whether in the forum or in another man's house.

Throughout this aimless day, let us note, Horace sees no one, or no one he sees fit to name (while Horace will elsewhere characterize his slaves, they are here no more than functional extensions of his house). His game of "three-cornered catch" obviously requires three players, but if Maecenas was one of the three (at *Satires* 2.6.48–9, Horace represents himself and Maecenas as playing together in the Campus), Horace does not let on. The entire day, as it turns out, is set in the key of the adjective *solus* ("solitary," 112) that accompanied the *flâneur* at the start of the passage. The envy-deflecting paradox of *Satires* 1.6, taken as a whole, derives from the conjunction of this celebration of solitude with the commemoration of Horace's entrance into high society.

In fact the paradox serves Maecenas' interests as well as Horace's. Had Horace concluded with a celebration of his happily befriended present ("How blessed I am in your favor, my generous patron," etc.), his effusions would have risked registering either as interested flattery or as payment for favors received. Direct tributes tend to be self-canceling, and Horace does best when he lets himself be overheard praising his patron. Horace manufactures the ideal conditions for one such "authentic" demonstration of his good faith in *Satires* 1.9. Like *Satires* 1.5, the poem is a narrative without a projected addressee. But this narrative has the character of an anecdote, designed to circulate among (unspecified) friends. And whereas Horace's contrastive strategy remains implicit in satires such as 1.5 and 1.6, Horace here stages a pitched battle between himself and his distorted double.[21]

In the *Epodes*, as we will see, such battles regularly bring the speaker face to face with his opponent. In *Satires* 1.9, the battle is circumscribed: framed in the narrative past tense and in the averted third rather than the confrontational second person. And it is Horace's unnamed interlocutor who initiates contact, not Horace. It is his assault that jolts Horace out of his decorously silent ruminations and into satiric speech: "I was walking, it chanced, on the Sacred Way, as is my habit, thinking over some trifle or other, totally absorbed in it (*Ibam forte via Sacra, sicut meus est mos, | nescio quid meditans nugarum, totus in illis, S.* 1.9.1–2). Perhaps Horace's medita-

---

[21] This is the third in a series of contests. On *S.* 1.7, see Henderson (1994); on the interconnections of *S.* 1.7, 1.8, and 1.9, see Anderson (1982) 79–83.

tions resembled the exemplary moral reflections, material for his satiric jottings, in which he describes himself as typically immersed at the end of *Satires* 1.4 (133–8). At any rate, Horace is soon interrupted by one outstanding example of how not to behave.[22] One consequence of this interruption is that a poem that opens in silence ends in a cacophony of "yelling" (*clamor utrimque, S.* 1.9.77).

The satire dramatizes Horace's efforts to distance himself, both physically and discursively, from his unwelcome companion. All Horace wants, it seems, is to return to his silence. Words – both the words he speaks to his companion and the words of the anecdotal satire that reports their conversation – are in this case a deviation from what Horace represents as the civilized norm.[23] The man who accosts Horace is eager to penetrate the circle of Maecenas – so eager, in fact, that he breaks the most fundamental rules of social intercourse.[24] Ignoring a first obvious cue, Horace's politely distancing farewell (*num quid vis?, S.* 1.9.6), and all his subsequent evasive maneuvers (speeding up, stopping short, etc. – gambits which allow the other to infer that his departure would be welcome), he persists in maintaining what is clearly an undesired contact, "chattering on, praising the neighborhoods, the city" (*cum quidlibet ille | garriret, vicos, urbem laudaret,* 12–13). When Horace responds to this demonstration of what might be termed "positive impoliteness" by maintaining an unresponsive silence, his companion calls his bluff, jocularly describing their real relation and implicitly challenging Horace rudely to confirm its truth: "you're desperately eager to be off, I've seen it all along, but it's no use, I'll cling to you to the bitter end" ("*misere cupis*" *inquit* "*abire, | iamdudum video, sed nil agis; usque tenebo,*" 14–15). Incapacitated by politeness, Horace evades the challenge, responding only with a feeble and ineffectual pretext for a parting of the ways ("I'm off to visit someone who lives far away...."). The satirist is unequal to the contest because he cannot find it in himself to be anything but civil.

There is one point, however, at which the outsider succeeds in cracking Horace's polite reserve. "How do you stand with Maecenas?" (*Maecenas quomodo tecum? S.* 1.9.43), he asks (it is significantly he and not

---

[22] The ruminations of *S.* 1.4 ("that way I'll be welcome when I run across my friends," *sic dulcis amicis | occurram,* 135–6, etc.) have a particular relevance to the "run-in" (*accurrit, S.* 1.9.3) of *S.* 1.9. We may see the kinship of Horace and his interlocutor; surely, as argued by Zetzel (1980) 71–2, Horace saw it too. One cannot draw a distinction without simultaneously drawing a likeness.

[23] On the passage in *S.* 1.9 from "civic frankness" to civility, see Henderson (1994) 152–3.

[24] For a detailed account of the (im)politeness strategies of this satire, see Henderson (1993).

Horace who introduces this name into conversation). Horace replies by answering what he takes to be the "real" question ("how do you think I would fare with Maecenas?"): "He's a man of limited acquaintance and of very sound mind" (*paucorum hominum et mentis bene sanae*, 44). The politely rude gist is that Maecenas will not be so mad as to admit this aspirant to friendship.[25] Horace's companion, who is not after all a fool, deflects the insult back onto his interlocutor in the form of an unsavory compliment. If Maecenas is so hard to get at, Horace must have been both lucky and clever to succeed: "No man has made more adept use of his opportunities [sc. than you have]" (*nemo dexterius fortuna est usus*, 45). Horace's companion is only following what he takes to be Horace's example, making the most of what his own good fortune has put in his way in the shape of Horace himself. Perhaps Horace can be prevailed upon to manage an introduction: "you'd have a strong ally to second your interests, if you'd just open the door for your friend here; I'll be damned if you wouldn't push all the others aside" (*haberes | magnum adiutorem, posset qui ferre secundas, | hunc hominem velles si tradere: dispeream ni | summosses omnis*, 45–8). He assumes, "naturally" (it is natural to him), that Maecenas' friends are images of himself – men frantically jostling and angling for their personal advantage.

Unlike the false friend of *Satires* 1.4, Horace immediately rushes to the defense of his friends and thereby also of himself. The spontaneity of this defense, which is represented as an outburst forced out of an otherwise reticent poet by his companion's intolerably offensive insinuations, is underwritten by the dislocated word order characteristic of authentic excitement (*S.* 1.9.48–52):

> non isto vivimus illic
> quo tu rere modo; domus hac nec purior ulla est
> nec magis his aliena malis; nil mi officit, inquam,
> ditior hic aut est quia doctior; est locus uni
> cuique suus.

Our way of life there isn't at all the way you think; no house is more free of those faults; it doesn't bother me, I tell you, if another man is richer or more cultivated than I am; each of us has his own place.

This staged rupture of discursive norms is rounded out by Horace's authoritatively and ungraciously curt reply to his interlocutor's incredul-

---

25 Similarly van Rooy (1972) 46. At *S.* 1.9.44 and 50, my punctuation follows that of Klingner (1959).

ity: " 'What an amazing story, I can hardly believe it.' 'But that's how it is' " (*"magnum narras, vix credibile." "atqui | sic habet,"* 52–3). A moment later, Horace regains his self-control, reverting to the distancing, ironic courtesy that his anger momentarily broke through. Horace's companion and many of Horace's readers may not be convinced by Horace's protestations, however rhetorically marked as "heartfelt" they may be. But what matters here is less the truth-value than the pragmatic value of Horace's idealizing description of Maecenas' circle. The encounter gives Horace a chance to act the part of a faithful friend – a man who knows both how to keep his mouth shut and when to open it.

In the tenth and final satire of the collection, the charges against Horace are resituated within the sphere of aesthetics. The poem is framed as a response to the anger aroused by the criticisms Horace leveled against Lucilius in *Satires* 1.4. Horace stands accused of literary insubordination – he has failed to show the proper deference to the man he identifies as the inventor of the satiric genre. Horace does not deny that he has publicly faulted Lucilius: "Sure, I said that Lucilius' verse stumbled over its own misfashioned feet" (*Nempe incomposito dixi pede currere versus | Lucili, S.* 1.10.1–2). Indeed, far from retracting his criticisms, Horace spends much of the satire fleshing them out. In *Satires* 1.4, Horace represented his aesthetics through the hostile lens of his detractors. Here he begins to spell out what he means by "writing properly" (*scribendi recte, S.* 1.4.13). One result is that this satire repeatedly exposes its predecessors' stratagems. Where the conclusions of *Satires* 1.4 and 1.6 relegated Horace's writing life to the slenderest interstices of his day, *Satires* 1.10 makes it clear – to anyone foolish enough to have been taken in by the pose of dilettantism – that Horace is a professional who takes his art seriously. And when Horace announces that the satirist needs to have at his disposal a variety of conversational styles, including that of the "urbane man who spares his strength and intentionally pulls his punches" (*urbani, parcentis viribus atque | extenuantis eas consulto, S.* 1.10.13–14), he invites us to appreciate the calculated self-depreciations of his own satires. It is appropriate that this *ars saturica* comes at the end of the collection. It is as if the magician had decided, at the conclusion of his performance, to display before the audience the devices that enabled his act.

Horace thus enters *Satires* 1.10 not as a moralist, not as the friend of Maecenas, but as an author and an authority, a self-assured master of the art of satire, with a reading public familiar with his work. Near the middle of the poem, Horace establishes what is in effect a contemporary canon and claims a place for himself within it. Fundanius excels in comedy, Pollio in tragedy, Varius in epic, Virgil in pastoral; as for Horace, "this was the kind of poetry, attempted in vain by Varro of Atax and certain others, that I could write better, though not as well as its inventor" (*hoc erat, experto frustra Varrone Atacino* | *atque quibusdam aliis, melius quod scribere possem,* | *inventore minor, S.* 1.10.46–8). Such a claim, however deferentially tempered, is bound to arouse resistance. In fact the bow to Lucilius provokes Horace's imagined interlocutor to point out what he views as an inconsistency: "But [you point out that] I said before that he was a muddy river, often carrying more mud than water" (*at dixi fluere hunc lutulentum, saepe ferentem* | *plura quidem tollenda relinquendis,* 50–1). Horace's response is that his respect for Lucilius may be heartfelt (and there is no reason to believe that he did not admire Lucilius for the qualities he names) without being all-consuming.[26] Contemporary authors, lacking the authorizing patina of time and the accumulated weight of a tradition of critical approval, are always at a disadvantage when it comes to asserting their literary authority. The *mos maiorum* rules literary as well as social values. Although Horace never makes the claim directly, what justifies his criticisms of Lucilius is his status as Lucilius' best and strongest descendant.

The new standards call for selectivity and refinement, and Horace accordingly stresses the labor not only of writing but of erasing. The emphasis is on exclusion – of unnecessary words that clutter up the meaning, and of imported words that contaminate the purity of the Latin. Ridiculing those who count Lucilius' use of Greek words a virtue, Horace rhetorically asks if they would likewise prefer their lawyers to "mingle imported words with their inherited vocabulary, after the fashion of a bilingual Canusian" (*patriis intermiscere petita* | *verba foris malis, Canusini more bilinguis,* 29–30). The erasure of the distinction between legal and poetic discourse suggests that the poet – so often, throughout Roman history, not a native of Rome – is henceforth to be judged by the same criteria as the orator whose place is at the very center of Roman political activity. Hence the admixture of Grecisms, often perceived as a mark of refinement and cultivation, is here categorized as déclassé, a betrayal of provincialism, characteristic of the "bilingual Canusian," the native of Horace's own Apulia who is not yet fully and thoroughly Roman.

---

[26] Horace's critique of Lucilius doubtless emboldened Ben Jonson to deliver his famous censure of an already-deified Shakespeare: "Would he had blotted a thousand [lines]."

The social implications of the key Horatian value of *brevitas* are no less striking. In *Satires* 1.10, Horace finally unites his own penchant for "few words" with his patron's preference for "few men" to produce a composite model of literary and social distinction. Horace explicitly connects the refined style with an elite audience near the end of the satire, where he counsels the aspiring poet to edit both his poetry and his readership: "use your eraser often if you hope to write poems worth rereading, and don't work for the crowd's applause; be content with a few readers" (*saepe stilum vertas, iterum quae digna legi sint | scripturus, neque te ut miretur turba labores, | contentus paucis lectoribus, S.* 1.10.72–4). Horace proceeds to fill out the end of the satire with the names of the "few readers" he himself aims to please, a list that includes some of the most eminent men of his day. What is conveyed is not so much that Horace is selective as that Horace has been selected, having achieved a success beyond the wildest dreams of those poets who are forced to scrape together an audience as best they can – in the baths, in the forum, etc. To be "content with a few readers" such as Maecenas, Pollio, and Messalla, is not at all the same as being "content with little" or "content with one's humble ancestry." Horace's boast is but thinly veiled by the characteristic language of satiric modesty.

But while Horace heaps derision on the unworthy readers who presume to criticize him – "as if I could be made miserable by the nasty things Demetrius says behind my back, or by the carpings of that fool Fannius, Tigellius' best friend!" (*men . . . cruciet quod | vellicet absentem Demetrius, aut quod ineptus | Fannius Hermogenis laedat conviva Tigelli? S.* 1.10.78–80) – he defers to the judgment of his distinguished friends. Horace not only claims the authority to criticize Lucilius, he recognizes the authority of men such as Virgil, Varius, and Maecenas to criticize him in turn: "It's these men I'd like my poems to please, such as they are; I'll be grieved if they enjoy them less than I hope" (*quibus haec, sint qualiacumque, | arridere velim, doliturus si placeant spe | deterius nostra*, 88–90). If the announced subject of *Satires* 1.10 is not social but literary standards, there is, as it turns out, no real difference between the two. Horace's refined poetry wins favor on behalf of its polished producer.

The self-incriminating satirist of Satires 2

Horace enters *Satires* 2 with the face he has acquired in *Satires* 1. His new status is on display in the first poem of the collection, where he claims the friendship not only of Maecenas but of Caesar himself, whose name, as if making up for its absence from *Satires* 1, appears three times within the poem's eighty-six lines. And he appears in *Satires* 2.6 as the happy pro-prietor not only of a town house but of a Sabine "farm," more properly termed (as contemporaries would have surmised) a villa.[27] For the reader who knows Horace only from his literary corpus (a reader Horace always has in view), the enhancement of Horace's social status is likely to be understood as a direct effect of the literary labors of *Satires* 1. The depen-dence of social on literary success, a dependence Horace labored to deny in poems such as *Satires* 1.4 and 1.6, is both aggressively advertised and defensively ruptured in Horace's second and final collection of satires.

Face-saving in *Satires* 2.1 and 2.6

At the outset of the collection, Horace represents his satire as bringing him nothing but grief. Attacked on one side by those who think his satire too forceful and on the other by those who think it flabby, Horace turns to his jurist-friend Trebatius for some mock-legal advice.[28] After failing to convince Horace to give up writing altogether, Trebatius counsels him to trade in his satire for a poetry celebrating "the deeds of uncon-quered Caesar" – a literary "labor" that will earn its author "great rewards" (*aude | Caesaris invicti res dicere, multa laborum | praemia laturus, S.* 2.1.10–12). When Horace claims to be unequal to this epic task, Trebatius recommends a laudatory portrait highlighting the leader's justice and bravery, on the model of Lucilius' praise of Scipio (*attamen et iustum poteras et scribere fortem, | Scipiadam ut sapiens Lucilius,* 16–17). Horace postpones this undertaking while satirizing his own poetic ambi-tion in language that recalls the social climber of *Satires* 1.9: "I won't fail myself, when circumstances are in my favor" (*haud mihi deero | cum res ipsa feret,* 17; cf. *haud mihi deero, S.* 1.9.56). Timing is crucial, for Caesar's ear is not always "pricked up" (*attentam,* 19) to receive verse, and botched intrusions earn his displeasure – or rather, as Horace puts it, drawing out the metaphor of the "pricked-up ear," "if you mishandle him, he kicks out, guarding himself on all sides" (*cui male si palpere recalcitrat undique tutus,* 20). Horace here succeeds in being at once deferential (by advertis-ing the care with which he approaches the great Caesar) and familiar (by likening the great Caesar to an irascible quadruped). Insofar as Caesar is proposed as one privileged overreader of this satire, the irreverent por-trait also advertises Horace's confidence in Caesar's good will (he will

---

[27] As Horace elsewhere makes clear; on the misrepresentation, see Leach (1993) 275–6; Frischer (1995).   [28] See further Muecke (1995).

respond to the image, we are to presume, not with an angry kick but with an amused smile). The reciprocally complimentary implication is that Horace is not a flatterer and that Caesar is above needing to have his ego stroked. But the surface message of this opening exchange is that Horace's chosen branch of poetry has brought and continues to bring no advantages.

If Horace continues in this unprofitable vein, it is, he claims, because he cannot help himself. Every man has his characteristic enthusiasm, and Horace's happens to be "enclosing words in metrical feet, in the manner of Lucilius" (*me pedibus delectat claudere verba* | *Lucili ritu*, S. 2.1.28–9). In *Satires* 1.10, Horace reproached Lucilius for being "content merely to fit something into six feet" (*si quis pedibus quid claudere senis*, | *hoc tantum contentus*, S. 1.10.59–60); here, he celebrates his pleasure in the same minimal accomplishment. The belittling of poetic labor recalls the close of *Satires* 1.4 and 1.6, where Horace posed as a poetic dabbler, with the difference that Horace now represents himself not as a dabbler but as a confirmed and indeed incorrigible versifier. Preoccupied as he is with the pleasures of poetic composition, Horace can hardly be accused of laboring to cultivate the friendship of important men.

Poetry both absorbs and represents the writer's life. The "manner of Lucilius," as Horace now depicts it, is essentially confessional. Lucilius "used to entrust his secrets to his books as if to trustworthy comrades, turning to them and nowhere else in bad times and good" (*ille velut fidis arcana sodalibus olim* | *credebat libris, neque si male cesserat usquam* | *decurrens alio, neque si bene*, S. 2.1.30–2). The paradox, one that is central to autobiographical poetry, including Horace's, is that the secrets Lucilius buried in his purportedly discreet books end up published to the world: "and so it is that the old man's entire life is open to view, as if depicted on a votive tablet" (*quo fit ut omnis* | *votiva pateat veluti descripta tabella* | *vita senis*, 32–4). This dialectic will recur at the end of *Epistles* 1, where a homebred book metamorphoses into a piece of public property.[29] What interests me here, however, is that the books that lend Lucilius a sympathetic and ostensibly leakproof ear are acting like good dependent *amici*, and that the friend of the great Scipio is thus figuratively situated at the center of his own circle of devoted "friends." Horace's writing likewise affords its author a measure of independence: "whether I'm rich or poor, at Rome or (if chance so decrees) in exile – whatever the color of my life, I will

---

[29] See further below, 174–6.

write" (*dives, inops, Romae seu fors ita iusserit exsul,* | *quisquis erit vitae scribam color,* 59–60). "Rich or poor, at Rome or in exile" could be para-phrased "whether in Caesar's favor or out of it." Forty years later, the exiled Ovid, writing determinedly on in Tomis, would live out the implied narrative of these lines – lines which must have struck Ovid with a painfully ironic force, issuing as they do from a poet destined so richly to enjoy Augustus' favor. But (as Ovid would probably have acknowl-edged) the fact that Horace's determination was never put to the proof does not in and of itself negate the value of his declaration of authorial independence.

What kind of writing does Horace's *scribam* imply? The immediate context of this declaration, which is separated from the passage about Lucilius' faithful books by about twenty lines, is a defense of satire's aggressive character. Every creature fights, Horace points out, with the weapons nature has supplied – the wolf with its teeth, the bull with its horns, Scaeva with poison. We would expect Horace to complete the analogy by claiming that his "natural" weapon is his satiric pen.[30] Instead, with his "whatever the color of my life, I will write," Horace reverts to and intensifies his earlier claim of poetic enthusiasm (*me pedibus delectat claudere verba,* S. 2.1.28). It is as if the intervening discussion of satiric belligerence were a screen for the more serious charge of literary toady-ism, a charge Horace labors to refute not only by refusing twice over to compose poetry in praise of Caesar but also by representing his poetry as a form of natural and irrepressible self-expression. The point is that it is not external but internal compulsion that drives Horace to write. Horace's poetry may please his friends, but he does not write to that end. He writes because he is a writer. Although the context is humorously self-deflating, this application of the argument from nature is not.

Lucilius is a model, however, not only of aesthetic independence but of social dependence. When Trebatius worries that Horace's satirical thrusts will annoy his important friends, Horace counters with the example of his great predecessor, whose vigorous satire earned not the wrath but the favor of "brave Scipio and wise Laelius" (*virtus Scipiadae et mitis sapientia Laeli,* S. 2.1.72; the laudatory hexameter may derive from the Lucilian portrait of Scipio to which Trebatius earlier alluded), who were wont to spend their moments of private leisure "relaxing and fooling around in his company while their greens were cooking" (*nugari*

[30] So Rudd (1966) 127.

cum illo et discincti ludere donec | decoqueretur holus, 73–4). Horace can boast the same intimacy with the great men of his day (74–8):

> quidquid sum ego, quamvis
> infra Lucili censum ingeniumque, tamen me
> cum magnis vixisse invita fatebitur usque
> invidia, et fragili quaerens illidere dentem
> offendet solido.

Whatever I am, however inferior to Lucilius in wealth and talent, still envy will have to confess that I've lived in the company of great men; when she tries to sink a tooth into me, she'll encounter something she can't crunch up.

The Lucilian parallel is as close as Horace comes within the satires to representing himself at dinner with his own "brave Scipio and wise Laelius," Caesar and Maecenas. The parallel may be skewed – Horace transforms himself, in the space of these lines, from a dinner-companion (*cum . . . vixisse* rendering *conviva*) into a dish, an indigestible morsel for gnawing envy – but it enables us nonetheless to glimpse the other dinner scene, the one that stimulates envy's appetite.

In *Satires* 1.10, Horace would have balanced his purported deficiencies in "wealth and talent" with the counterweight of superior art. In *Satires* 2.1, as we have seen, Horace prefers to strike a pose of Lucilian artlessness, resting his defense instead on the importance of his social connections. This offensive defense culminates in the satire's closing lines, as Trebatius (mock-) solemnly reminds Horace of the archaic law against casting *mala carmina* ("evil spells" but also "bad poems," *S.* 2.1.82), and Horace replies: "So be it; but what if someone composes *good* poems, earning Caesar's favorable judgment?" (*esto, si quis mala; sed bona si quis | iudice condiderit laudatus Caesare?* 83–4). Let us note that Horace invokes Caesar not as the foremost literary critic but as the most powerful man of his day; his literary "verdict" counts because his political preeminence is, by this time, essentially incontestable. But even this gesture of self-promotion by association is qualified by a second condition which focuses on the satirist's moral worth: "what if it's a case of someone who is himself blameless barking at a man who deserves reproach?" (*si quis | opprobriis dignum latraverit, integer ipse?* 84–5). Trebatius furnishes the answer, which punctuates the poem: "The case will dissolve in laughter, you'll be acquitted and dismissed" (*solventur risu tabulae, tu missus abibis,* 86). Caesar's favorable verdict does not so much establish (by imperial *fiat*, as it were) as recognize the aesthetic and moral excellence of Horace's *bona carmina*. Still, the balance between innate and socially ascribed value is difficult to sustain.

Satires 2.6 offers a similar blend of self-assertion and self-defense. Designed as a counterpart to *Satires* 1.6, the poem invites us to measure how far Horace has traveled since the momentous meeting with Maecenas described in the earlier satire.[31] Its occasion is Horace's delight in his newly acquired Sabine "farm," a rustic refuge that enables him to recapture the leisure he once enjoyed within the city of Rome. Once, but no more: unlike the author of *Satires* 1.6, the author of *Satires* 2.6 is a busy man and, in a small way, a public figure. The seven years that have elapsed since his admission into Maecenas' circle (Horace himself supplies the chronology at lines 40–2) have transformed Horace from a relative nobody into something of a somebody.

The transformation is registered in the account of a typical day at Rome that Horace delivers from the safe heights (social as well as geographical) of his "mountain citadel" (cf. *in montis et in arcem*, *S.* 2.6.16). In marked contrast to the day celebrated in *Satires* 1.6, Horace's new routine features not an aimless ramble but a frantic rush from one obligation to another. His headlong speed elicits a complaint from one irritated pedestrian (who introduces into the poem the name Horace has hitherto withheld): "Would you shove everything out of your way when you're racing to Maecenas' side, your mind only on him?" (*tu pulses omne quod obstat | ad Maecenatem memori si mente recurras? S.* 2.6.30–1). Horace is secretly delighted, he confesses, at being thus recognized and recognizable (*hoc iuvat et melli est, non mentiar*, 32); Maecenas too might take pleasure in this sketch of his friend's single-minded devotion. As he draws near his goal, (Maecenas' house on) the Esquiline (Horace discreetly elides the particular destination), he is pounced on by people who want something of him. Most insistent is the man who wants him to make sure that Maecenas puts his seal on some documents. If Horace replies "I'll try," the man insists "It's within your power, if you're willing to do it" (*"experiar": "si vis, potes,"* 39). Others, on the assumption that his proximity to the powers-that-be gives him access to privileged information (*nam te | scire, deos quoniam propius contingis, oportet*, 51–2), crowd around him in search of the latest news, greeting his protestations of ignorance with irritated incredulity. Horace may insist that the widespread belief in his power and his knowledge is ill-founded, but the overestimation is

---

[31] For the comparison, cf. Lejay (1911) 513; Muecke (1993) 194.

flattering nonetheless.[32] And of course Horace's published insistence that he is "out of the loop" itself goes to show that he deserves the trust everyone believes him to enjoy; his silence, here as in *Satires* 1.5, is an index not of his ignorance but of his discretion.[33] Horace thus not only displays but bolsters the world's flattering estimate of his social value at the very moment that he discounts it.

But this value is indexed against Maecenas'. Horace's acknowledged pleasure in being recognized not in his own right but as the friend of Maecenas itself serves as a deferential compliment to his patron. The compliment is enhanced by the echo of *Satires* 1.9. There, the man who latched on to Horace depicted Maecenas' household as a jostle of competitors and offered to help Horace "move all the others aside" (*summosses omnis*, *S.* 1.9.48); here, Horace depicts himself doing just that, elbowing everyone out of his path (cf. *pulses omne quod obstat*, *S.* 2.6.30) in his rush to get where he's going – and where he's going is where the social climber of *Satires* 1.9 wanted to be going, up the mountain "to Maecenas" (*ad Maecenatem*, 31). The key difference is that Horace is not running but "running back," duly returning (*recurras*, 31), to Maecenas' side; this is a portrait not of ambition but of energetic devotion, and as such highly flattering to Maecenas. Moreover, while Horace represents himself as valuing Maecenas' friendship, he does not suggest that the sentiment is reciprocated. Far from advertising how far in he is with the great Maecenas, Horace labors to depict himself as a mere minor sidekick, a companion with whom Maecenas discusses only such safely trivial subjects as sports and the weather (44–5) – a self-belittling self-characterization that may not be (and is not meant to be) entirely convincing, but does constitute a public act of homage. And although the once carefree *flâneur* is now beset by cares, he is at pains not to attribute his travails directly to Maecenas. It is others, not Maecenas, who make demands of him. It is others who plague Maecenas' friend with business; Maecenas only requires his participation in what Horace depicts as play, or at least not as work – his company on a journey, at the theater, at play on the Campus Martius (*quem tollere raeda | vellet iter faciens*, 42–3; *ludos spectaverat una, | luserat in campo*, 48–9). Horace races to join Maecenas; it is others, with their pestering demands, that he longs to escape.

It might seem as if the two central "facts" of this satire – Horace's

---

[32] Horace effects a similar transfer of discursive responsibility in *S.* 1.6, where, as remarked by Gold (1987) 117, it is Horace's detractors who identify him as the *convictor* of Maecenas.

[33] See Griffin (1984) 198–9.

recently acquired property and his confirmed and publicy recognized intimacy with Maecenas – were closely, indeed inextricably connected. But if Horace treats these two facts within a single poem, it is chiefly in order to sever their connection, thereby anticipating and disarming the slanders of the invidious, who will be likely to view Horace's villa as the long-awaited pay-off for his seven years of service. The flip side of Horace's self-belittling representation of his relations with Maecenas, accordingly, is his self-assertive disavowal of indebtedness. While the first epode makes it sufficiently clear that Horace owes his Sabine property to Maecenas' generosity,[34] *Satires* 2.6 attributes Horace's good fortune not to his patron but to "the gods" (*di*, *S.* 2.6.4), in particular Mercury (a deflection of gratitude reminiscent of *Satires* 1.6, where Horace gave thanks not to his patron but to his father). The pressure of Horace's unexpressed gratitude to Maecenas may leave its mark on his invocation of Mercury as *Maia nate* ("Maia's son," 5), a formula that faintly echoes the patronal name it displaces. But the displacement is sufficient to stave off the self-incriminating "thank you" (portraying Horace as a poet for hire) that we might have expected Horace to produce. Moreover, had Horace thanked Maecenas directly, the poem might read as an enforced or ungraciously punctual pay-off of Maecenas' generous gift.[35] As in *Satires* 1.6, the obliquity of Horace's "thank you" keeps the satire's value from being exhausted in the act of exchange.

The same displacement helps shape the second half of the poem. Although a portion of the satire is located on the Esquiline, at Maecenas' very door, Horace never crosses the threshold. Instead, at the satire's midpoint, he turns away from Maecenas and back toward the country, where this satire began: "Amid such distractions I wretchedly waste my day, often praying 'countryside, when will I see you again?'" (*perditur haec inter misero lux non sine votis:* | *o rus, quando ego te aspiciam? S.* 2.6.59–60; cf. "This was what I prayed for," *hoc erat in votis*, 1). After summarizing the pleasures of country leisure (61–2), Horace spends the rest of his satire describing a dinner party on his Sabine farm. One effect of the resultant asymmetry – instead of depicting two contrasting days, the two panels of this satire divide a single day between them, pairing a Roman day with a Sabine evening – is to draw attention to the elided conclusion of Horace's city day. As in *Satires* 1.6, so in *Satires* 2.6 Horace's day notably fails to culminate in a dinner party at the luxurious table of his generous patron.

---

[34] See *I.* 1.23–34.
[35] Cf. Kiessling and Heinze (1957) 297–8.

The displacement is a gesture not only of discretion (Horace will never publish the private interactions of Maecenas' circle) but also of authority, enabling Horace to represent himself as the master of his own *domus*. In Satires 1.6, Horace depicted himself dining alone at home in Rome; in Satires 2.6, he dines in company on his Sabine farm (*S.* 2.6.65–9):

> o noctes cenaeque deum! quibus ipse meique
> ante Larem proprium vescor vernasque procaces
> pasco libatis dapibus. prout cuique libido est
> siccat inaequalis calices conviva, solutus
> legibus insanis . . .

> O evenings and dinners of the gods, in which I dine with my own people before my own hearth, feeding my impudent slaves with the dishes we've sampled. Each according to his desire, the guest drains unequal cups, free from crazy rules . . .

The emphasis, in this dinner party of "the gods" (emphatically not "the gods" for news of whom Horace was pestered earlier in the poem),[36] is all on Horace's ownership: Horace's hearth, Horace's friends, Horace's slaves. In this house at least, Horace is not a parasite but a host, who entertains his own circle and sustains his own dependent house-slaves. Within Horace's circle, moreover, each guest is free to indulge his preferences, just as Horace himself in Satires 1.6 is free to wander wherever he likes (*quacumque libido est*, *S.* 1.6.111); "inequality," with its troublesome implications of rivalry, is displaced from the guests to their cups. Taken as a whole, the scene offers an antidote to the poisonous image the invidious may harbor of competitive scurrility at Maecenas' urban table.

The conversation at Horace's rustic symposium also bears obliquely and defensively on his relationship with Maecenas. Instead of gossiping about other people's villas, Horace's guests discuss timeless ethical questions, such as "whether wealth or virtue makes men happy, and what draws us into friendships, utility or moral rectitude" (*utrumne | divitiis homines an sint virtute beati, | quidve ad amicitias, usus rectumne, trahat nos, S.* 2.6.73–5). The proper answer to these semi-rhetorical questions is the second member of each pair – what makes a man truly happy is not immorally purchased wealth but virtuous poverty – and the implication, here as elsewhere, is that Horace seeks no material advantages from his connection with his great friend. This answer is amplified in the tale of

---

[36] See Bond (1985) 82.

49

the country mouse and the city mouse with which one of Horace's guests rebukes another guest who "ignorantly praises Arellius' care-laden wealth" (*laudat Arelli* | *sollicitas ignarus opes*, 79). The tale is familiar: unimpressed by the rustic hospitality of the country mouse, the city mouse prevails upon his friend to come sample the delights of urban luxury; back in the luxurious town house he calls home, the city mouse regales his guest with the leavings of the master's feast; all goes well until the master returns home with a pack of barking dogs, who drive the terrified mice from the table. Heading home, the country mouse has the last word, which is also the last word of the satire: "my woods and my hollow, safe from ambush, will console me with a bit of vetch" (*me silva cavusque* | *tutus ab insidiis tenui solabitur ervo*, 116–17).

Like the asymmetry in the satire's two panels, the imbalance in its dinner parties – two rustic (Horace's and the country mouse's) vs. one urban (the city mouse's) – serves to underscore the absence of a city dinner in the first half of the poem. Insofar as the city mouse's dinner does double duty for the dinner at Maecenas' house that Horace chooses not to represent, the country mouse's parting words would seem to express Horace's preference for his own over Maecenas' hospitality.[37] And yet, as indicated by the pendulum-swing of the next satire, which presents Horace in his morally bankrupt "city mouse" aspect (racing off to the very dinner *chez* Maecenas that *Satires* 2.6 so scrupulously evaded), the "country mouse" costume does not quite suit the poet of the Sabine farm.[38] The multiple oppositions that frame and structure the tale of the two mice – between wealth and poverty, vice and virtue, danger and safety, servile dependence and manly (mousely) independence, city and country – line up with a certain conventional neatness in parallel columns. But in Horace's case, the columns are not parallel but intertwined, and the accounting cannot be so simple. For Horace's country retreat is not just an alternative to but a gift from the city, a crumb, as it were, from the master's table. Unlike the country mouse, that is, Horace has chosen the path not of virtuous poverty but of (to give it its best construction) virtuous wealth – his relation with Maecenas involves *usus* as well as *rectum*. If Horace does his best to erase the first of these terms,

---

[37] The seeming ungraciousness is mitigated by the fact that it is not the master of the house (who never puts in an appearance) but his dogs – not the host but his invidiously barking attendants – that drive the country mouse out of the city.

[38] See Rudd (1966) 252; Leach (1993) 285–7 and Frischer (1995) 224–6 suggest that the inconsistent Horace is himself the target of Cervius' satiric tale.

one reason is that it is exceedingly difficult to break the conventional linkage of virtue with poverty and wealth with immorality. Within *Satires* 2.6, the only way Horace can defend himself from charges of unmanly subservience is to sever the connection between his services (whether poetic or strictly practical) and his "reward" (his Sabine villa). This is why, although the satire bounces back and forth between country and city, Horace takes care to situate the act of writing in the country: "And so, when I have removed myself out of the city and into my mountain citadel, what should I begin by celebrating in the satires of my prosaic Muse?" (*ergo ubi me in montis et in arcem ex urbe removi,* | *quid prius illustrem satiris musaque pedestri? S.* 2.6.16–17). Within this poem, satire is implicitly defined as a country activity, independent of city obligations. If Horace's farm comes with strings attached, his satires do not.

Mending misfortune with art: the satirists of *Satires* 2

Horace's withdrawal from Rome to the country is complemented by his retreat in *Satires* 2 from the very role of "satirist," as that role is constituted in poems such as *Satires* 1.1, 2, and 3. Indeed, if Horace shares the stage with Trebatius in the dialogue of *Satires* 2.1 and entrusts the concluding fable of *Satires* 2.6 to one of his dinner guests, in the remaining satires of Book 2 he effectively yields the stage, speaking relatively few words in propria persona and ascribing the bulk of his satire to someone else.[39]

We can gain insight into the significance of this discursive shift, which is one of the distinctive features of Horace's second satiric collection, by considering the characters who have taken Horace's place. In some cases, this speaker is little more than a proper name, a peg on which to hang a satiric discourse. All we know about Catius, the man who recites the culinary precepts that fill up *Satires* 2.4, is that Horace claims him as a friend (*per amicitiam, S.* 2.4.88); all we know about the garrulous Cervius of *Satires* 2.6 is that he is Horace's neighbor (*vicinus, S.* 2.6.77). About the book's three chief philosophizers – Ofellus, Damasippus, and Davus – we are more fully informed. And these three satirists, it emerges, have something in common. Ofellus, the rustic philosopher of *Satires* 2.2, has lost his farm to the resettlement program of the triumvirs, a fact that Horace reveals, as if incidentally, near the end of the poem: "You can still see him, with his livestock and his children, working undaunted as a tenant on the

---

[39] On the effects of Horace's abdication, see Labate (1981) 26.

little farm that was taken over by the surveyors" (*videas metato in agello* | *cum pecore et gnatis fortem mercede colonum, S.* 2.2.114–15).[40] Damasippus, the man who delivers the lengthy diatribe of *Satires* 2.3, is a dealer in antiques and expensive real estate[41] whose business has gone bust (*postquam omnis res mea Ianum* | *ad medium fracta est, S.* 2.3.18–19; cf. *male re gesta*, 37). And Davus, the featured speaker of *Satires* 2.7, identifies himself at the outset as one of Horace's slaves (*servus, S.* 2.7.1) – as a man, that is, deprived not of his property but of his *libertas.* The dispossessed farmer, the bankrupt businessman, the slave: all have suffered (or inherited) a reversal of fortune, a diminution of status.

And this is perhaps why they turn to satire – why they need satire. It is no accident that two of these satires take place during the Saturnalia, a festival which temporarily annuls status differences, granting the slave a "December license" (*libertate Decembri, S.* 2.7.4) that frees his tongue if not his person.[42] Like the Saturnalia, satire levels society by bringing the master down. For Ofellus, this leveling philosophy is a tonic that both fortifies and consoles. As he reminds his sons – sons who will not inherit their family farm – a man who lives modestly and moderately has little to lose: "Let Fortune rage and stir up new storms; how much will she take from our simple pleasures?" (*saeviat atque novos moveat Fortuna tumultus,* | *quantum hinc imminuet? S.* 2.2.126–7). They are not the first or the last to suffer dispossession, he adds; the new owner will be driven out in his turn, if not by another man then in the end by death, the ultimate leveler (129–32). Philosophy is also a comfort to Damasippus, who claims to have been rescued from the very brink of suicide by the Stoic philosopher Stertinius, who consoled him (*solatus, S.* 2.3.35) by proving that all men, with the exception of the Stoic sage, are equally insane. This lecture, which Damasippus proceeds to recite for Horace's benefit, not only restored the bankrupt businessman's self-respect, it also equipped him with a means (however ineffectual) of self-defense, "so that from now on if I'm abused I can take my revenge – whoever says I'm crazy will hear the same from me" (*posthac ne compellarer inultus.* | *dixerit insanum qui me totidem audiet*, 297–8). The equalizing thrust of satire is clearest in the case of Davus, who uses his moment of Saturnalian license to question

---

[40] This translation borrows from Rudd (1979) 93.

[41] On Damasippus, see Cic. *Fam.* 7.23.2; *Att.* 12.29.2, 12.33.1.

[42] It is significant that the slave awaits Horace's express granting of this license before launching into his tirade. On the practical limits of Saturnalian license, see D'Arms (1991) 176; on Horace's Saturnalian satire, see Freudenburg (1993) 211–23.

Horace's right to the title of "master" (*tune mihi dominus? S.* 2.7.75). Subject to "the biddings of circumstance and other men's orders" (*rerum imperiis hominumque,* 75), enslaved by "wretched fear" (*misera formidine,* 77), Horace is in effect, Davus claims, the "fellow slave" of his slave (*conservus,* 80) – which makes Davus the fellow master of his master. The fact that it is their own misfortune that opens the eyes of these philosophers to the equalizing truths they propound does not deprive their discourse of authority, but it does open it to the accusation of impurity. Misery – cynics might say – loves company. By situating his satirists as he does, Horace exposes satire for what it "really" is: not a disinterested revelation of timeless philosophical truths, but a consolation prize awarded to life's losers. Satiric leveling is how the satirist hopes to get even.

But stoic endurance, fortified by stoical reflections, is not the only way of responding to fortune's blows. The man laid low by fortune can also use his wits to better his lot. When Damasippus delivers his harangue, he may be angling not only for respect but also for sympathy and, perhaps, an invitation to dinner. The cheerful polypragmatist, who arrives uninvited at Horace's country retreat, is one of a long line of meal-cadging philosophers whose great original is Socrates, known to his enemies not as the father of philosophy but as "the *scurra* of Attica," as Cicero reports.[43] Perhaps Damasippus even hopes to win himself a position in Horace's household as a philosopher-in-residence. The former dealer in antiques is now marketing another kind of cultural capital.

How closely do these down-and-out philosophers resemble the man who records their words of wisdom? Very little, it would appear. The autobiography furnished by Horace's satires presents no "reversal of fortune" to be satirically faced down or corrected. Book 1 depicts Horace's life story as a relatively smooth ascent from humble beginnings, to the honor of the military tribunate (Horace does not specify the circumstances), to a well-deserved place within the exalted circle of Maecenas; Book 2 continues the curve, remarking Horace's intimacy with the young Caesar and establishing him on his new Sabine farm. Moreover, by aligning himself with the "country mouse" of *Satires* 2.6, who experiences two reversals in rapid succession – one "change of lot" (*mutata sorte, S.* 2.6.110) boosting him into city luxury, the other restoring him to his proper place in the country – Horace succeeds in representing his newly landed status not as a step up in the world but as a

---

[43] Cic. *Nat. D.* 1.93, cited by Corbett (1986) 3.

restoration of the status quo. Here as elsewhere in Horace's poetry, the Sabine farm figures as the ideal setting for the man who is "content with his lot" (*illa* [*sorte*] | *contentus vivat*, S. 1.1.2–3), an emblem of the disavowal of ambition, not its culmination.

I do not mean to suggest that we should take Horace's satiric autobiography at face value but to draw attention to what is missing from his earliest self-portrait. Horace insulates his autobiography and his satiric practice from the influence of fortune by erasing his own famous reversal of fortune, most memorably recorded in *Epistles* 2.2 (49–52):

> unde simul primum me dimisere Philippi,
> decisis humilem pennis inopemque paterni
> et laris et fundi, paupertas impulit audax
> ut versus facerem.

After Philippi discharged me, leaving me earth-bound, my wings clipped, stripped of ancestral house and lands, bold poverty spurred me to compose verse.

By displacing these autobiographical "facts" onto a series of surrogates in *Satires* 2, Horace retroactively exposes the satirist of Book 1. Like Ofellus, Horace forfeited his family property to the resettlement program of the triumvirs; like Damasippus, he has betaken himself to the profession of satirist; like Davus – and this is the hardest self-accusation of all – he has forfeited his freedom in the service of another man.

The last charge is explicit, leveled by the slave against his master in *Satires* 2.7. When Horace hasn't been invited anywhere for dinner, according to Davus, he praises "carefree cabbage" (*securum holus*, S. 2.7.30), posing as a devoted adherent of the simple life – a real Ofellus or country mouse, as it were. But the moment he receives an invitation from his patron Maecenas, however belated, he is off like a shot, leaving his parasites (*scurrae*, 36) to exit with empty stomachs, heaping curses on their host, who is himself a parasite at a richer man's table. For an overreading Maecenas, the slave's accusation, like the pedestrian's angry comment in *Satires* 2.6, serves as a gratifying index of Horace's devotion to his friend (misread by the slave, naturally enough, as his devotion to his friend's rich table). But the bitter culmination of Davus' tirade is harder to swallow: "The truth is that you, who give orders to me, are yourself someone else's wretched slave, and you dance like a wooden puppet on strings that another pulls" (*nempe* | *tu mihi qui imperitas alii servis miser atque* | *duceris ut nervis alienis mobile lignum*, 80–2). As Michael André Bernstein has pointed out, the image of the marionette seems designed to illustrate Horace's "enslavement" not to sexual desire (Davus' ostensible subject here) but to Maecenas.[44] And as Davus renews his attack, the slippage between sexual and social enslavement becomes still more apparent. No matter how badly he is treated, Horace is incapable, his slave accuses, of extricating himself from the toils of desire: "'I'm free, I'm free!' come, say the words! You can't do it; a harsh master rides your mind, applies sharp spurs when you're worn out, and reins you around, though you say no" (*"liber, liber sum" dic age. non quis; | urget enim dominus mentem non lenis et acris | subiectat lasso stimulos versatque negantem*, 92–4). Davus' point is that Horace, far from taming his appetites as a rider his horse, is himself "ridden" by his overmastering desire. But Davus' personification also helps confirm our suspicion that it is indeed the master who is in question here.

Horace's relation to Maecenas is likewise subjected to the stern scrutiny of Damasippus in *Satires* 2.3. The charge brought by the once-successful businessman against Horace is, appropriately, not servile self-abasement but self-inflating social ambition. "What's my particular form of madness?" Horace foolishly asks, after Damasippus has concluded his lecture. Damasippus has his answer ready: "First, you're busy building, which is to say imitating tall men, though you're hardly two feet from head to toe" (*primum | aedificas, hoc est, longos imitaris, ab imo | ad summum totus moduli bipedalis*, S. 2.3.307–9). Damasippus has in mind one "tall man" in particular: "Is it right for you to do whatever Maecenas does, you, who are so unlike him and so far out of his league?" (*an quodcumque facit Maecenas te quoque verum est | tantum dissimilem et tanto certare minorem?* 312–13). Damasippus drives his point home with the fable of the frog and the calf, the moral of which is that no matter how hard Horace works at puffing himself up, he'll never be as big a man as Maecenas (*non si te ruperis ... | par eris*, 319–20).

Damasippus' satire on Horace's "littleness" functions as an oblique compliment to the inimitable "bigness" of the great Maecenas. But it redounds to Horace's credit as well. Imitation is, after all, the sincerest form of flattery, and while Damasippus accuses Horace of emulating Maecenas, he might himself be accused of emulating Horace. It is finally Damasippus, not Horace, who is the overinflated frog of this puffed-up

---

[44] Bernstein (1992) 45–7. Cf. *S.* 1.8, likewise featuring a "wooden puppet" (the Priapus that guards Maecenas' gardens on the Esquiline), where a struggle for mastery against female opponents displaces the issue of the speaker's subordination to Maecenas.

poem. One of Horace's best jokes is that this outsized satire, which covers more than twice as much paper as its closest rival (*S.* 1.4, with 143 lines), opens with Damasippus charging that Horace writes too little (*sic raro scribis, S.* 2.3.1). And the content of the satire is correspondingly enlarged and exaggerated. The miser who insists on drinking vinegar has a cellar stocked, Damasippus reports, "with vintage Chian and Falernian, a thousand jugs full – that's nothing; make it three hundred thousand!" (*positis intus Chii veterisque Falerni | mille cadis – nihil est, tercentum milibus,* 115–16). The enthusiastic revision may be taken as a figure for the relation between this garish diatribe and the diatribes of Book 1, a relation encapsulated in the joke with which Horace finally silences Damasippus in the last line of the poem: "Let the greater lunatic spare the lesser!" (*o maior tandem parcas, insane, minori!* 326). But the joke does concede that the difference between the two is a difference only of degree.[45] Like the slave, the aspiring client at once paints and himself embodies a satiric caricature of Horace, the *amicus* of Maecenas. Such hyperboles overshoot the mark but describe its general location.

The analogy these satires put into play – Damasippus and Davus are to Horace as Horace is to Maecenas – holds not only for the content of these relationships but also for their discursive form. Like most of the other satires of the second book, they may be described as downward transpositions of this original discursive dyad – transpositions, that is, in which Horace takes the seat formerly occupied by his patron, passing the satiric megaphone to his social inferiors.[46] If Horace is less inclined to play the satirist in Book 2, one reason is that he has already repaired his fortunes. The fiction of the second book is that Horace, being a made man, no longer needs or deigns to wear the satiric mask. But this movement from the stage to the audience not only elevates the Horace of Book 2, it also and simultaneously demotes the Horace of Book 1, situating him among the horde of men displaced, declassed, or dispossessed by the vicissitudes of the civil wars, men on the make, men scrambling to repair their fortunes. Horace's satiric exposé of the upwardly mobile satirist in Book 2 effectively satirizes the satirist of Book 1.

---

[45] Hence perhaps the clustering of comparatives (*maiorem, minus, minorem, maior dimidio, magis atque | . . . magis, par*) and terms denoting size (*longos, moduli bipedalis, ingens, magna*) in 308–20.

[46] Pressed to its logical conclusion, this satiric argument would disclose Horace's patron as but one more puppet and parasite. This is a disclosure that Horace avoids but that Caesar, the ultimate puppet master, can treat as a joke, as in the letter to Maecenas preserved in Suetonius' life of Horace (*veniet ergo ab ista parasitica mensa ad hanc regiam*).

It is as if Horace winced, when rereading his first book of satires, at the occasional grossness of his self-defense; as if he came to feel that he had shown, in poems such as *Satires* 1.9, too much of the work that went into solving the problem posed by his individual reversal of fortune. In his second book, Horace is much more consistently self-conscious, anticipating and as it were inoculating himself, not without pain, against every charge of artful ambition and self-serving opportunism. The encounter with the social climber is recast, accordingly, in the mock-epic dialogue of *Satires* 2.5, a dialogue from which Horace is entirely absent. In this satiric addendum to the Homeric *nekuia*, Ulysses consults Tiresias not as a seer but as a financial prognosticator: "Add to your tale, tell me this too, Tiresias: what arts can I use to repair the fortune I've lost?" (*Hoc quoque, Teresia, praeter narrata petenti* | *responde, quibus amissas reparare queam res* | *artibus atque modis*, S. 2.5.1–3). Though set in the epic past, the poem is thoroughly topical. The generic "impoverished aristocrat" represented in the guise of Ulysses may well be, like Ofellus, a victim of the civil war – not an expropriated farmer, of course, but an impoverished senator. Unlike Ofellus, however, Ulysses does not view his poverty with the fortitude of a philosopher; "without assets," he complains, "breeding and character aren't worth a damn" (*et genus et virtus nisi cum re vilior alga est*, 8).[47] In response to the request of his money-hungry friend, Tiresias offers instruction in the fine and thoroughly Roman art of legacy-hunting, a specialized and degraded form of the art of friendship. The irony is blatant, but the alternative perspective of true friendship goes unexpressed. Is Horace an honest Ofellus, content with his lot, whose farm has been miraculously restored, or a Ulysses who has worked hard and deviously to accomplish such a restoration?[48] While Horace might like to fancy himself an Ofellus, he knows that others may accuse him of being a Ulysses. By making the implicit comparison first himself, Horace precludes their attack and shows himself to be nobody's fool.

In *Satires* 2.8, Horace's final variation on the theme of loss and recovery, the comic poet Fundanius regales Horace with a description of a dinner party at the house of one Nasidienus Rufus. This is in fact the most detailed such description in Horace's satires; Fundanius tells Horace not only what the guests said and what they ate but also just where they all reclined – information that conveys something about the guests' relative status (the various locations on the three couches of the Roman

---

[47] This translation borows from Rudd (1979) 110.
[48] On the echoes of S. 2.5 in 2.6, see Lejay (1911) 514.

dining room had various social values). By contrast, when Horace describes his Sabine dinner in *Satires* 2.6, or a dinner he enjoyed in company with Maecenas and others en route to Brundisium in *Satires* 1.5, he refrains from recording the seating arrangements. Guests at these other dinners, we are to understand, are too busy enjoying the true pleasures of conviviality to worry about who reclines where. Horace's defensive representation of Maecenas' *amici* as men who know and are happy with their assigned places (*est locus uni* | *cuique suus, S.* 1.9.51–2) similarly naturalizes the social hierarchy into invisibility. Against this blandly idealizing backdrop, Fundanius' specifications in *Satires* 2.8 serve perhaps as one index of Nasidienus' obsession with relative status.[49]

The diners of *Satires* 1.5 are diverted by the antics of two buffoons; the rustic company of *Satires* 2.6 enjoys a simple meal and ethically enriched conversation. In *Satires* 2.8, however, the dinner – the food and its elaborately theatrical presentation – is itself the entertainment, ready-made material for Fundanius' subsequent comic narration.[50] Nasidienus believes that a dinner party's success depends on the quality of the food and the artfulness of its preparation, and the conversation is accordingly dominated by the intrusive culinary glosses supplied by Nasidienus and his hanger-on Nomentanus, for example: "This eel was caught when it was pregnant; the flesh is not as good after they give birth" (*haec gravida* ... | *capta est, deterior post partum carne futura, S.* 2.8.43–4). These exquisitely irrelevant and unappetizing refinements might be comedy enough, but Horace cannot resist adding a bit of slapstick. Nasidienus has just finished describing his special recipe for fish sauce when a dust-laden tapestry suspended above the table falls down into the platter on whose virtues he was discoursing (*ruinas* | *in patinam fecere,* 54–5). At this tragic turn of events, the host covers his head and weeps as if at the death of a son. This is in effect Nasidienus' "reversal of fortune" – a domestic and hilariously trivial variation on the reversals suffered by Ofellus, Damasippus, and Ulysses.

Like its counterparts, *Satires* 2.8 is in part a meditation on the proper response to calamities (*casus, S.* 2.8.71; compare *casus dubios, S.* 2.2.108). Thus Nasidienus is consoled by the "sage Nomentanus" (*sapiens ...*

---

49 Nasidienus' arrangements are unusual – he yields the host's place to one of his hangers-on, as if unsure of his own ability to entertain his guest of honor. For a seating chart, see Wickham (1891) 199; on the ethos of equality vs. the reality of social discrimination at the *convivium*, see D'Arms (1990).

50 On actual performances of comedies at Roman dinner parties, see Jones (1991) 192–3.

Nomentanus, 60), who reads a universal significance in the host's debacle: "Alas, Fortune, what deity is more cruel to us than you? How you delight in making sport with the affairs of men!" (*heu, Fortuna, quis est crudelior in nos | te deus? ut semper gaudes illudere rebus | humanis!* 61–3). Nomentanus is seconded, with heavy irony, by Balatro, a hanger-on of Maecenas: that was just the way of things; here Nasidienus had labored so hard to be sure that everything would be just so; and then accidents like this happened (65–72). But even this dust-cloud, he reminds his disconsolate host, has a silver lining: "Adversity enables a host, like a general, to display talent that remains hidden when things are going well" (*sed convivatoris uti ducis ingenium res | adversae nudare solent, celare secundae,* 73–4). These edifying reflections are designed to recall the attitude of the second satire's stalwart farmer, who recognizes that Fortuna is a tempestuous goddess (*S.* 2.2.126) and counsels his sons to "answer adversity with fortitude" (*fortiaque adversis opponite pectora rebus,* 136).[51] But unlike Ofellus, Nasidienus does not resign himself to his misfortune. Nor does he have the sense to follow the lead of the fabled mice, whose dinner suffers from a similarly violent interruption, by abandoning his pretensions and retreating into the social shadows where he belongs. Revived by his philosophical counselors, rather as Damasippus is resuscitated by the sage Stertinius, Nasidienus rushes out of the room, only to return triumphant, a few lines later, leading a procession of slaves bearing platters laden with food no less extraordinary than that destroyed by the calamitous tapestry. Fundanius announces this return with a mock-epic apostrophe: "You reenter, Nasidienus, with a changed face, like a man bent on mending misfortune by means of art" (*Nasidiene, redis mutatae frontis, ut arte | emendaturus fortunam, S.* 2.8.84–5). Like Ulysses, Nasidienus seeks to restore his fortune with art, the art in this case not of false friendship but of gastronomy.

But the attempt is not successful, as Fundanius gleefully reports in the poem's (and the collection's) closing lines: "We paid our host back by taking off without even tasting his dishes, as if they'd been tainted by the breath of Canidia, more poisonous than the snakes of Africa" (*quem nos sic fugimus ulti, | ut nihil omnino gustaremus, velut illis | Canidia adflasset, peior serpentibus Afris, S.* 2.8.93–5). Canidia is one of the two witches encoun-

---

[51] Cf. further the ironic warning against complacency at *S.* 2.2.106: "naturally you will be uniquely blessed with constant good fortune" (*uni nimirum recte tibi semper erunt res*). At *S.* 2.7.88, Davus defines the man who is truly *liber* as one who cripples all attacks of fortune (*in quem manca ruit semper fortuna*).

tered by the figwood statue of Priapus in *Satires* 1.8, a poem which likewise ends with a hasty departure, viewed from the opposite perspective. For whereas Priapus takes his revenge (*non testis inultus, S.* 1.8.44) by driving the witches out of Maecenas' gardens, Fundanius and his friends take theirs by abandoning Nasidienus' table. The allusion to Canidia thus turns the dinner party of Nasidienus inside out, exposing the would-be insider as a double of the ultimate outsider, the witch who uses the art of magic, a kind of perverted cookery, in a vain attempt to win friends and influence people.[52] Unbeknownst to Nasidienus, the real party, the incrowd, can only be somewhere else.

The punishment meted out to Nasidienus is not only the desertion of his table. The *coup de grâce* is struck by Horace, whose satire publishes and fixes the host's exclusion from the company he so longs to keep. In this regard, the most obvious double for Nasidienus in the first book is not the witch of *Satires* 1.8 but the social climber who fastens onto Horace in *Satires* 1.9. Just as Nasidienus advertises the excellence of the food he serves, so this aspiring *amicus* promotes his wares, such as they are, with a blithe and almost endearing lack of finesse: "If I know myself, you'll value me as highly as your friends Viscus and Varius. After all, who can produce as much verse as I can, and in as little time?" (*si bene me novi non Viscum pluris amicum,* | *non Varium facies: nam quis me scribere pluris* | *aut citius possit versus? S.* 1.9.22–4). It is not just their dubious talents but their very eagerness to display their (dis)qualifications that renders men such as these unfit for Maecenas' friendship. In both poems, moreover, Horace's exposé of these inept pretenders is motivated. It constitutes his delayed vengeance – on the social climber, for persecuting him with unwelcome attentions, and on Nasidienus, contrariwise, for failing to invite him to dinner, a dinner whose guest list, as Horace gradually discovers, included not only Fundanius but also Maecenas, Varius, and Viscus. Why wasn't Horace invited, when so many friends of his were?[53] Perhaps the talented "freedman's son" is still not a big enough fish to merit a place at the table of the nouveau riche. The satire is, then, both Horace's revenge and his vindication. For if the house of Nasidienus was

---

[52] On Nasidienus' witchy feast, see Freudenburg (1995); for a comparison of the cuisine of Nasidienus and Canidia, see Gowers (1993) 176–7.

[53] Horace's mortification is sketched in just under the surface: it is after Fundanius incidentally reveals that Maecenas was one of the guests (16) that Horace interrupts to ask who else was there (18–19). On Horace as "the uninvited *scurra*," see Freudenburg (1993) 232–3.

graced by this eminent company on this one memorable and disastrous occasion, Horace enjoys a day-to-day intimacy with these men, an intimacy to which the easy interchange of *Satires* 2.8, with its assumption of shared values, itself testifies. .

But Horace is not only a frustrated guest, he is also, significantly, a frustrated host. The poem opens with Horace's question: "How did you enjoy your dinner *chez* Nasidienus the Blessed? Yesterday, you know, when I was hoping for your company, I was informed that you'd been drinking there since midday" (*Ut Nasidieni iuvit te cena beati?* | *nam mihi quaerenti convivam dictus here illic* | *de medio potare die*, S. 2.8.1–3). It was when Horace was trying to get Fundanius to come to dinner at *his* house that he learned of his prior engagement. The hospitality extended by Nasidienus displaced whatever entertainment Horace had in mind. If the witch of *Satires* 1.8 and the social climber of *Satires* 1.9 are close relations of Nasidienus, the third and last double for Nasidienus is Horace himself, in particular the eager-to-please Horace of *Satires* 1.10.[54] The second book of satires may shortchange us, offering a mere eight satires instead of the ten we might have expected.[55] But the missing satires are in a certain sense included all the same, rolled into the grand finale of *Satires* 2.8 – an exercise in compression that retrospectively reveals the latent affinities between the discrete protagonists (Canidia, the social climber, Horace himself) of the earlier satires.

In *Satires* 1.10, Horace identifies the select readership to whose delectation he offers up his satires. The list, which includes all the eminent names on Nasidienus' guest list and then some, has been characterized not unfairly as a "piece of blatant name-dropping."[56] Unsympathetic readers – among them perhaps Horace himself – might liken Horace's pride in his elite audience to Nasidienus' in the guest list he has succeeded in assembling. Such readers might argue, moreover, that the protagonists of these two closing poems have more in common than a propensity to self-promotion by association. As Fundanius remarks

---

[54] For different versions of this comparison, see O'Connor (1990); Gowers (1993a) 167–70; Freudenburg (1995) 217–18. A sense of Horace's divided loyalties in *S.* 2.8 generates the exculpatory reading offered by Baker (1988) (the satire's true target is not the inept host but the rude guests) and extended by Seeck (1991) 538–9 (Horace is implying that Maecenas should reimburse Nasidienus for the cost of the meal).

[55] The expectation is enhanced by the parallels between *S.* 1.6 and 2.6 – both autobiographical, both addressed (directly or indirectly) to Maecenas, each marking (as it seems) the start of its collection's second half.   [56] Rudd (1986) 139.

near the end of *Satires* 2.8, the dishes carried in by a procession of slaves might have been "delicious, if only their master hadn't lectured us on their origin and nature" (*suavis res, si non causas narraret earum et | naturas dominus, S.* 2.8.92–3). *Satires* 1.10 is also a didactic discourse, a collection of precepts on the proper way to write satire. The poem opens a door to the satiric kitchen, as it were, showing us how Horace prepares his poetic effects, and exposing his poetic *sprezzatura* for the calculated, cultivated illusion that it is.[57] One might imagine Horace's elite circle yawning in dismay: "Dear Horace, your poetry would be delightful, if only you didn't insist on telling us just exactly how it was done!" Like Nasidienus, the Horace of Book 1 reenters society with a new face, equipped with the art of satire, an art that mends both faces and fortunes.

It is in part the distressed recognition of this likeness that fuels the second book of satires. Horace's second book is the product of second thoughts, an attempt to write over and thus blot out his earlier production. And yet in the process Horace inevitably retraces the original design. If Horace no longer addresses his patron directly, it is nonetheless clear that the satires of the second book are designed for Maecenas' overreading. The proliferating screens of the second book shield Horace but do not render him invisible. Horace is still writing satire – still aiming to please the discriminating palates of his powerful friends. Nasidienus' dinner is served, after all, on Horace's page.

What is the relation between the art of satire and the art of dining? Why do discourses on dining, both theoretical and practical, preoccupy fully half of the eight satires of Horace's second book? At the end of his very first satire, Horace compares the wise man, the man who understands how life should be lived, to a *conviva satur* (*S.* 1.1.119), a dinner guest who knows enough to leave the table when he has eaten his fill. As many readers have remarked, the second book of satires comically misreads this image by taking it literally: whereas Book 1 purports to teach us how to live, Book 2 devotes much of its energy to teaching us how to eat.[58] One model for this shift is provided by an exchange between the stern father Demea and the slave Syrus in Terence's *Adelphoe*. In this scene, Demea's description of his son's moral education is punctuated by the slave's ironic congratulations (414–17):

---

[57] On the social significance of such "backstage" spaces as the kitchen, see Goffman (1959) 106–40.   [58] See above all Gowers (1993a) 126–79.

DE. I leave out nothing, I get him used to it, I bid him gaze, as if into a mirror, at the lives of men, and to profit from the example of others: "Do this!"

SY. That's the way!

DE. "Don't do that!"

SY. Brilliant!

After a little more of this, the slave finally interrupts (419–29):

SY. I swear I don't have time right now to listen. I've got hold of just the fish I was after: I must take care it doesn't get spoiled. For it's as much of a disgrace for us slaves not to do the things you just said as it is for you; so far as I'm able, I lecture my fellow slaves in just your style: "This is well-sauced, this is burnt, this isn't clean enough; that's right, now; next time, remember." I take great pains to advise them, as I can, with what wit I have: and then I bid them gaze, as if into a mirror, upon the platters, Demea, and I advise them what needs to be done.

The passage is often cited in connection with Horace's description in *Satires* 1.4 of the fatherly teachings from which he claims his satire derives.[59] As we have seen, we must take – we are expressly invited to take – that self-characterization, which plays a strategic role within the polemics of *Satires* 1.4, with a large pinch of salt. And yet it is only in Book 2 that Horace makes space for the kind of thorough-going parody that is delivered within Terence's play by the slave Syrus. Indeed, Syrus' response to Demea could be taken to epitomize the relation between Horace's two books of satires. Book 2 takes down or de-grades both the content and the speaker of Book 1, substituting gastronomy for philosophy and the slave for the master. This is not a gratuitous exercise but a defensive strategy. Having exposed his foundational satiric narrative of misfortune and its artful amendment – a narrative he will have the face to apply to himself only a decade later – Horace cannot but abandon the satiric role.

[59] See Leach (1971); Anderson (1982) 51–6.

2

Making faces at the mirror:
the Epodes and the civil war

Horace's first epode situates the collection on the brink of the battle of Actium, the final episode in Rome's prolonged civil wars. The poem, which is addressed to Maecenas, represents Horace in the act of resolving to accompany his beloved patron into battle: "I will gladly fight this and every war in the hope of earning your favor" (*libenter hoc et omne militabitur | bellum in tuae spem gratiae*, I. 1.23–4). We do not know whether Horace actually fought at Actium; most likely he did not. But the book of epodes is itself evidence of his readiness to do battle on the home front on behalf of Maecenas and the young Caesar. The epodes that follow Horace's declaration are blows struck in an ongoing "culture war." Horace is fighting at once to stabilize a disordered world by establishing its center and defining its periphery and to protect his own face by ruling himself in and others out. The collection is characterized, accordingly, by the divergent impulses of solidarity and division, with gestures of deference directed toward (what Horace represents as) the center and gestures of authority aimed at (what Horace represents as) the fringes.[1]

In his *Epodes* as in his roughly contemporaneous collections of satires, Horace combines attacks on enemies with a defense of his friends' and his own moral integrity. But there is an urgency about the epodes that is absent from the satires. Whereas Horatian satire aspires to universality, the epodes are figuratively located within a particular historical crisis and take the form not of philosophical reflections but of socially engaged and consequential acts. The heightened emphasis on exclusivity and hierarchy that is one consequence of this historical situatedness is written into their metrical form, which compresses and articulates the relatively expansive and even flow of the satiric hexameter into unevenly matched

---

[1] Cf. Nagy (1979) 251, characterizing "Archilochean *iamboi*" as "an affirmation of *philótes* in the community"; see further Mankin (1995) 6–9.

pairs of (predominantly) iambic lines. Moreover, whereas the satirist typically addresses himself to a friend who reflects his values and his value,
positioning himself more or less securely on the inside as he launches his
attack against a third person (in this regard the opening of Horace's first
satire may be taken to be exemplary), the invective poet tends to take his
stand on the threshold between inside and outside, confronting an enemy
"you" head-on. The battle he wages is accordingly both more violent
and more dangerous.

This violence makes the epodes difficult to read – these poems are less
palatable than their mild satiric cousins. Scholars have mostly responded
by drawing a sharp line between epodes deemed worthy of attention and
their less deserving neighbors. Thus Epode 9, which advances the Actian
narrative of Epode 1 to the eve of Caesar's victory celebration, is elevated
into the scholarly spotlight, while the immediately preceding epode, an
outrageously obscene invective leveled against an oversexed Roman
matron, is dismissed as an early exercise in the lowest manner of Greek
iambos.[2] No doubt the epodes were written over a period of years, some
perhaps during Horace's "schoolboy" days in Athens, before the
assassination of Julius Caesar rekindled the banked fires of civil war. But
what matters chiefly is that Horace has chosen to include these disparate
poems within a single collection that is framed, at the outset and again at
its midpoint, by the final crisis of the civil war. The obscene Epode 8 is, I
will argue, as closely bound up with this historical moment as the explicitly political Epode 9. Instead of segregating early from late, sexual from
political, private from public, and "trivial" from "serious" epodes, we
need to attend to what the various kinds of poems Horace included
within this relatively brief collection have to say to and about each other.[3]

The scholarly attempt to impose order on the collection by ranking
the epodes, in effect ruling some in and others out of the Horatian
canon, not only reflects Horace's epodic project of discrimination, it also
exposes his essential problem. The act of repelling intruders is itself
repellent; as he makes faces at the enemy, the invective poet defaces
himself. The margin at which Horace fights has an uncanny tendency to

---

[2] So, e.g., Fraenkel (1957) 58–9, 71–5. I do not mean to suggest that the polarity of "sexual"
vs. "political" epodes is the sole factor at work here; *I*. 10 wins attention because of its
Archilochean lineage, *I*. 13 because of its anomalously ode-like quality (on which see
further below, 96–8), *I*. 16 because of its much-debated relation to Virgil's (eminently
canonical) fourth eclogue, and so on.

[3] For exemplary investigations along these lines see Henderson (1987); Fitzgerald (1988).

turn into a mirror. If Horace can never quite succeed in cleansing the interior of undesirable elements, one reason is that he recognizes those elements in himself. The result is that the collection is riven by the infelicitous act of self-exorcism. Whereas in the satires Horace first labors to distinguish his unambitious self from the targets of his satire and then proceeds to expose himself as their kin, in the epodes there is no "first" and "then," no saving postponement of the moment of ironic truth. Far from helping to put an end to civil war, Horatian invective only internalizes its proliferating unstable distinctions. In the perpetual-motion machine of the *Epodes*, distinctions are no sooner drawn than confounded, no sooner confounded than redrawn.

This is nowhere more clear than in the first outright invective of the collection, a violent attack on an ex-slave who has risen from leg-irons to landed riches. The poem is distasteful, even disgusting, partly but not only because our prejudices have changed. Horace is not simply fulfilling the requirements of the genre; he claws at the face of the ex-slave in an attempt to eradicate its resemblance to his own. He begins, accordingly, by maximizing the distance between himself and his target: "The enmity of wolves and lambs is no greater than that I bear you" (*Lupis et agnis quanta sortito obtigit,* | *tecum mihi discordia est, I.* 4.1–2). An aggressive apostrophe sketches the grounds for this distinction: "You, with your flanks scorched by Spanish thongs and your ankles by the chafing chain" (*Hibericis peruste funibus latus* | *et crura dura compede,* 3–4). The purse-proud ex-slave may stroll about unfettered (*superbus ambules pecunia,* 5) and hide his scars beneath an extravagantly draped toga (*bis trium ulnarum toga,* 8), but the truth of his vile origins, indelibly inscribed on his body, remains immutable: "fortune does not alter the facts of birth" (*fortuna non mutat genus,* 6). If fortune dresses him up, Horace gives him a dressing-down, at once exposing and reinflicting the old wounds.

But the exercise exposes Horace's scars too. *Fortuna non mutat genus*: this succinct truism might be wielded not only against the rich ex-slave but also against the "freedman's son" – "Fortune's boy," as some would name him (*Fortunae filius, S.* 2.6.49) – who purportedly lucked his way into high society. Midway through the poem, as if sensing the danger to his own face, Horace turns it away and confronts the ex-slave instead with the "faces of passers-by" (*ora . . . huc et huc euntium, I.* 4.9). It is with the venting of their *liberrima indignatio* (10) – an expression suggesting not only disdain but freeborn status, and the privilege of outspoken free speech that this status confers – that the poem concludes. Where Horace attacked the ex-slave directly, these passers-by preserve their dignity by expressing their outrage only to each other. While repeating the substance of Horace's charges, what they stress is the poetic injustice of the ex-slave's transformation: a man once "furrowed by the triumvir's whip until the crier himself was sick of it" (*sectus flagellis hic triumviralibus | praeconis ad fastidium*, 11–12) now plows (*arat*, 13) a vast estate, trots his ponies up and down the Appian Way, and takes his place at the theater in the rows reserved for Roman knights (13–16). They conclude with a more particular complaint (17–20):

> quid attinet tot ora navium gravi
>   rostrata duci pondere
> contra latrones atque servilem manum
>   hoc, hoc tribuno militum?

> What's the good of launching so many beak-faced ships of massive
> weight against the pirates and bands of slaves, when such a man as
> this is a military tribune?

This sets the poem in the context of the war against Sextus Pompey and draws the relevant moral (what is the point of fighting Pompey's army of slaves if the same rot has invaded our own side?). The mention of the severe "faces" of the warships reminds us that the poem is itself a skirmish in the battle it describes: a face-off between a community "face" and a defaced servile opponent.

For readers of Horace's first book of satires, however, the final squib inevitably recalls the promotion, scandalous in the eyes of many, of Horace himself to the post of military tribune (*S.* 1.6.45–8). It is true that the criminal ex-slave has little in common with the virtuous, simple-living Horace who strolls across the stage of the satires, and one could argue that Horace is here implicitly distinguishing the undeserving ex-slave from his deserving freeborn self, the wrong way of responding to a change of status from his own right way of modesty and moderation. By invoking the community to repeat his charges, moreover, Horace effectively authorizes himself as a spokesman for community values. And yet Horace betrays some discomfort with his role. In the same satire that reports his achievement of the military tribunate, Horace remarks that his father would not have minded if Horace had grown up to be a *praeco*, a "crier" or auctioneer (*S.* 1.6.86). In this epode Horace does indeed take on the role of the crier who delivers the tongue-lashing that in this case not only accompanies but displaces the slave's whipping. The weariness of the crier is perhaps the nausea of the poet who is beginning to recognize himself in his victim. Less a member of a different species than his distorted twin, the ex-slave reflects Horace in the mirror of other people's blame. If Horace begins by proclaiming absolute difference, the structure of the poem, a diptych composed of two reflecting ten-line panels, reintroduces the concept of sameness – as though betraying at the level of form what Horace had ruled out at the level of statement.[4]

Canidia, Canicula, and the poetry of impotentia

The consummate outsider, the ultimate "other," of Horace's early poetry is the witch Canidia. She has a starring role in three poems. In *Satires* 1.8, a figwood statue of Priapus narrates her intrusion into his garden, a converted graveyard in which shades of the past still lurk, waiting to be conjured up by her spells; in Epode 5 she concocts a love-potion to lure a wandering lover back home, while the little boy whose liver and marrow are to furnish her secret ingredients pleads and threatens in vain; and in the dialogue of Epode 17 Horace himself pleads for mercy and Canidia, enraged by his earlier poems, refuses to grant it.[5] Elsewhere (*S.* 2.1, *S.* 2.8, *I.* 3), Horace alludes to Canidia in passing as if to establish her as a fixture in his poetic world. Most astonishing perhaps is Canidia's assumption of the place of honor at the end of Horace's early collections. Her name breaks into the last line of Horace's last satire (*S.* 2.8.95) as suddenly as the banquet described in that poem breaks up. And Canidia not only dominates but actually speaks the closing lines of the book of epodes.

Like the ex-slave of Epode 4, Canidia epitomizes the perversion of traditional Roman hierarchies. A compendium of female vices and the very antithesis of a modest housewife, Canidia is distinguished by her loose tongue and unbridled sexuality. This bad character is implicit in her name. The old age written there (*canities*) casts her as the first in a series of Horatian hags (Chloris in *C.* 3.15, Lyce in *C.* 4.13) who are represented as unfit but still hungry for the arms of a lover.[6] This hunger is also legible: like "Scylla" (traditionally derived from σκύλαξ, "puppy"), "Canidia," who often appears in the company of dogs, herself resembles a ravenous

---

[4] On the boomerang-effect, see Henderson (1987) 111; for a description of the "double structure," see Carrubba (1969) 57–60.

[5] For detailed commentary on the magical practices described in these poems, see Ingallina (1974).

[6] On the social factors underlying invective against old women in antiquity (and beyond), see Bremmer (1987).

canine. And yet by making his hag not just a hag but a witch, a producer of incantations not unlike his own, Horace activates, however grudgingly, the musical suggestion of the name (*canere*).[7] Not only the target but the producer of poetry, Canidia embodies an indecorous poetics against which Horace tries to define his own poetic practice.

Canidia is associated with dogs because, throughout the classical tradition, dogs form part of a misogynistic depiction of female powers and desires.[8] In *Satires* 1.8 Canidia descends to a bestial low as, accompanied by her fellow-worker Sagana, she scrabbles in the graveyard earth and tears at a lamb with her teeth (*scalpere terram | unguibus et pullam divellere mordicus agnam | coeperunt, S.* 1.8.26–8). Invoking Hecate and the Fury Tisiphone, both figures linked and often identified with dogs, the witches succeed in conjuring up "snakes and hell-bitches" (*serpentis atque . . . | infernas . . . canis*, 34–5).[9] And before the satire ends the quaking Priapus will term the witches "two Furies" (*Furiarum . . . duarum*, 45), a description extended in Epode 5, where Canidia wears her hair in the style of the Furies, with short snakes knotting her tresses (*brevibus illigata viperis | crinis et incomptum caput, I.* 5.15–16). At the close of *Satires* 2, when Nasidienus' guests flee as if her breath had tainted the meal (*velut illis | Canidia adflasset, S.* 2.8.94–5), Canidia joins the ranks of the Harpies, surnamed "the dogs of Zeus" (Διὸς κύνες, *Argon.* 2.289) by Apollonius of Rhodes.[10] In the ritual cuisine of Epode 5, bones snatched from the jaws of a ravenous bitch (*ossa ab ore rapta ieiunae canis, I.* 5.23) top off the list of the ingredients to be added to Canidia's magic fire, while the she-dogs who bark at "old man" Varus as he roams the Subura (*senem . . . adulterum | latrant Suburanae canes*, 57–8)[11] function as Canidia's representatives *in absentia*. Canidia thus belongs in the line of vindictive hags epitomized by Hecuba, the aged "bitch" who ends her life as a dog.[12]

---

[7] Varro (*Ling.* 7.32) proposes an etymological link between *canis* and *canere*. On the multiple suggestions of *can-*, see Ahl (1985) 31–3. The association of Canidia with *canities* is the most generally accepted because of the quantity of the *a*, but there is no need to rule out other possibilities simply on this basis. Horace was a poet, not a linguist. As Ahl (1985) 56 comments, "wordplay across vowel quantities abounds in Latin literature."

[8] The evidence on dogs in ancient Greek poetry is collected and discussed by Lilja (1976).

[9] The scene is modeled on Jason's supplication of Hecate in Ap. Rhod. *Argon.* 3.1214–17, where Hecate herself appears, crowned with δράκοντες and escorted by χθόνιοι κύνες.

[10] *Harpyia* is a dog's name at Ov. *Met.* 3.215.

[11] Following Bain (1986), I read *latrant* at *I.* 5.58.

[12] Cf. Plautus' comically "rationalized" Hecuba, who heaps abuses on everyone she meets and thereby earns the title of "dog" (*omnia mala ingerebat, quemquem aspexerat. | itaque adeo iure coepta appellari est canes, Men.* 717–18).

But Canidia's rage, unlike Hecuba's, is always mixed with desire. The proximity of these emotions, well analyzed by John Winkler,[13] is clearly visible in Canidia's magical practices. In the ritual puppet-show of *Satires* 1.8, Canidia stages her vindictive triumph over a recalcitrant lover, representing herself with a puppet of wool, her victim with one of wax (*S.* 1.8.30–3):

> lanea et effigies erat, altera cerea: maior
> lanea, quae poenis compesceret inferiorem;
> cerea suppliciter stabat servilibus ut quae
> iam peritura modis.

There was one puppet of wax, another, larger one of wool to crush the lesser with punishments; the wax one stood suppliant, as if about to die like a slave.

As she casts the wax puppet into the fire (cf. *imagine cerea | largior arserit ignis*, 43–4), Canidia at once punishes and melts her lover's resistance. In Epode 5, the slow starvation of the little boy the witches have kidnapped is not only a prelude to but a figure for Varus' erotic torments; the boy's "dried-up liver" (*aridum iecur, I.* 5.37) foretells the parching of Varus in Canidia's fire (81–2).[14] The drama of Epode 17 brings the wax puppet of *Satires* 1.8 to life in the shape of Horace himself, a supplicant (*supplex . . . oro, I.* 17.2) consumed by flames (*ardeo*, 30). The exemplum he invokes to move his torturer to mercy –"The Trojan matrons anointed man-slaying Hector, the prey of fierce birds and dogs" (*unxere matres Iliae addictum feris | alitibus atque canibus homicidam Hectorem*, 11–12) – not only suggests the coincidence of desire and rage but insinuates that Canidia resembles the ravenous scavengers as much as the angry Achilles. In the archaic traditions analyzed by Emily Vermeule, scavenging dogs are an alternative to the funeral pyre, and both methods of corpse-cleaning have an erotic dimension.[15] They are the misogynistic counterpart, as it were, to the conventional imagery of "consuming" love.

Connoting brazen shamelessness about the use of those parts which are particularly associated with shame, dogs often appear as the other or under-side of female beauty. When the scholiast Porphyrio identifies an estranged mistress named "Gratidia" behind the poetic alias "Canidia,"

---

[13] Winkler (1990) 71–98.

[14] The liver is commonly the seat of sexual desire; cf. *C.* 1.25.15, *C.* 4.1.12, *E.* 1.18.72.

[15] Vermeule (1979) 104–9; cf. Putnam (1982) 97–8 on the dangerous eroticism of the aptly named "Pyrrha" of *C.* 1.5.

he renders the tension in the doubleness of the female, who should by rights bear two separate names indicative of these fair and foul selves.[16] But Gratidia does not figure in our poems, nor is there any trace of her attractions left in Canidia. If she exists anywhere, it is in the literary past; the Canidia of the Horatian present might be described as a debased version of Catullus' Lesbia. The relation between the two is evident in Epode 17, where Horace gives an ugly turn to Catullus' love poems. Having fallen under Canidia's devastating spell, Horace confesses the witch's power and pleads for a release. But the plea lapses easily into mockery: "I have paid the penalty enough and to spare to you, much loved by sailors and salesmen" (*dedi satis superque poenarum tibi,* | *amata nautis multum et institoribus, I.* 17.19–20). *Amata nautis* ("loved by sailors") echoes the earlier poet's *amata nobis* ("loved by me," Catull. 8.5)[17] while offering a bitter answer to Catullus' only initially rhetorical questions (16–17): "Who will think you're beautiful? Whom will you love now?" Adding insult to injury, Horace includes a heavy-handed allusion to Catullus 42, a verbal assault on a brazen-faced bitch (*catuli ore Gallicani,* 42.9; *ferreo canis . . . ore,* 17) which culminates in the flagrantly ironic address "chaste and honest woman" (*pudica et proba,* 24). Cited within Epode 17 to the accompaniment of a "lying lyre" (*mendaci lyra, I.* 17.39), the phrase retains its Catullan barb, as Horace declares himself ready to atone for his sins by singing Canidia's praises: "chaste and honest woman, a golden star you will stroll among the stars" (*tu pudica, tu proba* | *perambulabis astra sidus aureum,* 40–1).[18] Horace goes on to invite Canidia to imitate the Dioscuri, who forgave Stesichorus' slanders of their sister, "ill-famed Helen" (*infamis Helenae,* 42), after the poet composed his famous palinode. But while Horace casts Canidia here not only as the wrathful brothers but also as the beautiful and maligned sister, the compliment is vitiated by the ambiguous adjective "ill-famed": is Helen a spotless matron or the scheming bitch she calls herself in the *Iliad* (κυνὸς κακομηχάνου ὀκρυοέσσης, 6.344)?

In this context, neighboring on Catullus' bitch and doglike Helen, Canidia's "golden star" is drawn into the orbit of the Dog Star, in Latin

---

[16] For an illuminating if literal-minded account of Horace's "affair" with Canidia, see Hahn (1939).

[17] For this and other echoes of Catullus here, see Fedeli (1978) 134; Bushala (1968) 8.

[18] It is interesting that the woman Catullus attacks has hold of his writing tablets (hence the reiterated demand *redde codicillos,* Catull. 42.11, 12, 19, 20, 24); a similar accusation could be leveled against Canidia, who effectively usurps Horace's poetic authority in the closing lines of *I.* 17. See further below, 94–6.

known as "Canicula." The kinship between the witch's passion and the star's fever-inducing heat is registered in a curious reference to Canicula in Satires 2.5: "whether ruddy Canicula splits the speechless statues" (*seu rubra Canicula findet | infantis statuas*, S. 2.5.39–40) – a pseudo-vatic circumlocution for high summer that elegantly summarizes the action of Satires 1.8, where an encounter with Canidia causes a figwood Priapus to split (*diffissa nate*, S. 1.8.47), thereby transforming him from a "speechless statue" into a garrulous one.[19] Whether or not Horace had the identification of Canidia with Canicula in mind,[20] his poetry betrays the contiguity of their associative spheres.

As Hesiod's famous description of the dog days suggests, the season dominated by the Dog Star globalizes the perversion of sexual hierarchy embodied by Canidia (*Op.* 582–8):

ἦμος δὲ σκόλυμός τ' ἀνθεῖ καὶ ἠχέτα τέττιξ
δενδρέῳ ἐφεζόμενος λιγυρὴν καταχεύετ' ἀοιδὴν
πυκνὸν ὑπὸ πτερύγων, θέρεος καματώδεος ὥρη,
τῆμος πιόταταί τ' αἶγες, καὶ οἶνος ἄριστος,
μαχλόταται δὲ γυναῖκες, ἀφαυρότατοι δέ τοι ἄνδρες
εἰσίν, ἐπεὶ κεφαλὴν καὶ γούνατα Σείριος ἄζει,
αὐαλέος δέ τε χρὼς ὑπὸ καύματος.

When the golden thistle flowers and the chirping cicada sitting on the tree pours out its shrill song continually from under its wings in the season of grueling summer, then goats are fattest and wine at its best, women are most lustful, and men are weakest, since Sirius dries out their heads and knees, and their skin is parched by the heat.

In this season of maximal sexual discrepancy, when (in R. B. Onians' succinct formulation) "both sexes feel the want" of vital fluids,[21] female desire peaks just as male potency hits its all-year low. The parataxis of the clauses describing this discrepancy conceals, moreover, a causal connec-

---

[19] This story of the passage from silence to speech via a heating encounter with an aggressive "other" will be retold in the next satire (S. 1.9); see above, 36–9. For the association Canidia/Canicula, cf. also the symmetrical structure of I. 3, pairing Canidia (I. 3.8) with Canicula's "starry heat" (*siderum . . . vapor*, 15), and the sequence of S. 1.7 and 1.8, the first depicting Persius' defeat of the hateful "Dog Star" Rex (*canem illum | invisum agricolis sidus*, S. 1.7.25–6), the second Priapus' rout of Canidia. On these parallel battles see Anderson (1982) 79–81.

[20] At I. 17.41 the star in question must be, as argued by Barchiesi (1994b) 208–11, the stellified Helen, a star that signals death to sailors – more bad news for the ship of state and perhaps also for the epodic ship launched in I. 1.   [21] Onians (1951) 178.

tion: it is the woman's heat as well as Sirius' that saps the man's strength.[22] The rise of the Dog Star heralds an indecorous reversal of the sexual hierarchy, a resurgence of female heat at the expense of male potency. It is significant that the passage opens with the music of the cicada, mythical consort of the dawn-goddess, withered counterpart of her eternally renascent desire. Eos herself appears in a triple anaphora in the lines immediately preceding (578–81). Eos and Tithonus, youthful goddess and debilitated male, provide the paradigm for human sexual relations during this season.[23] If, as Canidia boasts in Epode 17 (62–73), Horace's efforts to escape her control through suicide are destined to fail, it must be because Canidia has granted him the dubious distinction of immortality. Like Tithonus, it seems, Horace is doomed to endure the heat of his mistress for all eternity.

Female heat, male debility: in Latin, these canicular extremes may be expressed by a single word, *impotentia*. The twinned meanings of *impotentia*, "violence" (the failure to master oneself) and "weakness" (the inability to master another), are played out in the three poems dominated by Canidia. In *Satires* 1.8 Priapus' jutting post (*palus*, *S*. 1.8.5; this is Horace's rendition of the Greek φαλλός) notably fails to do its apotropaic job.[24] Although Priapus does finally succeed in scaring the witches out of his garden, it is through no gesture of potency. Instead Priapus temporarily loses control of his body, letting fly a terrified fart that startles the witches into flight – an unintended act of self-assertion that splits open the statue rather than the intruders.[25] In Epode 5, neither the helpless little boy onstage nor "old man" Varus offstage offers a type of virile manhood. And in Epode 17, Horace is himself reduced to parched skin and bones (*ossa pelle amicta lurida, I.* 17.22) by Canidia's relentless heat. It is thus ultimately not (only) Canidia but Horace who is marked by the *canities* of enfeebled old age (*tuis capillus albus est odoribus*, 23).

But canicular heat is not the exclusive property of the lustful woman.

---

[22] Cf. Detienne (1977) 121–2; on the significance of the head and knees here, see Onians (1951) 110–11, 177–8.

[23] The same paradigm may inform the famous Homeric simile likening the Trojan elders to cicadas (*Il.* 3.151–2). Commentators identify the tenor of the simile as the garrulousness or eloquence of the elders without remarking Helen's presence on the scene. It is perhaps the fiery beauty of Helen, an avatar of Eos, that transforms the elders into Tithonuses. This would suggest an early date for the story of Tithonus' transformation, on which see King (1989).

[24] Cf. Anderson (1982) 76–7. On the Priapic satirist, see Richlin (1992) 58–9, 66–7.

[25] On Priapus' self-"rape," see Hallett (1981).

In each of these confrontations, male helplessness is shored up by the violence of invective. The gas bomb launched by Priapus in *Satires* 1.8, the "Thyestean curses" (*I.* 5.86) vented by the little boy of Epode 5, the withering ironies of Epode 17: in each case, impotence generates a compensatory invective heat. But impotence remains part of the story. What distinguishes the epodes is precisely this failure to erase the origins of invective in impotence.[26] This lineage is a joking matter in Epode 15, where the threat with which Horace menaces his fickle mistress – "Neaera, my manly vigor will really make you suffer" (*o dolitura mea multum virtute Neaera! I.* 15.11) – is instantly undercut by a conditional clause that signally fails to maintain a tough posture: "if there's anything of the man in Flaccus, he won't endure your giving night after night to his rival, and in his anger he'll seek out a mate" (*nam si quid in Flacco viri est, | non feret adsiduas potiori te dare noctes, | et quaeret iratus parem,* 12–14). The use of the cognomen "Flaccus" (cf. "flaccid") not only etymologizes Horatian impotence[27] but draws attention to the absent sting in Horace's promised vengeance. If Neaera has left him for a man who can satisfy her night after night (cf. *potiori,* 13), she is unlikely to be greatly disturbed by Horace's threatened departure.

But in Epodes 8 and 12 Horace's twofold *impotentia* is less easily laughed off.[28] Epode 8 begins by responding to what was probably an insultingly rhetorical question about the reasons for Horace's sexual inadequacy (*I.* 8.1–6):

> Rogare longo putidam te saeculo
> viris quid enervet meas,
> cum sit tibi dens ater et rugis vetus
> frontem senectus exaret,
> hietque turpis inter aridas natis
> podex velut crudae bovis?

You, rotted by long age, ask me what unstrings my strength, when you have a black tooth, and old age plows your forehead with wrin-

---

[26] Similarly Fitzgerald (1988) 189. Aiming to rescue Horace from recent "misreadings" which attribute impotence (which Watson interprets in the narrowest sense as sexual incapacity accompanied by sexual desire) to Horace's iambic persona, Watson (1995) succeeds chiefly in repeating and indeed bolstering the case he sets out to overturn; Watson's "toothless iambist" ([1995] 194) is nothing if not impotent.

[27] See Babcock (1966) 413–14 and in general on the discourse of impotence in the collection Büchner (1970) 74; Henderson (1987) 112–13; Fitzgerald (1988).

[28] On the tradition of invective against old women, see Richlin (1984).

kles, and between your shriveled buttocks your disgusting hole gapes like a sick cow's?

Like the attack on the ex-slave, this poem tells what Horace claims to be the body's ugly truth. But although the phrase modifying "you" already suggests the form of Horace's answer, the poem nevertheless begins as a defense of the poet's "enervation" – Horace badmouths this woman's private parts after she slanders his. The dynamic of Epode 12 is similar (*I.* 12.1–3):

> Quid tibi vis, mulier nigris dignissima barris?
> munera quid mihi quidve tabellas
> mittis nec firmo iuveni nec naris obesae?

> What do you want, woman most worthy of a black elephant? Why do you keep sending presents and messages to me, I who am no firm youth and whose sense of smell is not blunted?

Although later in the poem Horace offers indirect proof of his sexual prowess by quoting the woman's complaint – a complaint which is really a back-handed compliment: "you can do it with Inachia three times a night; with me you're always soft at the first go" (*Inachiam ter nocte potes, mihi semper ad unum | mollis opus*, 15–16) – this boast should not make us forget that Horace originally blamed his impotence on himself first (*nec firmo iuveni*) and on the woman second (*nec naris obesae*). Impotence, not disgust, is the premise of both poems. In a defensive reversal, the hideousness of the woman is manufactured to excuse the incapacity of the man.

While Horace might like to describe himself as fighting in a virtuous cause, driving out those who are guilty of disorderly conduct, attacks such as these bring the invective poet uncomfortably close to his targets. We cannot separate Horace's poetry from the misconduct it details; the ugliness that Horace describes is the ugliness of his description. The veneer of metrical and rhetorical form[29] does not contain Horace's violence, any more than his lover's cosmetic surface withstands the heat of her lust (*I.* 12.9–11); his sarcasms are as coarse a disguise for his intentions as her pretensions to Stoicism are for hers (*I.* 8.15–16). Nor can we wipe these poems clean by reading them allegorically. If Horace is criticizing not only sexual but literary excesses,[30] the critique has not managed to stay above the mud of its metaphors. As Emily Gowers has pointed out,

---

[29] Valiantly demonstrated by Carrubba (1969) 44–52.   [30] So Clayman (1975) 78–80.

the disgusting bodies of Epodes 8 and 12 are less the antithesis than the incarnation of Horatian invective.[31]

The polar opposition between Horace's epodes and Canidia's incantations is likewise complicated and compromised. On the one hand, Horace is at pains to distinguish his speech acts from hers. This may be one reason he calls his invectives *iambi* (*I.* 14.7, *E.* 1.19.23, *E.* 2.2.59), avoiding the term "epodes" (ἐπῳδοί), which might suggest their kinship with the witch's magic charms (ἐπῳδαί). Although in the middle of *Satires* 2.1 Horace cites Canidia's poisons as an analogue for his own satiric practice, at the satire's end he is careful to distinguish his "good poems" (*bona [carmina]*, *S.* 2.1.83) from the "evil spells" (*mala . . . carmina*, 82) a Canidia might cast. The clinching image of the satirist as a morally irreproachable hound (cf. *opprobriis dignum latraverit, integer ipse*, 85) may figure the attack-poet as a dog, but it also insists on the distance separating Horace from malignant biters such as Canidia. The alert sheep dog who wards off intruders in Epode 6 and the hunting dog who sniffs out the ugly truth of a woman's body in Epode 12 are likewise introduced as paradigms of canine virtue, no kin to the various bitches encountered elsewhere in the collection.[32] A similar contrast underlies the brief history of "Fescennine license" in Horace's letter to Augustus (*E.* 2.1.145–55), where Horace describes how this traditional form of entertainment, involving an exchange of rustic insults (*versibus alternis opprobria rustica*, 146), eventually turned vicious, like a rabid dog (*saevus apertam | in rabiem coepit verti iocus*,148–9), until the law against *mala carmina* was passed (the law to which Trebatius refers at the end of *Satires* 2.1), and the dog changed its tune, fearing the master's staff (*formidine fustis*, 154). If Canidia represents rabid *licentia*, Horace is evidently on the side of decently leashed and trained *libertas*.

But the deeply rooted kinship of the witch and the invective poet cannot be so easily dismissed.[33] The kinship of their discourses is on display in Epode 17, which pits Horace's exempla ("Achilles forgave Telephus") against Canidia's ("Tantalus suffers eternally for his sins"). As the dialogue-form of Epode 17 suggests, moreover, Horace's poems and Canidia's spells are alike enmeshed in the seemingly inescapable symmetries of revenge.[34] As Canidia insists that Horace will not go unpunished

---

[31] Gowers (1993a) 288.

[32] On the dog as a figure for the invective poet in *I.* 6, see Dickie (1981).

[33] On their affinities, see Barchiesi (1994b).   [34] See Gowers (1993a) 282, 288–9.

for his slanders (*inultus ut tu riseris Cotyttia* | *vulgata, I.* 17.56–7), so the invective poet undertakes to bite back when bitten (*an si quis atro dente me petiverit,* | *inultus ut flebo puer? I.* 6.15–16; note the repetition, with semantic variation, of *inultus ut*).[35] Horace dramatizes this symmetrical progression in Epode 5, where one vengeful speech (Canidia's against Varus) begets another (the little boy's against Canidia). A similar chain reaction is ignited in Epode 17, where Canidia punishes Horace for prior acts of poetic malice by heating him to the boiling point, thereby providing fuel for his subsequent attacks. The fact that no such attacks follow provides a crucial exception, one to which I will have occasion to return, to the general rule of the epodic game. Someone is bound to end up in tears, someone else in laughter. The only question is who, and for how long.

Canidia, Maecenas, and the cloak of Nessus

The misogyny of the *Epodes* is readily processed as a variation on a traditional and familiar theme which attributes the decline of Rome to the sexual misconduct of Roman women. One foreign woman plays directly into this story – Antony's ally and mistress, the seductive queen of Egypt, whom Horace eyes askance in Epode 9; Canidia is in a sense Horace's personal Cleopatra. But it would be a mistake to reduce the sexual epodes to allegories or moralizing diagnoses of the contemporary political scene.[36] The author of the *Epodes* is no more omnipotent than his various personae; Horace is not a detached analyst of current events but an enmeshed participant – sharing, let us recall, the social stigma of the upstart of Epode 4 and the bed of the woman of Epode 8. The dynamics of Horatian misogyny may be better understood in terms of what Neil Hertz has called "male hysteria under political pressure."[37] In the *Epodes*, sexual *impotentia* and civil war are intertwining instances of the canicular scenario. The same virile goods are at stake in the zero-sum games of sexual and social intercourse. The Dog Star is a cosmic projection not

---

[35] Cf. the call for vengeance at *I.* 5.74, *I.* 15.11, and *S.* 2.1.44–8.
[36] For this strategy (not so much incorrect as inadequate), cf. Manning (1970) (Horace is attacking the vicious practices of actual witches); Nisbet (1984) 9 ("Canidia" as Canidius Crassus); Fitzgerald (1988) 189 (Horace's impotence is "a metaphor for the inadequacy the poet feels in the political context"). The claim of authorial omnipotence is often a justification for our own interpretations. But why should we believe that Horace has absolute control over all the recoverable meanings of his text – any more than we believe that his intentions are irrelevant to those meanings?   [37] Hertz (1985) 161.

only of the parching heat of desire but also of the devastating glare of the evil eye – that desiccating, invidious energy that threatens all growing, prospering things, and that is unleashed above all in times of civil war.[38] Horace's erotic sufferings are one symptom of the *impotentia* that afflicts all Romans with its debilitating heat.

Horace proposes a drastic cure for this encompassing *impotentia* in Epode 16. He begins by lamenting the devolution of Rome, whose very name bespeaks virile power (Greek ῥώμη, Latin *virtus* or *vis*), into the impotence of headlong violence (*ruere*, "rushing"): "Another generation is being worn down by civil wars, and Rome herself is rushing to ruin through her own power" (*Altera iam teritur bellis civilibus aetas,* | *suis et ipsa Roma viribus ruit, I.* 16.1–2).[39] Riven by civil war, Rome will accomplish what no other power could, her own destruction, and triumphant barbarians will trample her ashes (*barbarus heu cineres insistet victor,* 11). In the *Works and Days* Hesiod bids the farmer shun the heat of the dog days and seek "the shade of a rock and wine from Biblis" (*Op.* 588–9); in Epode 16, Horace extends this annual retreat into a permanent holiday, inviting his countrymen to abandon Rome to "soft" men (*mollis,* 37) and to assert their manly vigor (*virtus,* 39) by fleeing to the mythical Isles of the Blest, where they can reconstruct a harmonious community far from the turmoil of Rome.

If Rome has become an intemperate mistress who saps her citizens' strength, Horace's temperate paradise is a model of female virtue. Absorbed into the landscape, female sexuality remains safely under control (*I.* 16.43–6):

> reddit ... Cererem tellus inarata quotannis
> et imputata floret usque vinea,
> germinat et numquam fallentis termes olivae
> suamque pulla ficus ornat arborem.

> Earth unplowed renders grain each year, the vine always flourishes unpruned, the shoot of the ever-faithful olive buds, and the dark fig adorns its own tree.

---

[38] Canidia herself wields the evil eye; in *I.* 5, the little boy who has lost his apotropaic locket (*insignibus raptis, I.* 5.12), shrinks from the invidious glare (*quid ut noverca me intueris,* 9) with which she initiates the process of canicular desiccation; cf. Gowers (1993a) 285–7. On *invidia* and civil war, see Barton (1993) 95 ("envy is civil war") and *passim.*

[39] The same verb opens the despairing *I.* 7 (*Quo, quo scelesti ruitis?* 1). On the pun, see Macleod (1983) 218–19, and cf. the gnomic formula at *C.* 3.4.65 (*vis consili expers mole ruit sua*). On the key Solonic subtext of *I.* 16, see Cavarzere (1994).

No plowing, no pruning, no grafting: the moral excellence of these plants mirrors the original virtue and integrity of the human race before the corruption of desire. It should not surprise us, then, that the purity of Horace's "fortunate fields" is guaranteed by the absence of the Dog Star: in the promised land, Horace insists, "no star's blazing *impotentia* consumes the flock" (*nullius astri | gregem aestuosa torret impotentia*, 61–2). Occurring only here in Horace's poetry, *impotentia* is rightly associated with the Dog Star,[40] the source of all the varieties of impotence that Horace hopes to leave behind.

But these hopes are stifled by Epode 17, which offers in effect another version, in a different register, of the canicular story.[41] Whereas in Epode 16 Horace promises his fellow Romans relief from the trials (*malis . . . laboribus*, I. 16.16) of civil war, in Epode 17 he is himself seeking a respite from the labor imposed on him by Canidia (*nullum ab labore me reclinat otium*, I. 17.24) – only to be promised an unending series of new labors (*novis ut usque suppetas laboribus*, 64). And while Horace may banish such mythical voyagers as "the shameless Colchian" witch Medea (*impudica Colchis*, I. 16.58) and "Ulysses' hard-working company" (*laboriosa . . . cohors Ulixei*, 60) from the untrodden utopia of Epode 16, these characters seem quite at home in the dystopia of Epode 17 (cf. *Colchicis*, I. 17.35; *laboriosi remiges Ulixei*, 16).[42] One particularly ominous echo associates Canidia with the victorious "barbarian horseman" of Epode 16 (*barbarus . . . | eques*, 11–12), whom Horace imagines "arrogantly scatter[ing] the buried bones of Quirinus" (*ossa Quirini | . . . dissipabit insolens*, 13–14). The apocalyptic vaunt of Canidia, who is also wont to disturb the bones of the dead (cf. *S.* 1.8.22), paints a similar picture: "I'll ride horseback one day on enemy shoulders, and the world will yield before my unheard-of arrogance" (*vectabor umeris tunc ego inimicis eques, | meaeque terra cedet insolentiae*, I. 17.74–5). In this climactic perversion of hierarchy, Horace's Cleopatra asserts a dominion at once sexual, social, and imperial, "riding" her enemy as a knight his mount and compelling the world

---

[40] The identification is supported by the scholia here and at *I.* 1.27, where Horace is not interested in being rich enough to move his cattle to summer pastures *ante sidus fervidum* (Ps.-Acro glosses *ante caniculares dies*). More interesting evidence is afforded by a comparison of the idyllic landscape of *I.* 16, complete with ilex and down-leaping waters (47–8), to that of *C.* 3.13, Horace's great sublimation of canicular *impotentia* into Callimachean refinement; see further below, 98–101.

[41] On the juxtaposition, see also Armstrong (1989) 64; likewise Fitzgerald (1988) 177–9 on the parallel "plots" of *I.*15 and 16.

[42] On the erotic tenor of *laboriosus* here, see Bushala (1968).

(including Rome – but Canidia's mythic victory is not susceptible to such specifications) to acknowledge her power.

Within the *Epodes*, Horace envisions not one but two possible exits from Rome's grim canicular romance. One, the subject of Horace's harangue in Epode 16, involves the obliteration of proper names and the eradication of differences within the virile community. The other, represented by Epodes 1 and 9, involves by contrast the introduction of proper names such as Maecenas and Caesar, names that specify, differentiate, and offer a possible telos for the narrative. Civil war will only come to an end, in other words, when distinctions are either altogether abolished or firmly reestablished. While the first solution is marked as utopian – and blocked, in any case, by the resurgence of Canidia in Epode 17 – the second seems more promising. If Horace's subjection to Canidia perverts the proper order of things, his subordination to Maecenas appears to be an instance of the kind of coupling which holds Roman society together.

This is the message of the programmatic exercise in epodic hierarchy with which Horace broaches his collection (*I.* 1.1–14):

> Ibis Liburnis inter alta navium,
>   amice, propugnacula,
> paratus omne Caesaris periculum
>   subire, Maecenas, tuo.
> quid nos, quibus te vita si superstite
>   iucunda, si contra, gravis?
> utrumne iussi persequemur otium,
>   non dulce, ni tecum simul,
> an hunc laborem, mente laturi decet
>   qua ferre non mollis viros?
> feremus et te vel per Alpium iuga
>   inhospitalem et Caucasum
> vel Occidentis usque ad ultimum sinum
>   forti sequemur pectore.

You will go on Liburnian galleys, my friend, amid high-fronted ships, ready to undergo every peril, Maecenas, at Caesar's side. What of me, to whom life is sweet if you survive, a burden otherwise? Shall I, as bidden, pursue a life of leisure, leisure which does not please unless shared with you, or this work, taking it on with a spirit befitting the endeavors of men who are not soft? I will take it on, and will follow you undaunted across Alpine ridges and the inhospitable Caucasus or all the way to the most distant western bay.

Maecenas' pledge to Caesar, encapsulated in the speech act of allegiance "I will go" (*ibo*, represented with minimal distortion by Horace's *ibis*) and elaborated in "ready to undergo" (*paratus . . . subire*), serves as the model for Horace's pledge: he too is ready to follow his friend into battle and to suffer its travail (*feremus, et . . . sequemur*).[43] The hierarchical design of the epodic distich is underlined here, at the outset of the collection, by the placement of the prefixes *sub-* (*subire*, 4) and *super-* (*superstite*, 5) in the lower and upper lines of their respective distichs, where they help to define Maecenas' position relative first to Caesar and then to Horace.[44] Or, alternatively (taking Horace's first person plurals literally), not only to Horace but to the plurality of friends and supporters Horace here purports to represent – a broadening base that further stabilizes this social pyramid. That this pledge is voluntary and not coerced is underscored by *iussi* ("as bidden," 7), a qualification that paradoxically casts Horace's determination to follow Maecenas as an act not of obedience but of defiance – love triumphing over duty, as it were. In this well-articulated chain of command, we are given to understand, it is the indissoluble bond of affectionate friendship that guarantees the loyalty of inferior to superior – of Horace to Maecenas, and also, by extension, of Maecenas to Caesar.

The same linkage is on display in Epode 9, at the midpoint of the collection, by which point Horace is anticipating not the battle of Actium but the party in honor of Caesar's Actian victory (*I*. 9.1–4):

> Quando repostum Caecubum ad festas dapes
>   victore laetus Caesare
> tecum sub alta – sic Iovi gratum – domo,
>   beate Maecenas, bibam?

> When will I, rejoicing in Caesar's victory, drink the Caecuban wine
> saved for holiday feasts, under a high roof again (such is Jove's plea-
> sure), in your company, blessed Maecenas?

---

[43] The chiastic link (*feremus* picking up *subire, sequemur ibis*) is reinforced by the patterning of simple and compound verbs (*ibis/subire, persequemur/sequemur*). See Babcock (1974) 20–1 (comparing *C*. 2.17); Williams (1994) 397–8.

[44] This hierarchical design is appropriately disrupted by Canidia, whose *adynaton* in *I*. 5 – "sooner will the sky sink below the sea, with the earth stretched out above" (*priusque caelum sidet inferius mari, | tellure porrecta super, I*. 5.79–80) – enacts the inversion it describes; the incantatory triple rhyme that knots this distich to its neighbors (cf. *tibi*, 77; *mari*, 79; *uti*, 81) is further evidence of Canidia's tendency to refute difference with likeness, a tendency that culminates in *I*. 17, where the distich dissolves into a series of formally indistinguishable trimeters.

If in Epode 1 Horace was gathering moral and social authority for his upcoming war of words, in Epode 9 he proceeds to wield this authority against Caesar's unnamed but readily recognizable enemies. The differentiation proceeds according to a familiar pattern: the enemy stands accused of perverting the natural order of things, mistaking slaves for citizens and women for men – Sextus Pompey by "threatening the city with chains removed from the faithless slaves he befriended" (*minatus Urbi vincla, quae detraxerat | servis amicus perfidis*, 9–10), Antony by turning Roman soldiers into the slaves of a "woman" (as Horace chooses to term Egypt's queen) and her eunuchs (*emancipatus feminae*, 12; *spadonibus | servire*, 13–14). Rehearsing the kind of propaganda favored by the Octavian party in this period, Horace thus projects disorder outward, away from the purified and reconstructed Roman community represented here by the hierarchy Horace–Maecenas–Caesar.[45]

I will have occasion to return to the putative success of Epode 9. For now, let me note that the amicable chain of Epode 1 is itself visibly under strain. Horace's gesture of deference extends not only to his position in the hierarchy but to the very mettle of his manhood. Unlike the unhesitatingly manly and martial Maecenas – this is the image that emerges from Horace's representation of Maecenas' pledge in the epode's opening lines – the poet harbors doubts about his own capacity to perform a labor that befits "men who are not soft" (*non mollis viros*, *I.* 1.10) and ascribes similar doubts to Maecenas: "you may ask how I could help your labors with my own, unwarlike and shaky as I am?" (*roges, tuum labore quid iuvem meo, | imbellis ac firmus parum?* 15–16). This conventional gesture of self-deprecation bolsters the value of Horace's valiant friend.[46] Yet in the context of this canicular collection, the vocabulary of impotence is troubling. As in Epodes 8 and 12, a question is raised about the poet's capabilities, and once again Horace seems not to be man enough for the job.

Horace is not, after all, perfectly comfortable with the subordinate status displayed in the opening lines of his first epode. His discomfort surfaces in the peculiar simile with which he answers Maecenas' imagined question (*I.* 1.17–22):

> comes minore sum futurus in metu,
> qui maior absentis habet;

[45] On Caesarian propaganda in *I.* 9, see Watson (1987).
[46] On the implied compliment to Maecenas, see Watson (1995) 201.

> ut adsidens implumibus pullis avis
> serpentium allapsus timet
> magis relictis, non, ut adsit, auxili
> latura plus praesentibus.

Accompanying you, I'll be less afraid, since fear increases in absence
– just as a bird guarding her unfledged young fears the gliding attack
of snakes more when she is away from them, not that she could
defend them better if she were there.

The simile is potentially unflattering not only to Horace, the futilely
fluttering mother bird, but also to his patron, here represented not as a
protective parent but as the helpless chicks – a reversal signaled by the
placement of *minor* in the longer and *maior* in the lesser line of their
distich. While we can certainly dismiss this figurative waywardness, or
read past it,[47] it is instructive to dwell on it for a while first. An illuminating parallel is provided by Book 9 of the *Iliad*, where Achilles complains
of the ingratitude of the Atreidae by likening himself to a mother bird
who "carries all the food she gets to her unfledged young but fares ill
herself" (*Il.* 9.323–4).[48] Like the Horatian simile, to which it has contributed the phrase "unfledged young" (ἀπτῆσι νεοσσοῖσι, replicated in
implumibus pullis, I. 1.19), the Homeric simile illustrates a relation
between men, and more particularly between men of unequal status.
Like Horace, moreover, Achilles is contemplating entering battle on
another, higher-up man's behalf. The immediate point of Achilles' simile
is that he labors to provide booty for the Atreidae while himself remaining empty-handed. But by casting himself as the self-sacrificing mother
bird, the Atreidae as his perpetually hungry and helpless chicks, Achilles
also sends a powerful message about his status (not child but parent) and
character (not lazy and selfish but hard-working and generous), implicitly distinguishing his praiseworthy self from his blameworthy (so-called)
"superiors." This subtext inflects the course of Horace's epode. It is true
that Horace is hardly an injured Achilles – unlike the hero of the *Iliad*,
our latter-day hero has little to offer (far from begging him to join the

---

[47] E.g., Cavarzere (1992) 122 limits the exemplum to illustrating Horace's affection. But it
would have been easy enough for Horace to achieve the same effect with a less problematic
image – likening himself to an old but faithful dog, for example, or a weak but eager puppy.
The parallel passages in Aesch. *Sept.* and Mosch. *Meg.*, regularly noted by commentators,
supply the terms of the Horatian simile but cast little light on its cross-identification. On the
programmatic significance of the simile, see Schmidt (1990) 134–5.

[48] On the echo, cf. Hierche (1974) 163–4.

campaign, Maecenas has apparently ordered him to stay behind) and nothing to complain of (as Horace goes on to underline). But it is also true that Horace is, like Achilles, in the process of negotiating his status in relation to men who are his social superiors. Although Horace has emptied out the content of the Homeric simile, refilling it with his own deferential blend, enough dissonance remains to remind us that the mother bird can figure not only helplessness but nurturing generosity in relation to her young. The simile may thus serve as an emblem, albeit highly compressed and imperfect, of Horace's characteristic career trajectory, from recipient of benefits to source.[49]

At the very least, the cross-identification saves Horace's face by rescuing him from an intolerable identification with the hungry chick, beak open for the patron's sustaining daily dose. In the closing lines of the poem, Horace rebuts this vulgar interpretation of his friendship with Maecenas more directly. Horace is eager to fight in the hope of earning Maecenas' favor (*in tuae spem gratiae*, I. 1.24) and not – as some might suspect – for the sake of more tangible rewards, whether in the form of more extensive lands, larger herds, or a fancier villa (25–30). Lest this disclaimer be read as an index of his patron's stinginess,[50] Horace hastens to add, by way of conclusion, that if his desires are moderate, that does not mean that Maecenas is not generous: "your generosity has enriched me enough and to spare" (*satis superque me benignitas tua | ditavit*, 31–2). In retrospect, it is easy to see that Horace could not have begun the poem with this grateful acknowledgement without suggesting that his devotion was purchased. The perfect tense of *ditavit*, which locates Maecenas' act of generosity in the past and its continuing effects in the present, also helps shield Horace's behavior in this poem from the charge of materialism.[51]

It is surely not an accident that Horace's next epode is a fantasy of perfect self-sufficiency. Although the speaker is retroactively identified as a usurer, the poem sounds more like the pipe-dream of one of his debtors (*I.* 2.1–8):

> Beatus ille, qui procul negotiis
> ut prisca gens mortalium,

---

[49] For this trajectory in *C.* 1–3, see Santirocco (1986) 153–68.

[50] This is a recurrent rhetorical problem for Horace; cf. the sequence of thought at *C.* 3.16.33–8, also to Maecenas ("I don't enjoy a luxurious life – but I'm not pinched by poverty – and at any rate if I did want more you would be glad to give it to me").

[51] See White (1993) 15 on large occasional gifts as a way of avoiding the appearance of a quid pro quo.

> paterna rura bubus exercet suis,
>   solutus omni faenore,
> neque excitatur classico miles truci,
>   neque horret iratum mare,
> forumque vitat et superba civium
>   potentiorum limina.

Blessed is he who, remote from toil and moil, like the human race of yore, works family lands with his own oxen, quite debt-free, nor starts up, soldiering, at the harsh trumpet, nor shudders before an angry sea, nor frequents the forum and the proud stoops of powerful citizens.

Securely ensconced in his proper place, this lucky farmer remains outside all systems of exchange. He stays put, and his land stays in the family. He is his own man and his own master, indebted to no one, competing with no one, inferior to no one. He is everything, in other words, that the grateful friend of Maecenas whom we met in the previous epode is not. The contrast operates in detail. As the close of Epode 1 makes clear, Horace's oxen and Horace's lands are not inherited family property but the gift of another man;[52] if not literally in debt, he is in a condition of perpetual gratitude, the analogue of debt in the sphere of friendship; he has just undertaken to play the soldier; and rather than shunning the stoops of powerful citizens, Horace (we must assume) seeks them out – Maecenas' stoop, at any rate.

Reading Epode 2 as the fantasy of Maecenas' friend helps bring one of its more curious features into focus: the total erasure of other farmers from its georgic landscape. If Epode 16 dreams of a world without women, Epode 2 envisions a world without men. Whereas Hesiod praises the good strife that makes a man "long to work when he sees a rich man who hastens to plow and plant and set his household in good order" (*Op.* 21–3), in the fantasy of Epode 2 there is no competitor, rich or poor, and for that matter no other free man, anywhere in sight. Insulated from strife, whether the good kind or the bad (and at this historical juncture the good kind was perhaps increasingly hard to imagine), Horace's model farmer reigns unchallenged in a solitude

---

[52] The run of the thought here ("I am interested in winning your favor, not in increasing my property; your generosity has enriched me enough; I am content with what I have") seems quite unambiguous, pace Bradshaw (1989) 162 (arguing that these lines do not indicate that the villa was Maecenas' gift).

fundamentally at odds with the hierarchical, intermeshed society represented within Epode 1.

I do not mean to suggest that Epode 2 is simply a Horatian fantasy of independence from Maecenas, a potentially offensive fantasy rendered "plausibly deniable," as it were, by the Archilochean surprise ending. In retrospect at least, it emerges that there are several things wrong with Horace's rustic picture.[53] Although the speaker of Epode 2 longs for a world without money – the only form of exchange envisioned here is an offering to Priapus and Silvanus, *tutor finium* (*I. 2.22*), gods who guarantee the inviolability of the farmer's property – it is increasingly apparent that he has no interest in a world without wealth. It is true that Roman artists (Horace and Virgil among them) are wont to depict agricultural prosperity as a natural and inevitable side-effect of moral excellence. But this dreamer seems to value the rustic ethos not as a good in itself but as a means to an end. It is one thing for Virgil to write of the farmer surrounded by his "dear children" (*dulces . . . nati*, G. 2.523) and supported by his "chaste house" (*casta . . . domus*, 524; the metonymy has absorbed the self-effacing wife). It is something else for Horace's farmer to imagine what an asset it would be to have "a modest wife," "on the Sabine model, or the sunburnt kind a nimble Apulian weds" (*pudica mulier, I. 2.39; Sabina qualis aut perusta solibus | pernicis uxor Apuli*, 41–2).[54] By contrast with the frivolous creatures (male or female) he might waste his money on in Rome, this hard-working helpmeet "does her part" (*in partem iuvet*, 39) to contribute to the domestic economy, enabling her husband to enjoy feasts which don't cost a penny (*dapes inemptas*, 48). The model farmer may be doing his own plowing at the start of the poem (*rura bubus exercet*, 3); he may be tired (*lassi*, 44) when he returns to his wife near the middle of the poem – tired presumably from tending the animals his wife now helpfully shuts into their pens. But by the poem's end all the labor is being performed by unspecified others (they are invisible; only the animals catch the farmer's eye) while the farmer relaxes over his supper, enjoying the spectacle of his rustic properties (61–6): sheep returning from the pasture, oxen from the fields, and – a significant addition – "homebred slaves, the swarm of a wealthy household, around the gleaming Lares" (*vernas, ditis examen domus, | circum renidentis Lares*, 65–6). In the satires, Horace accuses himself of vacillating between simplicity and luxury, country and city. Epode 2, with its slide from labor to leisure, from poverty to riches, por-

---

[53] See Cavarzere (1992) 125–6 on the irony in the usurer's praise of a way of life that his own profession has gone a long way toward eradicating.

[54] As Henderson (1987) 111 remarks, the place-names point to Horace.

trays with more accuracy the schism between moralizing depictions of life on the farm and the relatively hedonistic reality of life on a villa.[55] As usual, the poet who claims to owe both his leisure and his villa to Maecenas finds the fantasy of rustic autonomy difficult to sustain.

And in fact the free lunch of Epode 2 is paid for in Epode 3, a poem which shows Horace in the throes of acute indigestion, brought on by a meal laced with that paradigmatic peasant foodstuff, garlic.[56] The poem is constructed out of a series of hilarious hyperboles, making comedy out of Horace's base physical complaint. And yet there are points of stress in the arc of Horace's humor. Horace's opening joke announces the new malodorous penalty for parricide (*I.* 3.1–3):

> Parentis olim si quis impia manu
> senile guttur fregerit,
> edit cicutis alium nocentius.

If ever a man breaks his father's aged throat with undutiful hand, let him eat garlic, more deadly than hemlock.

But Horace's garlic not only punishes but produces a kind of civil disorder; as William Fitzgerald has pointed out, Horace's stomach forms the battleground for an internalized *bellum intestinum*.[57] Everything excluded in Epode 2 is now reintroduced. Whereas the farmer eats alone in Epode 2 (no guests are mentioned in the description of his ideal dinner), in Epode 3 Horace is, as we learn in the poem's closing lines, at table with Maecenas. And if the farmer's chaste wife embodies female desire safely under control, the witches who invade Horace's thoughts in Epode 3 bring canicular heat back into the picture.

Although Horace begins by complaining of indigestion, his allusions to Canidia, Medea, and Deianeira suggest that his garlicky meal has brought on something resembling a bout of sexual overheating. As one tightly interwoven passage suggests, the canicular heat that parches Apulia is a cosmic version of the cloak of Nessus that consumed Hercules (*I.* 3.15–18):

> nec tantus umquam siderum insedit vapor
> siticulosae Apuliae,
> nec munus umeris efficacis Herculis
> inarsit aestuosius.

---

[55] Cf. Virgil's oddly counterpoised images of the gentleman's leisure (*latis otia fundis*, G. 2. 468) and the peasant's labor (513–22).

[56] For a full discussion of *I.* 3, see Gowers (1993a) 280–310.   [57] Fitzgerald (1988) 181–2.

> Never did such intense astral heat hang over thirsty Apulia, nor did
> the gift burn more fiercely on the shoulders of capable Hercules.

The irony of the epithet "capable" is underscored retroactively when
Horace surrenders, in the first line of Epode 17, to the "capable art" of
Canidia (*Iam iam efficaci do manus scientiae, I.* 17.1). It is precisely the
capacity of "capable Hercules" that Deianeira destroys; the cloak of
Nessus is a hyperbolic figure for the hero's sexual humiliation.[58] The perversion of proper sexual roles is further illustrated by the star that "sits
on" Horace's home territory of Apulia, an image that not only heralds
but depicts female sexual dominance, prefiguring Canidia's posture
astride Horace's shoulders near the end of Epode 17 (*I.* 17.74). In the
battle of the sexes, the witches seem to be winning.

The final distichs of Epode 3 reveal, however, that it is Maecenas, not
Canidia, who has "poisoned" his friend's meal. Epode 3 is, it emerges, not
a piece of invective but a joking response to a practical joke. Its banal
denouement suits its banal premise, anchoring Horace's hyperbolic treatment of garlic in the quotidian context of a dinner party. Horace's last
words are thus inevitably anticlimactic.[59] Instead of producing the
expected "If you pull such a stunt again, Maecenas, may you burn for it!,"
the invective poet pulls his punchline, modifying Maecenas' punishment
to the more respectable pangs of unrequited desire (*I.* 3.19–22):

> at si quid umquam tale concupiveris,
> iocose Maecenas, precor
> manum puella savio opponat tuo,
> extrema et in sponda cubet.

> If you ever long for such a thing [again], my playful Maecenas, may
> your girlfriend raise a hand against your kiss and recline at the other
> end of the couch.

The modification reflects the friends' unequal status. Unlike Canidia and
the little boy of Epode 5, or Horace and the dog of Epode 6, or Horace
and his rival in Epode 15, Horace and Maecenas are not symmetrical
figures who can simply exchange places in the invective scenario. Even in
jest, Horace cannot envision his powerful friend in the role of underdog.
Maecenas is not mastered by his resistant girlfriend, as Horace by Canidia
or Hercules by Deianeira, and he thus retains his superiority relative to

---

[58] The sexual note is amplified at *I.* 17.30–5, where Hercules reappears as a foil for the overheated poet, in a passage that is a veritable résumé of *I.* 3.

[59] Fraenkel (1957) 69; Watson (1995) 198.

both his girlfriend and his friend. The difference Maecenas makes is evident in the eerily similar poses depicted in the opening and closing lines: a son with his hand on his father's throat, a girlfriend with her hand against her lover's garlicky mouth. By translating parricide into an erotic mishap, impious insubordination into conventional mock-resistance – a translation assisted by the intervening stories of destructive female desire, which displace political with sexual violence – Horace drains off the disturbing energy of civil disorder. Epode 3 may accordingly be read as a demonstration of the survival, in the midst of the civil wars, of an enclave of good fellowship that guarantees the eventual restoration of good order.[60]

Yet this happy prospect is complicated if we read the framing vignettes not as the two poles of a metamorphosis but as mirror images: first of aggression, punishable with garlic; and second of self-defense against the garlic-eater. In either case, Horace figuratively raises a hand – his writing hand, as it were – against his patron. Is the dominance of Maecenas in their friendship analogous to the dominance of Canidia over her lovers (including Horace)? Is the forceful desire implied by the verb *concupiveris* related to the aggressive eros of the witches? The social network in which, exiting the utopia of Epode 2, Horace here finds himself enmeshed, is itself a kind of Nessus' cloak. Within the *Epodes*, all gifts – the *munus* of Deianeira, the *dona* of Medea, the *munera* of the importunate woman of Epode 12, the gift of the Sabine farm – seem to be poisoned. The generous Maecenas, dedicatee of the collection and donor of "enough and to spare" (*satis superque me benignitas tua | ditavit*, I. 1.31–2), may be intended to form an exemplary antithesis to the vengeful witch who demands of her lover-victim punishments "enough and to spare" (*dedi satis superque poenarum tibi*, I. 17.19) in the final epode of the collection. But the patron's generosity causes Horace almost as much grief as the witch's insatiable appetite.[61]

The patron and the witch who bracket Horace's *Epodes* come closest to converging in Epode 14, where Horace responds to a familiar accusation, leveled now by Maecenas himself (*I.* 14.1–5):

> Mollis inertia cur tantam diffuderit imis
>   oblivionem sensibus,
> pocula Lethaeos ut si ducentia somnos
>   arente fauce traxerim,
> candide Maecenas, occidis saepe rogando.

---

[60] So Gowers (1993a) 309.   [61] Cf. Fitzgerald (1988) 182.

Why soft inertia has poured such a profound forgetfulness over my senses, as though I had drained with thirsting throat cups full of Lethean sleep: my good-natured Maecenas, you kill me by repeatedly asking this.

Horace goes on to blame his "soft inertia" on Phryne, a freedwoman he is stewing over (*macerat*, 16) – a state of affairs that Maecenas should greet not with reproaches but with sympathy, being himself in love with a charmer "as fair as the flame [that] set Troy ablaze" (*non pulchrior ignis | accendit obsessam Ilion*, 13–14). The poem thus ends by sorting the two friends out into parallel but decorously unequal couples.[62] But its opening lines contain traces of another story, one that illustrates the conjunction of social and sexual inadequacies. Maecenas' reiterated questioning (*rogando*, 5) of Horace's indolence recalls not only Epode 1, where he is imagined as questioning (*roges, I.* 1.15) his friend's capacity for military service, but also Epode 8, where Horace's bedmate demands to know (*rogare, I.* 8.1) what has unstrung his capacity for sexual service. And the opening phrase "soft inertia" echoes the complaint of the woman of Epode 12, who likewise finds Horace too "soft" and "inert" (*mollis, I.* 12.16; *inertem*, 17) to satisfy her needs. But it is above all Canidia who hovers dangerously close to these lines. The allusion to drugged *pocula* brings the witch's love potions into play, while the reference to "forgetfulness" recalls the "ointment of forgetfulness" that Canidia claims in Epode 5 to have smeared on Varus' bed.[63] The language suggests a connection between Canidia and Phryne, who is evidently adept at bringing her lovers under her debilitating spell. But the resonance of the witch's name in Maecenas' epithet *candide* ("good-natured" – a somewhat surprising choice in this context) suggests that Maecenas must also bear some of the blame.[64] It is as if the reiterated patronal "demand" were itself the cause of Horace's "soft inertia."[65] With his apostrophe to *candide Maecenas*, Horace comes as close as he ever will to revealing (perhaps inadvertently) that Canidia and Maecenas form in effect a single corporate whole. Horace's relation to Maecenas is not the solution to *impotentia* but part of the problem.

---

[62] Cf. the decorous parallelisms that close *C.* 2.17, a poem that likewise opens with the friends closely knotted together.

[63] Cf. *amoris . . . poculum* (*I.* 5.38), *poculum* (*I.* 5.78), *desideri . . . pocula* (*I.* 17.80), *unctis . . . cubilibus | oblivione* (*I.* 5.69–70; I follow Bain [1986] 129–31 in taking this "ointment of forgetfulness" as Canidia's concoction); these are the only other instances of *poculum* and *oblivio* within the collection.

[64] For a study of this kind of "lyric cryptography," see Shoptaw (forthcoming).

[65] Cf. *I.* 8.1, where the woman's "question" (*Rogare*) about Horace's inadequacy echoes the language of her sexual solicitation; see Grassmann (1966) 48.

Potent silences

What Maecenas wants from Horace, it emerges, is the completed book of epodes; what Epode 14 offers is Horace's excuses for not being able to oblige. A powerful god stands in the way – the god of love, who prevents Horace "from rolling up my iambic undertaking, my long-since promised poem" (*deus, deus nam me vetat | inceptos, olim promissum carmen, iambos | ad umbilicum adducere, I.* 14.6–8). Horace's *mollis inertia* thus combines impotence with art-lessness (*in-artia*).[66] The combination suggests that poetic mastery is founded on self-mastery and that the achievement of closure is itself an expression of potency.

Horace's inability to put a period on the book of epodes is symptomatic of his involvement in a civil war that jeopardizes the very distinctions that underwrite closure. The disconcerting recognition of the proximity of oneself and the despised other – in Girardian terms, a recurrent "crisis of difference"[67] – complicates the course not only of individual poems such as Epode 4 but of the collection as a whole. The crisis is played out in a series of poems across the collection's (off-) center. In Epode 9, as we have seen, Horace produces an image of Caesarian order that contrasts sharply with the perverted hierarchies espoused by Caesar's enemies. But the project of differentiation turns out to be incomplete. The fugitive Antony may be borne hither and thither on an "uncertain sea" (*fertur incerto mari, I.* 9.32), but so is Horace. At the poem's close, the celebratory Caecuban to which Horace looked forward in the poem's opening lines is converted to a medicinal use, as Horace orders a slave to "dose us with Caecuban to check the fluid nausea" (*vel quod fluentem nauseam coerceat | metire nobis Caecubum,* 35–6). Caesar's battle may have been won, but Horace's anxieties are not yet quelled: "it's a comfort to dissolve our worries and fears for Caesar's affairs with sweet Bacchus, the Loosener" (*curam metumque Caesaris rerum iuvat | dulci Lyaeo solvere,* 37–8). The same unsteady waters heave under Horace's ship as under Antony's.[68] Horace may be seasick, but his "fluid nausea" is also a symptom of the blurring of clear boundaries, both corporeal and moral.

It is significant that the verb *solvere* ("dissolve," "release," "launch")

---

[66] I owe this point to Denis Feeney. Schmidt (1990) 153–4 identifies the unnamed god with Jupiter, arbiter of the poet's lapsed moral authority, an identification that works better when the poem is viewed as part of the collection than when it is read on its own terms. By leaving the god unnamed, Horace perhaps makes space for both readings.

[67] See, e.g., Girard (1977) 49–67.

[68] While Horace is perhaps to be imagined as far from the battle and on dry land (so Williams [1968] 212–18), his concluding bout of "nausea" (literally "seasickness") may be taken to suggest that his concern for Caesar has effectively transported him to the scene.

recurs in the opening line of Epode 10, which attempts to clarify these boundaries once and for all. In this almost ridiculously confident invective, Horace attacks one Maevius, who figures here as a kind of low-class Antony: "Under an evil omen is the ship bearing smelly Maevius launched and on its way" (*Mala soluta navis exit alite,* | *ferens olentem Maevium, I.* 10.1–2). In Epode 9, Antony is described as traveling "with unfavorable winds," or more literally "with winds not his own" (*ventis . . . non suis, I.* 9.30); in Epode 10, Horace takes it upon himself to ensure Maevius an equally difficult journey.[69] Assuming the Caesarian role of commander-in-chief, Horace assigns his various winds – material extensions of his invective spirit – their roles in the upcoming campaign. First Auster is reminded to "whip both sides with bristling waves" (*ut horridis utrumque verberes latus,* | *Auster, memento fluctibus, I.* 10.3–4), reducing Maevius' ship, and by association Maevius himself, to the status of a slave.[70] Then, after Eurus rips off rigging and oars, Aquilo is to crash down on the ship "as forcefully as when on high mountains he shatters the trembling oaks" (*quantus altis montibus* | *frangit trementis ilices,* 7–8), disabling and as it were castrating both ship and passenger.[71] When Maevius reappears, he is sweating and pale with terror and venting an unmanly howl (*illa non virilis eiulatio,* 17); and in a final twist, as Alberto Cavarzere has pointed out, he is transfigured into the "randy goat" (*libidinosus . . . caper,* 23) Horace promises to the storm gods.[72] By contrast with his pathetically reduced foe – stripped of his status as a free man, a man, even finally a human – Horace maintains a pose of almost Jovian omnipotence.

With this downing of the ship of anti-state, along with its Antonian passenger, the book achieves a plausible ending. Ten is a good round number for a poetry book, favored by Horace in *Satires* 1 and by Virgil in the *Eclogues*. With poems to Maecenas in first and penultimate position, this abbreviated iambic collection would anticipate the design of two subsequent Horatian collections, *Odes* 1–3 and *Epistles* 1. The closural effect is enhanced by the polar opposition between enemy Maevius setting out on his ship (*exit, I.* 10.1) and friend Maecenas setting out on

---

[69] Compare *fertur incerto mari, I.* 9.32 with *quietiori nec feratur aequore, I.* 10.11. On the "imbricat[ion]" of *I.* 9 with *I.* 10, see Henderson (1987) 115–16.

[70] The magical efficacy of Horace's tongue-lashing is underscored by the proximity of *verbera* and *verba,* exploited again in the resonant phrase *verbera linguae* at *C.* 3.12.3.

[71] Cf. *I.* 12.19–20, where an unfaltering erection is compared to a young tree.

[72] Cavarzere (1992) 183–4.

his (*Ibis*, *I.* 1.1). Maevius' ill-fated exit would thus form Horace's happy ending.

But the absolute difference between the torrential invective poet and his battered target cannot be sustained, and Horace's triumph over Maevius does not conclude the collection, which goes on to append a suite of seven poems to its initial self-contained ten, producing a book that might be described as an epodic distich writ large. The failure of the "original" *finis* (and what we are dealing with here is, of course, not the history but the drama of composition) is flagged by the very fact that the book continues, and continues in such a way as to acknowledge the failure. At the start of Epode 11, the poet plummets from his Olympian heights into the depths of amorous subjugation, no longer the master but the victim of stormy passions. Elegiac dactyls now begin to break up his invective iambs (*I.* 11.1–4):

> Petti, nihil me sicut antea iuvat
>   scribere versiculos amore percussum gravi,
> amore, qui me praeter omnis expetit
>   mollibus in pueris aut in puellis urere.

> Pettius, writing poetry does me no good at all, just as before, hard hit
> as I am by love – love which requires me, beyond all others, to burn
> for soft boys or girls.

The metrical irregularity, varying as if drunkenly between stern iambs and soft dactyls, is thematized in Horace's memory of amorous nights past when he would "wander with unsteady foot" (*ferebar incerto pede*, 20; compare Antony, wandering on an unsteady sea, *fertur incerto mari*, *I.* 9.32) from the company of friends to the hostile door of a fair enemy (*ad non amicos heu mihi postis*, *I.* 11.21).[73] Horace's inability to hold his tongue after the strong finish of Epode 10 is replicated within the erotic narrative, as he recalls how the indiscreet wine-god used to draw forth his heart's secrets (*simul calentis inverecundus deus | fervidiore mero arcana promorat loco*, 13–14). In mid-lament, he would long to burn with "free-spirited resentment" (*quodsi meis inaestuet praecordiis | libera bilis*, 15–16) – with the iambic spirit that would free him from writing soft poems such as this.[74] In the present of this poem, Horace claims to have given up the fight, recognizing that neither the outspoken advice nor the harsh

---

[73] See Barchiesi (1994a) for a detailed demonstration of the dialogue between elegy and *iambos* in *I.* 11.   [74] Cf. Barchiesi (1994a) 132.

chiding of his friends can loosen the bonds which bind him to his new lover Lyciscus (*unde expedire non amicorum queant | libera consilia nec contumeliae graves*, 25–6). In this weighing of love against friendship (cf. *amore . . . gravi*, 2), the scale tips toward passion; Horace can be freed only by another erotic entanglement, "another passion, for a blonde girl or a smooth boy knotting/unknotting his long hair" (*alius ardor aut puellae candidae | aut teretis pueri longam renodantis comam*, 27–8). One knot unties another, a paradox summed up in the ambiguity of *renodantis*.[75]

Although Epodes 9, 10, and 11 are superficially very different poems, they operate within a single logic that opposes masculine self-mastery to effeminate subjection. But whereas Epodes 9 and 10 locate effeminacy in the reviled other (Antony, Maevius), Epode 11 brings the charge home to Horace. Horace's indiscriminate fever may be a benign variation on a standard erotic theme (unlike the elegists, Horace is not fixated on a single beloved). But within the context of the collection Horace's serial passions may also recall the darker indistinguishabilities of the civil war, the recurrent and seemingly incurable eruptions of fratricidal rage mourned in Epodes 7 and 16. If in those poems Horace is the doctor whose *libera consilia* and *contumeliae graves* are doomed to failure, in Epode 11 he is himself the hopelessly impassioned patient.[76]

It is fitting that the poem that reopens the collection takes the impossibility of closure as its theme. Like the history of Rome, Horace's erotic history is constructed as a series of episodes, always to be continued: *Altera iam teritur. . . .* When the collection does finally end, it is not with a solution but with an exacerbation of passions. In Epode 17, the erotic subjection of Epode 11 is intensified into sexual abjection,[77] as Horace, no longer issuing elegiac laments at the threshold of a hard-hearted beloved, grovels in desperate supplication before his vengeful dominatrix. The book ends with Canidia's rhetorical question, one that blocks the exit it announces. A witch capable of drawing the moon down from the sky and rousing the cremated dead (*I.* 17.77–9) will hardly fail to work her will against Horace: "am I to lament that my arts have no effect against you?" (*plorem artis in te nil agentis exitus? I.* 17.81).

But Epode 17 does nonetheless furnish the book with an ending, in part by at once replaying and inverting the scenario of the pseudo-

---

[75] Cf. Armstrong (1989) 66.
[76] On the political resonance of *I.* 11, cf. Fitzgerald (1988) 189, followed by Mankin (1995) 193.
[77] On *I.* 11, 14, and 17 as related treatments of desire interfering with *iambos*, see Schmidt (1990) 158.

closural Epode 10. In Epode 10, Maevius' ship is "launched and on its way" (*soluta . . . exit, I.* 10.1); in Epode 17, Horace's prayer for release (*solve, solve, I.* 17.7; *solve*, 45) is answered by Canidia's refusal of an exit (*exitus*, 81). If a seemingly omnipotent Horace once whipped Maevius into submission, it is now Canidia's turn to vaunt the potency of her spells (note her reiterated *possim* at lines 78 and 79), giving Horace a taste of his own medicine. Shipwrecked Maevius' terrified "pleas to an unsympathetic Jove" (*preces . . . aversum ad Iovem, I.* 10.18) are avenged, as it were, by Canidia's rejection of Horace's prayers (*I.* 17.53–5):

> Quid obseratis auribus fundis preces?
> non saxa nudis surdiora navitis
> Neptunus alto tundit hibernus salo.

> Why flood with pleas ears that are locked shut against them? The rocks beaten by wintry Neptune's rising surge are no deafer to denuded sailors [than my ears to you].

The ghost of the "denuded sailor" Maevius could not but be pleased by the fate of his quondam tormenter. But what needs emphasizing here is that it is Canidia who now occupies the quasi-Olympian heights earlier (if fleetingly) held by Horace. The book of epodes thus ends with not Horace but Canidia at the helm.

One reason for this displacement is that Horatian invective has no inherent closural mechanism. Like the civil war, one attack seems to generate another in a self-perpetuating cycle. Horace's solution is to let the vehicle of *impotentia* crash, with Canidia inside it. Epode 17 functions at once as a piece of invective and as a disavowal of invective, both of the epodic metrical form and of the epodist's role.[78] The epode's pervasive ironies, which cast blame as praise and victory as defeat, enable Horace to project the heat of invective onto Canidia while himself remaining, for all his proclamations of fiery distress, perfectly cool. The silence that follows Canidia's final rhetorical question may signal her ultimate triumph over the poet, who is struck dumb, like the accursed civil warriors he addresses in Epode 7 (*tacent, et albus ora pallor inficit | mentesque perculsae stupent, I.* 7.15–16). But it also coincides with Horace's achievement, at long last, of an ending. The poem thus reverses the story line of *Satires* 1.8 and Epode 5, where exposure to Canidia respectively

---

[78] Cavarzere (1992) 233. On Horace's epodic "self-destruction" via the figure of Canidia, cf. Barchiesi (1994b) 212–13.

transforms a dumb statue into a satirist and a soft little boy into an invective-spewing fury.[79] Having the last word may be a form of victory, but it is a victory that leaves the victor vulnerable to a symmetrical reversal. By yielding the field to Canidia, by declining to respond to her outburst with an outburst of his own, Horace puts an end to the endless game and arrests the perpetual motion of the invective machine. What follows Canidia's final vaunt is the silence of potency – the silence of a mended Priapus, unsplit by Canidia's furious heat.

The significance of this silence is amplified in the only poem that escapes Canidia's baneful influence almost entirely, the finely tuned thirteenth epode, where Horace rewrites the canicular scenario so as to exclude female desire altogether. The party that Horace recommends to his disconsolate friends is for men only – and for men, moreover, whose "knees are strong" (*dumque virent genua*, *I.* 13.4), not parched like the knees of Hesiod's heat-parched men. Unlike the drug-laced perfumes manufactured by Canidia (*I.* 5.59, *I.* 17.23), the garlic of Epode 3, and the disgusting secretions of the woman of Epode 12 (7–8), the nard in which these drinkers are drenched (*nunc et Achaemenio | perfundi nardo iuvat, I.* 13.8–9) is a true restorative.[80] It is no accident that at the end of the poem Horace chooses Chiron as his spokesman. Chiron – the "good" centaur, the famous healer – is the antithesis of the centaur Nessus, whose gore (consuming Hercules in the literalized flames of Deianeira's desire) is featured in two epodes, in both instances parallel to Canidia's drugs (*I.* 3.17–18, *I.* 17.31–2).

The success with which Epode 13 detoxifies the invective atmosphere may be gauged by comparing the poem with its utopian counterpart, Epode 16.[81] As in Epode 16, Horace refrains from specifying an addressee; this harmonious virile community is premised on the erasure of the status distinctions implicit in proper names. But the one name that remains, that of the consul Torquatus, invoked to date the vintage of Horace's chosen wine, anchors Epode 13 securely within history. Whereas Epode 16 envisions the vast periodization of the gold, bronze, and iron ages, Epode 13 finds cause for hope in the more human-scaled cycle of seasonal alteration: winter storms pass, and this too shall pass. In

---

[79] For this reading of the "educational" value of *I.* 5 I am indebted to Maurizio (1989).

[80] On the significance of unguents, see Onians (1951) 209–12; on the odors of the *Epodes*, Henderson (1987) 115–16; on the various interrelated "poisons" (garlic, drugs, blood), Porter (1987) 255–9.

[81] On the relation between *I.* 13 and 16, see further Schmidt (1990) 155–6.

Epode 16 Horace himself takes on the role of *vates*, undertaking to lead his people into the promised land: "encircling Ocean awaits us; let us seek those blessed fields and fortunate isles" (*nos manet Oceanus circumvagus; arva, beata | petamus arva, divites et insulas*, I. 16.41–2). Within the modest limits of Epode 13, Horace transfers the vatic function to Chiron, who tells Achilles of a landscape from which he, like the fugitive remnant of Epode 16, will never return: "the land of Assaracus awaits you" (*te manet Assaraci tellus*, I. 13.13). If Epode 16 imagines sailing right out of history, the *ut* that introduces Chiron's exemplary wisdom at the center of Epode 13 acknowledges the unbridgeable distance between our world and the world of the heroes. Chiron knows the future; Horace only knows the past. The symposium Horace offers his careworn companions may be a short-lived anodyne, but it is worth more than the patently utopian vision of Epode 16, which only highlights the horror of the inescapable present.

Within the *Epodes*, as we have seen, the inability to repress speech itself comes to figure *impotentia*. Horace's redoubled invective in Epode 4 only doubles back on its author, and the verbal flood of Epode 11 at once enacts and describes a failure of virile self-control. The narrator of Epode 5 prefaces Canidia's long speech with the tag "what did she say, or rather what leave unsaid?" (*quid dixit aut quid tacuit?* I. 5.49) – a tag that might also serve to introduce Horace's own extravagant invectives in Epodes 8 and 12. Epode 13 is by contrast full of silences. Horace does not disclose the source of the gloom that clouds the company (I. 13.3–8):

> rapiamus, amici,
> occasionem de die, dumque virent genua
> et decet, obducta solvatur fronte senectus.
> tu vina Torquato move consule pressa meo:
> cetera mitte loqui: deus haec fortasse benigna
> reducet in sedem vice.

Let us snatch, friends, our chance from the day, and, while there is spring in our knees and no disgrace, let old age melt away from furrowed brows. Do you bring out wine pressed in the year Torquatus was consul, my birth year. Leave the rest unspoken; a god will perhaps, with a kindly turn of the wheel, restore things to their proper place.

With a kind of temporal foreshortening, this passage brings the poles of death (*senectus*) and birth (*consule . . . meo*) close together, and one message of the poem is certainly the familiar symposiastic injunction to drink up your allotted wine before your time is up.[82] But these drinkers evidently have a more particular complaint to make against their time. What needs to be set to rights is something both more profound than the weather and less universal than the condition of mortality. It is not my purpose here to identify that "something" but only to point out that Horace explicitly decrees that it shall remain shrouded in silence: *cetera mitte loqui*. Had Horace said more – had he, for example, replaced the *deus* with Caesar, the man appointed to set the world to rights, and included a few hits aimed against a particular enemy such as Antony – the poem might have taken shape as a reprise of Epode 9. As it is, Horace censors himself, bridling speech at the verge of invective. It is the potency of this achieved silence that sets Epode 13 apart from its iambic neighbors and gives it the appearance of a misfiled ode.

I will close this chapter not with an epode but with Horace's ode to the Bandusian spring (*Odes* 3.13), a poem that illustrates at once the survival and the transformation of epodic canicularity within the odes. By the time Horace publishes his collected odes, the civil war is over, Cleopatra is dead, and Octavian has become "Augustus." Times have, indeed, changed. No longer advising all virile Romans to flee their homeland, Horace relocates the pastoral utopia of Epode 16 in the Italian countryside. The Bandusian spring celebrated in *Odes* 3.13 is the twin of the ever-flowing spring near which Hesiod's holiday-makers take their ease during the dog days. The world of heat and labor, of battles and vengeance, seems very far away (*C.* 3.13):

> O fons Bandusiae, splendidior vitro,
> dulci digne mero non sine floribus,
>   cras donaberis haedo
>   cui frons turgida cornibus
> primis et venerem et proelia destinat;
> frustra: nam gelidos inficiet tibi
>   rubro sanguine rivos
>   lascivi suboles gregis.
> te flagrantis atrox hora Caniculae
> nescit tangere, tu frigus amabile
>   fessis vomere tauris
>   praebes et pecori vago.

---

[82] On the *carpe diem* theme here, see Davis (1991) 146–50; Lowrie (1992).

fies nobilium tu quoque fontium
me dicente cavis impositam ilicem
saxis, unde loquaces
lymphae desiliunt tuae.

O Bandusian spring, more brilliant than glass, worthy of sweet wine
and flowers, tomorrow you'll be given a kid, marked by its brow,
swelling with the beginnings of horns, for love and battle – in vain,
for it will dye your cold streams with red blood, this scion of the
lascivious herd. The fierce season of blazing Canicula cannot touch
you, you offer your lovely coolness to plow-weary oxen and the
wandering herd. You too will be one of the famous springs, when I
tell of the ilex above the hollow caverns from which your chattering
streams leap down.

No overheated women trouble this pastoral refuge; no amorous heifers
pursue these weary oxen. The parching heat of canicular desire is reme-
died by the spring's "lovely coolness" (*frigus amabile*),[83] and if the brisk
feminine waters (*lymphae*) that issue from the spring are garrulous, their
untranslatable musical "chatter" remains perfectly chaste. The waters the
usurer Alfius imagines dozing by – "springs clamor with splashing
waters, inviting light naps" (*fontesque lymphis obstrepunt manantibus,* |
somnos quod invitet levis, I. 2.27–8) – derive from the same source. Such
water music is a charming lullaby, not a love-charm.

But Horace's *fons* is a source of poetry as well as refreshment. By
replacing the more conventional "I will become *nobilis* when I drink
from your waters" with "you will become one of the noble springs when
I tell of your waters," Horace bypasses the traditional fiction of inspiration for a claim of intrinsic poetic power. Instead of deriving his authority from a famous spring, Horace claims to confer renown upon his own
source; the local spring is ennobled by the famous poet, not the poet by
the spring. Horace mitigates the audacity of the claim here by using his
power to promote not himself but the spring. But the favor is reciprocal.
By canonizing the spring, Horace effectively canonizes himself.

As poems such as *Odes* 3.30, *Epistles* 1.20, and *Odes* 4.3 acknowledge,
this canonization is predicated on the poet's death – the displacement of
his mortal, perishable body by his corpus of immortal poems. In the ode
to the Bandusian spring, it is the death not of Horace but of a kid that is

---

[83] Cf. Vessey (1986) 388–9.

envisioned. Whereas the future promised by the kid's swelling brow is destined to be cut short, Horace's future has no date. It is significant that the sole appearance of the first person in this ode is in the phrase *me dicente*, "with me saying" (*C.* 3.13.14) – a participial construction or "ablative absolute" that absolves the poet from the grasp of time. The triumph over time is supported by the tenses (future main verb and present participle), which enable Horace's "telling" to fill both the present and the future of the poem. Horace's perfectly self-reflexive participial construction thus harbors its own semantic turgidity, like the kid's brow and like the spring itself, forever brimming over into the future.

The relation between the death of the kid and the life of the poet is also expressed as the difference between writing and voicing, book and music. As D. W. T. Vessey has remarked, the kid, with its "brow" and "horns" and red blood, sports the distinctive features of a bookroll, which also has a "brow" (the roll's edge), "horns" (the knobs at either end), and rubricated titles.[84] The poet, by contrast, survives above all as a speaker: *me dicente*. This is, famously, one of Horace's most musical odes – from the thickly-textured opening lines, resonating the sonic signature of the *fons*, to the liquid, clattering music of its onomatopoetic close.[85] When we pronounce these syllables, we revive Horace's *dicente*. The kid has lost its life to the spring, but Horace's words still leap off the page.

If Horace wards off canicular heat at the center of the poem, it is so that he can incorporate its power. In this ode, Horace does not match himself against Canidia, he becomes Canidia; the spell he weaves here is taken from the witch's "book of powerful charms" (*libros carminum valentium, I.* 17.4). Thus it happens that the ode effectively restages Epode 5 with different actors in the same roles. In the epode, Canidia is busy preparing a love potion; in the glassy mixing-bowl of the Bandusian spring, Horace is concocting his own magical potion.[86] Where Canidia plots to channel the vital energies of a little boy into her brew, Horace plans to sacrifice a young goat to his. In Epode 5 Horace claims that the sight of the boy's childish body could soften even the hardest hearts – all but Canidia's (*impube corpus, quale posset impia | mollire Thracum pectora, I.* 5.13–14); in *Odes* 3.13 it is Horace who hardens his own heart to the pathetic image of the humanized kid. Canidia's "uncommon potion"

---

[84] Vessey (1986) 391; Vessey associates this dimension of the kid with epic and suggests that the image is in effect a *recusatio*, an argument I find less convincing.

[85] See Wilkinson (1963) 57.

[86] On the spring as a precious glass utensil, see Vessey (1986) 386.

(*non usitatis . . . potionibus, I.* 5.73) is designed to rekindle her lover's desire and to renew her own youthful attractions. The potion of *Odes* 3.13 is also out of the ordinary, a philter of immortality. The blood that pours into the spring is metamorphosed into the *lymphae loquaces* that power Horatian lyric; and this source of power is never used up.

3

Acts of enclosure:
the ideology of form in the Odes

The aim of this chapter is to explore the combination of boldfacedness and self-effacement that characterizes the imperial poet of the *Odes*. By "imperial poet" I mean both the poet who claims imperial authority over his own "empire," his lyric domain, and the poet who celebrates the achievements of the emperor. As we will see, these two senses are closely intertwined. Horace correlates Rome's passage from civil war to the Augustan principate with his own progress from a poetics of *impotentia* to a poetics of potency; and he founds his newly secure lyric domain on the same conjunction of spatial and moral mastery that underwrites Roman imperialism. It is at the borders of poems, especially at their endings (both provisional and final), that the question of mastery is posed most acutely, and I will focus, accordingly, on Horace's thematics and pragmatics of closure – formal, spatial, moral, and ideological. Horace's poetic principate is not only dependent on but compromised by the centralization of *imperium* in the figure of Augustus. I will close with a discussion of the ways Horace adjusts his face when he invites the emperor into his lyric domain. Here I will be taking up the much-debated issue of Horace's "Augustanism" (whether "pro" or "anti") from the perspective of the rhetorical economy – the set of exchanges that regulates the interaction of the poetic *ego* and the emperor.

The poetics of potency

The distance Horace has traveled in the interim between the *Epodes* and *Odes* 1–3 may be gauged by comparing or rather contrasting the poet's posture in the poems that furnish their respective conclusions. For the groveling surrender of Epode 17 and the triumphant elevation of *Odes* 3.30 compose, it emerges, a maximally antithetical pair. It is almost as if Horace's lyric triumph were designed to eradicate all traces of his epodic humiliation. And it has done so with remarkable success. The self-canonizing *Exegi monumentum* instantly achieved the status of a classic; but how many readers, then or now, could recite the opening words of the seventeenth epode?

Where Horace's last epode made an exemplary display of poetic *impotentia*, the finale of his collected *Odes* advertises the lyric poet's newfound potency (*ex humili potens*, C. 3.30.12). In the epode, Horace pleaded on his knees (*supplex . . . oro*, I. 17.2) before an exultant Canidia, undone by her powerful arts (*efficaci . . . scientiae*, 1; *carminum valentium*, 4); in the ode it is Horace who exults, Horace who is celebrating the victory of his art. The triumphant lyric poet anticipates not a living death but a glorious afterlife, as the ghastly corporeal immortality Canidia inflicted on her victim yields to the imperishable corpus of Horace's immortal poems. Canidia's magical *carmina* may have dried Horace up (cf. *ossa pelle amicta lurida*, I. 17.22), but Horace's lyric *carmina* ensure that their author will "grow forever fresh in the praise of posterity" (*usque ego postera | crescam laude recens*, C. 3.30.7–8).

The exclusion of Canidia is confirmed by the welcome Horace extends to two other female figures in this final ode. At its center, Horace boasts that his fame will remain green "so long as the high priest accompanied by the silent virgin climbs the Capitoline hill" (*dum Capitolium | scandet cum tacita virgine pontifex*, C. 3.30.8–9). In Epode 17, Canidia accused Horace of posing as the "high priest of Esquiline sorcery" (*Esquilini pontifex venefici*, I. 17.58; this is the only other appearance of singular *pontifex* within Horace's poetry), which is to say of presuming to have the authority to regulate her magical practices. In *Odes* 3.30, the authority is, indeed, all Horace's. The ascent of the high priest with his properly subordinated, chaste, and silent female companion underscores the decorous reallocation of sexual and verbal powers that has cleared the way for Horace's triumph. At the end of the ode, accordingly, Horace pairs himself with his own silent virgin. The poet who once begged Canidia for his release (*solve*, I. 17.45) closes his collected odes by inviting Melpomene to bind his brow with Apollo's laurel (*cinge*, C. 3.30.16).[1]

One measure of the difference between the epode and the ode is the very finality with which Horace writes his lyric *finis*, declaring his monument complete. As we have seen, the poet of the *Epodes* figures himself as incapable of such a gesture; the *impotentia* that infects the

---

[1] These two "Muses" sport similarly songful names ("Melpomene" deriving from μέλπομαι, "Canidia" suggesting, albeit with a lengthened *a*, *cano*).

atmosphere of that collection regularly thwarts the imposition of absolute closure. I do not mean to fault the collection on this score. Some readers may in fact prefer the litotic, ironic, and unstable ending of the *Epodes*, where Canidia's rhetorical question, "Am I to lament that my arts have no effect against you?" (*plorem artis in te nil agentis exitus?* 81), frames the "exit" it refuses, to the relatively hyperbolic triumph of *Odes* 3.30. Nor is the difference between these closing poems unmixed with likeness. The epode stakes its own claim to poetic immortality, albeit in an ironically inverted form (this deathless poet is not inspired but incapable of drawing breath: *neque est | levare tenta spiritu praecordia, I.* 17.25–6). And the ode mounts its own indecorous resistance to closure: "I will not wholly die" (*non omnis moriar, C.* 3.30.6), might be paraphrased "I will not completely close." Canidia clings to the materiality of the body, but so does the poet of the ode, whose quantifications – "I will not *wholly* die, a *good part* of me will escape the funeral goddess" (*non omnis moriar, multaque pars mei | vitabit Libitinam,* 6–7) – blur the qualitative distinction between mortal body and immortal corpus.[2] Although the ode begins in the manner of an epitaphic inscription, it ends with an imperative addressed to the Muse from this side of the grave, substituting for the enclosing tomb the closural ring of the laurel garland – an emblem of completion that gives the poet more breathing room.[3] Still, unlike the trick exit of the *Epodes,* a door forever swinging open and slamming shut, this figural resolution enables *Odes* 1–3 to come to rest.

Horace proudly submits himself here to the Muse, and to no other. Certainly not to Maecenas, nor even to Augustus. Near the beginning of his lyric collection, Horace invited a quasi-deified Augustus to linger on earth to enjoy "great triumphs" and the "name of father and *princeps*" (*C.* 1.2.49–50); by its close, the poetic *princeps* is celebrating his own triumph, having displaced Augustus altogether. Virgil's "triumph" in the *Georgics* offers, in this regard, a striking contrast. While Virgil envisions himself leading the Muses in triumph from Helicon to Italy (*Aonio rediens deducam vertice Musas, G.* 3.11), he is quick to install Caesar at the very center of his projected temple (*in medio mihi Caesar erit templumque tenebit,* 16). Virgil may pose as a poetic "victor," "brilliant in Tyrian purple," but his activity is entirely oriented to and delimited by the figure

---

[2] See Rubino (1985) 107; Connor (1987) 9; Woodman (1974) 121 resolves the tension by substituting the qualitative term "essence" for Horace's quantification.

[3] Horace may have had in mind the garlanded hair (ἐστεφάνωσε ... χαιτάν, Pind. *Ol.* 14.35; cf. *cinge . . . comam, C.* 3.30.16) that furnishes the closing image of Pindar's collected Olympian odes.

of "that man" or rather "that god" (*illi victor ego et Tyrio conspectus in ostro*, 17); it is Caesar's wars, Caesar's fame that Virgil pledges to propagate through the ages (*pugnas | Caesaris et nomen . . . ferre per annos*, 46–7). Where Virgil dedicates his pride to Caesar, Horace offers up his, in a gesture of celestially qualified modesty, only to the self-reflecting figure of the Muse (*sume superbiam*, *C.* 3.30.14).

I will return to the stresses that complicate Horace's lyric relations with Augustus in the final section of this chapter. What I would like to underscore here is the extent to which Horace does indeed owe his poetic laurels to the emperor. As Caesar becomes "Augustus," Horace consolidates his own poetic *auctoritas*. Where the epodes dramatized a crisis of difference within the Roman community, the odes dramatize, over and over again, the restoration of order and the end of civil war.[4] The achievement of *potentia* in the self-contained measures of Horace's odes is coextensive with the restoration of the distinctions between self and other, man and woman, inside and outside, that the epodes recurrently fought and failed to maintain. Granted, this historical and poetic rupture is incomplete, and Horace will repeat within the odes the characteristic gesture of the epodes – relapsing from order into disorder, overriding closure. But these relapses are now contained within the security of a relatively well-delineated poetic, historical, and ideological frame.

It may be an accident of history that Horace turned to writing Aeolic lyric in the post-civil-war period, but it is an accident that he has taken pains to weave into his story. In *Odes* 1.2, the first poem after his introductory priamel, Horace situates his odes at the edge of that period (an edge marked by the poet's first words: *Iam satis*, "enough now," *C.* 1.2.1) by retracing, as if for the last time,[5] the journey from civil war to civil order, from the *Epodes* to the *Odes*, from the leveling, indiscriminate flood to the singular, distinguished name of Caesar. It is significant that the closing lines of the poem couple this name with that of a foreign enemy: "do not allow the Medes to ride unpunished while you are our general, Caesar" (*neu sinas Medos equitare inultos | te duce, Caesar*, 51–2). At the frontier of the ode, this apotropaic prayer aims, with Caesar's help, to distinguish inside from outside and friend from enemy. From here on in, violence will be channeled outward to the margins of the empire, where

---

[4] On the relatively (and surprisingly) limited scope of opposition to Augustus in the 20s, see Raaflaub and Samons (1990).

[5] I stress the "as if": see below, 118–27, and cf. Lyne (1995) 89–93 on the relapse of *C.* 2.1.

Roman youths will die – the argument is a familiar one – fighting not each other but the Parthians.

It is, moreover, the history described in *Odes* 1.2 that makes possible the thoroughly ahistorical *Odes* 1.1, whose Italy, floating in a timeless present tense, is disrupted by nothing more seditious than a boar that has torn free of the hunter's smooth nets (*seu rupit teretes Marsus aper plagas, C.* 1.1.28). In this priamel, men compete for political distinction, farmers work their ancestral lands, merchants sail the seas, and soldiers wage wars, as if the civil war had never disrupted, prohibited, or perverted these pursuits. The Republican status quo has been restored so perfectly that not a crack remains to recall its shattering. This erasure of history is the precondition for the self-portrait of the artist with which Horace's bird's-eye overview of men's various enthusiasms concludes. Secluded within his "cool grove" (*gelidum nemus*, 30), separated from the vulgar crowd by an ethereal throng of nymphs, satyrs, and Muses, the poet is the very epitome of aesthetic detachment.[6] This detachment is underwritten not only by Maecenas, invoked in the poem's opening and closing couplets, but also and primarily by Augustus, who clears a space for the poet's grove within a pacified Italy.[7] It is within this figurative grove, a space founded but not occupied by Augustus, that the poet exercises the *imperium* which will eventually earn him his laurel crown.

There is another sense in which Horace's triumph is dependent on Augustus'. In the years following Actium, when Horace was writing his odes, the honor of triumphing – the greatest glory to which a Roman could aspire – was coming to be reserved for Augustus and (Augustus permitting) members of the imperial family.[8] Let us recall that the equestrian Gallus, first prefect of Egypt, doomed himself through a display not of poetic but of military arrogance. If Gallus had been content to carve his name on papyrus, he might have survived to sing the praises of Caesar.[9] Horace can claim the status of *princeps* because he is not competing in the emperor's sphere. The dignity of the traditional *cursus honorum*

---

[6] On the figure of the *nemus*, see Troxler-Keller (1964) 40–3, and *passim* on the significance of Horatian landscapes.

[7] Cf. Santirocco (1995) 231–4 on the relation between Horace's "private joys" and Augustus' "public achievements." On Horace's "integration" of Epicureanism and Roman political ideology, see Müller (1985). On the relation between *C.* 1.1 and 2, see further below, 127–8.

[8] This de facto restriction was not yet the rule (the last non-imperial *triumphator* was Cornelius Balbus in 19 BCE), but the process must already have been under way; see Eck (1985) 138–40.

[9] Cf. Hardie (1993) 128.

may be compromised, the rewards of aristocratic competition circumscribed, by the supremacy of Augustus. But there is no corresponding
limit on the poet's ascent to glory.[10]

Lyric and empire

Horace's claim to the imperial bays may seem ill-founded. It is epic, after
all, which is the genre par excellence of military conquest and imperial
expansion; epic, not lyric, is the natural home of the *triumphator*.[11] While
it is true that Horace will in fact sing often enough of wars and empire-
builders, it is also true that the lyric poet – and especially, as Don Fowler
has pointed out, the lyric poet who espouses Callimachean values – is in
key respects ill-suited for this imperial role.[12] The characteristic expression of Horace's poetic power is not expansion but condensation, not
conquest but restraint. Filtering its subject matter through its form,
Horatian lyric matches the aesthetics of containment with an ethics of
contentment that would seem to leave little room for imperial ambitions. If the indefinitely extendable hexametric form suits the Jovian and
Virgilian theme of "empire without end" (*imperium sine fine*, Virg. *Aen.*
1.279), Horatian lyric, with its multiple articulations and recurrent
arrests, tends to concentrate instead on *fines*.[13]

And yet it is just this emphasis on limit that lends Horatian lyric an
"imperial" character.[14] The peculiar energy that charges Horace's lyric
fines both derives from and feeds a larger cultural preoccupation with the
masterful articulation of space. Rome's imperial expansion was bound up
with the proper regard for boundaries; the *triumphator* who ascended the
Capitoline hill would find within the temple not only Jupiter but the
deified boundary-stone, Terminus. Beyond the sacred *pomerium* that
encircled the city of Rome (a boundary that could be moved outward
only by the man who had extended the bounds of the empire), the army

---

[10] Cf. on this theme Brisson (1988).

[11] When Virgil imagines his "triumph" at the start of *G.* 3, he is seemingly anticipating a turn
to epic. As Zetzel (1982) 96 remarks, with *C.* 3.30 Horace's "poetry has become the virtual
equivalent of epic." When Propertius casts his elegiac muse as a *triumphator* (3.1.7–12), it is
in the context of a *recusatio* of martial epic.   [12] See Fowler (1995) 252–6.

[13] On Horatian *modus*, see Reckford (1969) 50–6.

[14] This argument is anticipated by Fowler (1995) 256–8, and one aim of this chapter is to show
the extent to which Horace is aware of (and labors to evade) the problem of "bad faith" to
which Fowler draws attention. On the relation between Horace's lyric enclosure and its
imperial enlargement, the "circumscribed and protective" space of the empire, see Traina
(1986) 248–9.

on campaign methodically constructed its own simulacrum of settled order in the shape of the Roman military camp, a masterpiece of formalist invention to which an admiring Polybius devoted a good-sized chapter of his history. The land-surveyors who designed and gave form not only to these camps but to towns, colonies, and provinces, were masters of the traditional and ritualized art of ordering space. Under Augustus, the labor of measuring the land intensified.[15] While the surveyors parceled out tracts within new colonies, imperial geographers mapped the *orbis terrarum*, including much unconquered territory, as a set of Roman "provinces."[16] *Divide et impera*. The labor of the *finitores* supported the ethos of *imperium sine fine*; the ideal of terminal stability enabled the outward displacement of the *termini* of both city and empire. By as it were swallowing the primordial boundary-stone, Rome incorporated boundlessness within her own bounds: "other nations are granted land with a fixed boundary; the circuit of Rome is the circuit of the world" (*gentibus est aliis tellus data limite certo:* | *Romanae spatium est urbis et orbis idem*, Ov. *Fast.* 2.683–4).[17]

Imperial expansion depended on not only spatial but moral order. Rome's strength was regularly attributed to her adherence to the traditional virtues of frugality, discipline, and self-restraint, a topos famously encapsulated in Ennius' "Rome stands upon old-fashioned ways and men" (*moribus antiquis res stat Romana virisque, Ann.* 5.156 Skutsch).[18] And her decline was ascribed, conversely, for example by Livy, to the want of the "ways" and "men" through whose efforts the empire was both won and increased (*qui mores fuerint, per quos viros quibusque artibus domi militiaeque et partum et auctum imperium sit*, Livy *Praef.* 9) – to the ascendancy of "extravagance and avarice" (*luxuria atque avaritia*, Sall. *Cat.* 5.8), in Sallust's version of the story. At the religious festival of the Terminalia, neighbors paid homage to the incorruptible boundary-stone that marks off one man's property from another's, keeping greed within bounds. The virtue of continence was embodied for the commonwealth as a whole by the Terminus worshipped in Jupiter's temple on the Capitoline hill – especially if, as Giulia Piccaluga has argued, this primordial boundary-stone literally rested on a foundation of gold.[19] It is certainly suggestive that among Augustus' donations to the temples of Rome Suetonius singles out his depositing "sixteen thousand pounds of gold," along with a trea-

---

[15] On the geography of empire in this period, see Nicolet (1991).
[16] See Whittaker (1994) 15–19.   [17] See Piccaluga (1974) 196–200.
[18] Cf. Brunt (1990) 294.   [19] Piccaluga (1974) 166.

sure of assorted precious stones and pearls, in the *cella* of the temple of Jupiter (Suet. *Aug.* 30). Such public, noncirculating, centralized treasure forms a counterweight to the centripetal corruption of private fortunes.

The dependence of imperial potency upon moral restraint, outward expansion upon inner limitation, is a keynote of Juno's speech before the divine council of *Odes* 3.3. At the very origins of Roman history (the occasion is the apotheosis of Romulus), the once-hostile goddess concedes empire to Rome on one moral condition: Rome "may spread her name to the most distant shores" (*nomen in ultimas | extendat oras,* C. 3.3.45–6) and "reach with her armies every boundary that fences in the world" (*quicumque mundo terminus obstitit, | hunc tanget armis,* 53–4) only if she has the fortitude to shun the lure of gold (*aurum . . . | . . . spernere fortior,* 49–50).[20] Her worldwide voyages are to be motivated, accordingly, not by greed but by intellectual curiosity, a blameless desire to view the uninhabitable zones at the ends of the earth (*visere gestiens,* 54). Juno's hapless attempt to sever the link between conquest and enrichment by ascribing an Ionian, scientific impulse of exploration to Rome[21] effectively discloses the tragic paradox of Roman imperialism: imperial expansion destroys its own moral foundations. But the moral message is traditional enough. If Rome has the self-discipline to turn away from gold, to hide it away again in the earth (for example by consecrating it, anticipating the example of Augustus, in the temple Terminus will one day share with Jupiter on the Capitoline hill),[22] then no *terminus* in the world will stand in her way.

The same argument, *mutatis mutandis,* underpins Horace's assertion, at the start of *Odes* 1.22, that a man of blameless character (*Integer vitae scelerisque purus,* C. 1.22.1) will be safe in the armor of his virtue, however far he ventures beyond the edge of the Romanized world. Horace claims to know this truth from personal experience (9–12):

> namque me silva lupus in Sabina,
> dum meam canto Lalagen et ultra
> terminum curis vagor expeditis,
> fugit inermem.

---

[20] The stanza about continence, which comes between the two variously "imperial" stanzas, is joined to its predecessor by Wickham and Garrod (1912), to its successor by Klingner (1959), which suggests that this conditional stanza may apply to both.

[21] On this "surprising motive," cf. Fraenkel (1957) 270.

[22] Juno's allusion to the Capitolium a few lines earlier (*stet Capitolium | fulgens triumphatisque possit | Roma ferox dare iura Medis,* C. 3.3.42–4) suggests that this preeminently golden and preeminently imperial site underlies the (antithetical) pairing of *aurum* and *terminus* here.

> For in the Sabine woods, while I am singing my Lalage and straying carefree beyond the boundary-stone, a wolf fled before me, unarmed as I was.

The levity of this illustrative anecdote provides a nice antidote to the initial sermonizing.[23] What protects Horace from the fearsome enemy that lurks "beyond the boundary-stone," moreover, is not (only) moral but lyric purity. Behind this episode lies the phrase *lupus in fabula* (used by one speaker to alert another that the subject of their conversation is approaching), which derives from the folk belief that a man who fails to spot a wolf before it spots him will be struck dumb. In this encounter between man and wolf, Horace is, of course, anything but dumb. His stream of song suffices to counteract the wolf's fascinating gaze. The lyric campaigner, a light-armed soldier of love, routs his enemy and conquers the wilds by sheer force of musical enchantment.

Safe within the protective aura of his song, Horace is ready to travel to the same uninhabitable zones Juno held out to her morally temperate Romans – the sluggish, sunless north (*C.* 1.22.17–20), the heat-scorched south (21–2). Wherever you put me, Horace concludes, "I will love Lalage of the sweet laugh, the sweet voice," *dulce ridentem Lalagen amabo,* | *dulce loquentem* (23–4). While the echoes of Sappho (fr. 31 LP) and Catullus (poem 51) are unmistakable here, what is more significant is the depth of the difference between Horace and his models. Desire breaks Sappho's tongue – so her elegant verses declare; desire confounds Catullus. But Horace is precisely not undone by desire. His bodily integrity is not violated but shielded by his amorous song; his Sapphic verses are not a symptom of the *otium* that dooms great civilizations but an imperious and imperial expression of civilization. "My Lalage" may be a representative Horatian beloved, but she is also the hypostasis of Horatian song; to "sing my Lalage" is to chant the very syllables of musicality. If Horace wanders beyond the boundary-stone, and indeed to the ends of the earth, he is constantly reconstructing his own boundaries, designing his own traveling *fines*, in the articulations of his meter.

Here as elsewhere, the meters of Horace's verse measure off not only time but space. If imperial expansion is enabled by the proper regard for boundaries, in the "Lalage" ode Horace marks these boundaries in the metrical form of his verse. When he writes *ultra* | *terminum*, "beyond | the boundary-stone" (*C.* 1.22.10–11), he activates the symbolic potential

---

[23] On Horace's teasing of his Stoic friend Fuscus here, see Harrison (1992).

of his lyric space; as he passes beyond the *terminus* of the line-ending, he ritually performs the act of territorial transgression that produces the hyperbolic travels imagined in the poem's closing stanzas.[24] In Juno's speech in *Odes* 3.3, the adjective *ultimas* ("the most distant," 45) likewise occupies the iconic edge of the line. And when Horace imagines Caesar's campaign against Britain in *Odes* 1.35, he again sets his line-break to mark a territorial extreme: *serves iturum Caesarem in ultimos | orbis Britannos*, "keep Caesar safe when he sets out against the Britons at the edge | of the world" (*C.* 1.35.29–30). What sanctions these transgressions is the absence of an accompanying transgressive desire. The rich builder of *Odes* 2.18, who seeks to postpone the temporal *finis* of death by expanding the *fines* of his property, provides an instructive contrast (*C.* 2.18.23–6):

> quid quod usque proximos
> revellis agri terminos et ultra
> limites clientium
> salis avarus?

> And what about the way you pull up the boundary-stones of one neighboring field after another and leap greedily across your clients' hedges?

The man spurred by avarice leaps at once across the hedge that divides his land from his neighbor's and across the space that separates one line of verse from the next. In this episode of debauched imperialism, formal, spatial, and moral boundaries all give way at once.

While limit-words such as *ultra* and *ultimus* gravitate toward the end of the line, distant peoples are sometimes exiled to the edges of the poem. Horace marks the entrance to the pleasure-garden of *Odes* 2.11 with a line of foreign names, advising Quinctius not to worry about "What the warlike Cantabrian and Scythian may be plotting" (*Quid bellicosus Cantaber et Scythes, | . . . cogitet, C.* 2.11.1–2) – a (spatial and intellectual) marginalization of the enemy that makes the ode into an emblem of the empire, internally at peace, with enemies roaming its remote borders. More often enemies mark not the entrance but the exit of the ode. One example I have already had occasion to discuss is the prayer that closes

---

[24] The recurrent figuration of extremes in Catullus 11 provides an important model; but if Catullus is the flower at the field's edge (*prati | ultimi flos*, 11.22–3), Horace has more in common with the indifferent passing plow.

Odes 1.2, which establishes the border between inside and outside by matching the new representative of internal order against an irregulated enemy at the margins of the empire (*neu sinas Medos equitare inultos | te duce, Caesar, C.* 1.2.51–2). A similar apotropaic gesture concludes *Odes* 1.21, where a chorus of boys is instructed to entreat Apollo to drive war and hunger and disease away from Rome and onto the Persians and Britons (*a populo et principe Caesare in | Persas atque Britannos, C.* 1.21.14–15). The integrity of the poem as of the empire depends on the relegation of violence to the outskirts.

A comparable purgation is enacted at the difficult conclusion of the prayer to Fortuna, *Odes* 1.35. Horace's first closural gesture, which dispatches Caesar to Britain and a fresh army of young men to "eastern parts and the Red Sea" (*Eois . . . partibus | Oceanoque rubro, C.* 1.35.31–2), signally fails to seal the poem. It is as if the image of the Red Sea, too fluid to mark the boundary, only succeeded in evoking the civil wars that reddened the entire Mediterranean with Italian blood.[25] As the poem reopens, a flood of memories surprises Horace, who vents a lament that spills, as if uncontrollably, over line and stanza breaks. Imperial expansion is compromised when moral lines are crossed (33–8):

> eheu, cicatricum et sceleris pudet
> fratrumque. quid nos dura refugimus
>   aetas? quid intactum nefasti
>   liquimus? unde manum iuventus
> metu deorum continuit? quibus
>   pepercit aris?

> Oh for shame, the scars and the crimes of brothers! What has our hardened generation recoiled from doing? What sin have we left unattempted? What have the young, in fear of the gods, refrained from grasping? What altars have they spared?

The breach of the verse enclosure in enjambment conveys the collapse of the difference between inside and outside, brothers and barbarians, sacred and profane, which is not so much tranquilly recollected as relived. We have seen similar crises enacted in the *Epodes*. Here, Horace succeeds in pulling himself up with a second and final apotropaic prayer: "Reforge on a new anvil, against the Massagetes and the Arabs, the dulled iron blade !" (*o utinam nova | incude diffingas retusum in | Massagetas Arabasque*

---

[25] As Horace laments elsewhere: "What sea has Italian slaughter not discolored? what shore is free of our blood?" (*quod mare Dauniae | non decoloravere caedes? | quae caret ora cruore nostro? C.* 2.1.34–6). On the close of *C.* 1.35, see Schrijvers (1973) 154–5.

ferrum! 38–40). The poem achieves its sharp edge by reforging the "hardened generation" into an iron sword turned now not against itself but outward, away from the interior of both the poem and the empire.[26]

If Horace can align the boundaries of his odes with the edges of the empire, he can also figure the empire as a Horatian ode writ large. In *Odes* 2.9, Horace represents Augustan imperialism as an analogue of his own lyric practice – the imposition of order on unruly materials. This imperial theme will, so Horace hopes, arrest the unmeasured flood of "tearful measures" (*flebilibus modis*, C. 2.9.9) emitted by his elegist-friend Valgius, who is mourning a lost love (17–24):[27]

> desine mollium
> tandem querelarum, et potius nova
> cantemus Augusti tropaea
> Caesaris et rigidum Niphaten,
> Medumque flumen gentibus additum
> victis minores volvere vertices
> intraque praescriptum Gelonos
> exiguis equitare campis.

At long last leave off those soft laments, let's sing instead of Augustus' latest trophies, of stiff Niphates, and of how the Median river, added to the number of conquered peoples, rolls with diminished crests, and of the Geloni cantering within set bounds in narrow fields.

The wit of the poem springs from the unlikely alliance it forges, in the cause of measure, between lyric and epic. This alliance is enabled by the transfer to elegy of the measurelessness usually associated with epic; Valgius' flood of elegiac couplets is the moral and (measured against Horace's tight stanzas) formal equivalent of the continuous verse (*carmen perpetuum*) Horace elsewhere rejects.[28] Doubly reduced, at once conquered and miniaturized, Rome's enemies will fit nicely within the frame of the lyric stanza, figured in the "narrow fields" of the final line.[29] As

---

[26] As in C. 1.2, closure coincides with the displacement of an opening universalism (Dacians, Scythians, and Italians united and undifferentiated in their fear of Fortuna, C. 1.35.9–12) by a differentiated, Rome-centered perspective.

[27] On the dynamics of this *recusatio*, see Davis (1991) 50–60.

[28] See Nisbet and Hubbard (1970) 97, commenting on C. 1.7.6 *carmine perpetuo* – a phrase that occurs within a poem that itself mimics hexametric unbrokenness (coupling dactylic hexameter and pentameter) while recommending lyric interruptions (*finire*, 17).

[29] See Davis (1991) 60 with n. 53; Fowler (1995) 257 ("Augustus will make good Callimacheans of the Geloni if it kills them").

Michael Putnam has pointed out, if Valgius' endless laments are old and effeminately "soft" (*mollium*, 17) the imperial theme Horace recommends is at once "new" (*nova*, 18) and bracingly hard, like the "stiff Niphates." Valgius' soft complaint will be cured when he joins in singing of, and thereby internalizes, Rome's mastery of the world.[30] The inconspicuous adverb *potius* also plays its part here. Potency, whether aesthetic, moral, or imperial, depends on proper management of the boundaries.

Horace offers an exemplary demonstration of this manifold potency in the four stanzas that compose *Odes* 3.18:

> Faune, Nympharum fugientum amator,
> per meos finis et aprica rura
> lenis incedas abeasque parvis
>   aequus alumnis,
> si tener pleno cadit haedus anno,
> larga nec desunt Veneris sodali
> vina craterae, vetus ara multo
>   fumat odore.
> ludit herboso pecus omne campo,
> cum tibi Nonae redeunt Decembres;
> festus in pratis vacat otioso
>   cum bove pagus;
> inter audaces lupus errat agnos;
> spargit agrestis tibi silva frondis;
> gaudet invisam pepulisse fossor
>   ter pede terram.

Faunus, lover of fugitive nymphs, through my domain and sunny countryside step gently, and depart in kindness toward my little younglings – if a tender kid falls at the full of the year, and wine in abundance does not fail the jug, comrade of Venus, and the ancient altar smokes with abundant incense. The whole herd romps on the grassy field, when your Nones of December come round again; on holiday in the meadow, the village idles in company with the leisured ox; the wolf strays among bold lambs, the forest scatters the tribute of her rustic leaves for you, the ditchdigger rejoices in striking the hated earth with triple stomp.

The rapacious goat-god may bring with him the disruptive forces of desire and panic fear, but his December festival is characterized by an

---

[30] Putnam (1990) 223; on the language of virility here, see Minadeo (1982) 141.

almost miraculous calm, as the rustic community reverts to the undifferentiated equality of the golden age.

Instead of digging a ditch to keep trespassers off, the laborer dances a dance. But the activities are related. The *fines* of Horace's property are congruent with the measures of the poem; the ditchdigger's foot at once beats the ground and marks the time. Indeed, to channel the god's energy Horace marshals all his formal art. If Faunus crosses *fines*, Horace counters by drawing the line over and over. In this intensely delimited, unenjambed ode, each stanza is a self-contained unit, and practically every line (if we take the adonic as part of the preceding line, the sole exception is line 6) presents a complete image, if not a complete sentence. The prevailing modesty of the diction and the perfect simplicity of the syntax (after the first stanza, the poem deploys nothing but present-tense third-person indicative verbal forms) contribute to the effect of aestheticized primitivism. The effect is enhanced by the asyndetic, paratactic final stanza, which juxtaposes lines of almost identical metrical shape and sentences of almost identical grammatical shape. In the closing frame of this highly ordered representation of festive disorder, Faunus' transgressive step yields to the rhythmic stomp of the ditchdigger's foot, a foot that goes nowhere. Horace's final phrase, *ter pede terram* (C. 3.18.16), is little more than a formula for the adonic, the equivalent of our *dum da da dum dum*. The potential violence of Faunus is thus reduced, within the golden circle of the poem, to the beat of the meter.

But this peace comes at a price. Violence is internalized here in the form of a sacrifice; the appeasement of Faunus costs Horace a "tender kid." One could argue, moreover, that it is not just an individual kid but individuality itself that is sacrificed here, as in the sixteenth epode, for the benefit of the collectivity. "Faunus" is the only true proper name within the poem ("Venus" in the second stanza names not the goddess but, by a familiar metonymical substitution, her sphere of expertise). The only identifiable individuals of the ode are the poet-speaker, the divine addressee, and the anonymous dancing ditchdigger who transfigures them both. Although the poem furnishes most of the ingredients of a Horatian party, no friend is invited to partake. "Herd," "ox," and "village" are generic or collective nouns; "wolf," "lambs," "forest," and "ditchdigger" could populate any rural landscape. Not only the characters but the circumstances of the poem are generic. While the poem mentions a particular date, the Nones of December, as the occasion of Faunus' rustic festival, the "now" of the poem is unspecified. Horace's omnipresent indicatives create an all-purpose present which can be repeated ad infinitum, with new individuals in the undifferentiated roles.

What is banished, along with such specifications, is individual desire. Although the second stanza promises to fill the jug, "comrade of Venus," with generous quantities of wine, the following stanzas present neither seductive individuals nor amorous couples, human or animal, but, as befits this holiday break from agricultural labor, presexual golden-age collectivities. It is a mild and diffused eros that holds the rustic community together, yoking laborer and farm animal, wolf and lamb, in an aimless, amicable union. But this is a union, let us note, from which the poet is excluded. Horace may retain his mastery of the world, but he loses his place within it. Like Faunus, he exists on another plane, high above the peasant merrymakers.

The well-defined *fines* of the ode to Faunus prefigure the secure Italy Horace celebrates in *Odes* 4.5. Like the ode to Faunus, albeit on a different scale, this ode pairs an individual deity, here the quasi-deified Augustus, with a series of collectivities (the *gens Romula*, the *patria*, the *quisque* of stanzas 8 and 9, the reverent first person plural of the final stanza). Desire is here translated into what Putnam has termed a "spiritual eroticism": in the extended simile that fills the third and fourth stanzas, the fatherland (*patria*, C. 4.5.16) longs for the return of Caesar as a mother for the return of a beloved son.[31] Aesthetic, moral, and territorial integrity once again go hand in hand, although it is now Augustus, long-absent landlord of all Italy, whose perfect control is mirrored in Horace's crystalline stanzas. The poet cedes his godlike heights and takes his place below, among the undifferentiated rustic folk.

The fatherland may be likened to a mother, but the communal voice Horace adopts here is that of a child (C. 4.5.17–24):

> tutus bos etenim rura perambulat,
> nutrit rura Ceres almaque Faustitas,
> pacatum volitant per mare navitae,
>   culpari metuit fides,
> nullis polluitur casta domus stupris,
> mos et lex maculosum edomuit nefas,
> laudantur simili prole puerperae,
>   culpam poena premit comes.

---

[31] Putnam (1986) 107.

For the ox in safety makes his rounds of the land, the land is nursed
by Ceres and nourishing Prosperity, sailors fly across the calmed sea,
good faith fears the finger of blame, the purity of the home is defiled
by no sexual crimes, custom and law have tamed spotted sin,
childbearers win praise for offspring that bear their father's image,
punishment follows close upon crime.

These stanzas, in which the prayers of Horace's *Carmen saeculare* are
represented as realized, seem well suited to performance by a chorus of
boys and girls.[32] The style (end-stopped stanzas, self-contained lines,
simple syntax) recalls the lucid parataxis of Horace's hymn to Faunus, but
in this case the content is just as chaste as the form. The spotless household, modeled on the maternal, doting *patria*, is home to women whose
sexuality is entirely absorbed in the faithful reproduction of offspring.
Even agricultural labor is chastened here. If the ox is plowing the earth in
preparation for the seed, we would hardly know it from this description.[33] Again, the travelers who "fly across" – not furrow[34] – the
becalmed surface of the sea may well include merchants engaged in
trade, but Horace does not tell us so. These merchants would in any case
be a reformed breed, exponents of the scrupulous *fides* heralded in line
20. The reward of virtue is the eradication of labor, and Caesar's Italy,
scrubbed clean of every trace of moral turpitude, enjoys what seems to be
a year-round holiday – an implication spelled out in the representative
prayer with which the ode concludes: "may the holiday you confer on
Hesperia last long!" (*longas o utinam, dux bone, ferias* | *praestes Hesperiae!*
37–8).

But this holiday carries restrictions absent from Faunus' December
revels. *Mos* and *lex* may have triumphed over sin, but the battle is not
over. The new order keeps the restrictive forces of fear, censure, and
retribution close at hand. As if to check the incipient luxuriance of Italy's
renewed leisure, Horace caps his description of the rewards of peace with
a warning (*culpari metuit fides, C.* 4.5.20) and balances the praise meted
out to virtuous childbearers with the penalty that constrains the sinful
(*culpam poena premit comes*, 24). Horace seems to be thinking back to *Odes*

---

[32] On Horace's "metronomic ... manner," see Collinge (1961) 7–9; on the ode's choral character, DuQuesnay (1995) 134–5, 143–50 (suggesting that the ode was designed for performance as part of the festivities surrounding Augustus' return in 13 BCE).

[33] On *rura perambulat*, see Kiessling and Heinze (1958) 416; if the subject were not animal but
human, the phrase would suggest a landowner making the leisurely rounds of his property.

[34] Contrast *C.* 1.1.14 (*secet mare*), 1.7.32 (*iterabimus aequor*).

3.24 in particular, where he advised the man eager for the title "father of cities" that complaints do no good "if sin is not pruned by punishment" (*si non supplicio culpa reciditur*, C. 3.24.34), and that legislation is vain where morals are unreformed (*quid leges sine moribus | vanae proficiunt?* 35–6). Indeed the morally upright seafarers of *Odes* 4.5, sailing easily across a peaceful ocean, answer point for point the "sharpwitted seafarers" who "vanquish the bristling sea" in the earlier ode (*horrida callidi | vincunt aequora navitae*, C. 3.24.40–1), ready to do and suffer anything in their desperate quest to avoid poverty (*magnum pauperies opprobrium iubet | quidvis et facere et pati*, 42–3). In the new Augustan era, sailing and agriculture, the arts of the fallen world, are to be practiced in a manner befitting the golden age.

Peace and prosperity at home, imperial domination abroad: so long as Caesar is safe and sound, Horace proclaims, no Roman need fear the rebellious nations at the borders of the empire. While Caesar brings the world to its knees, his virtuous Roman retreats to a private kingdom, where he pays homage to the godlike ruler who is responsible for his rustication (*condit quisque diem collibus in suis*, etc., C. 4.5.29ff.).[35] In the final stanza of the ode, Horace shifts from this representative third person to the communal first person plural (37–40):

> "longas o utinam, dux bone, ferias
> praestes Hesperiae!" dicimus integro
> sicci mane die, dicimus uvidi,
>   cum sol Oceano subest.

"May the holiday you confer on Hesperia last long, brave commander!" we say, dry at daybreak, when the morning is new, and say again, wine-soaked, when the sun is under Ocean.

The communal voice, the self-reflexive inscription of prayer, the progress from dawn to nightfall, all conspire to fashion this unproblematic close, a poetic counterpart to the well-settled affairs of Italy and the empire.

But the seal on Horace's *carmina* is not always this tight. While capable of rebuking Valgius for his erotic and poetic excesses, Horace is also ready to rehearse his own. One particularly elegant performance along these lines is *Odes* 4.1, where Horace first disavows and then relapses into both love and lyric poetry. Assailed by Venus, the poet pleads his advanc-

---

[35] On the farmer as a mini-Augustus, see Putnam (1986) 110.

ing years and recommends in his stead the youthful Fabius Maximus, who will welcome the goddess and repay her attentions with a beautiful new shrine. As for Horace (*C.* 4.1.29–32):

> me nec femina nec puer
> iam nec spes animi credula mutui
> nec certare iuvat mero
> nec vincire novis tempora floribus.

> As for me, neither woman nor boy, nor gullible hope now of mutual affection, nor drinking-contest gives me pleasure, nor binding my brow with fresh flowers.

With this nostalgic expression of resignation, which paints in some detail the scene its repeated *nec* crosses out, the poem achieves a viable conclusion. Venus is snugly enclosed within her shrine, and desire is safely confined within the frame of matrimony (for Maximus) or within the circle of the past (for Horace).[36] The lines are, accordingly, laden with closural devices: the contrastive self-reference, the multiple negations, the return to the opening theme of unfitness for love, and finally the encircling garland, emblem of the closed circle of ring-composition.[37] A similar garland binds the end of Horace's second ode to Bacchus (*cingentem viridi tempora pampino, C.* 3.25.20). But another closural wreath, the one Horace demands of Melpomene at the end of his first lyric collection (*mihi Delphica | lauro cinge volens, Melpomene, comam, C.* 3.30.15–16), seems, in this context, more to the point. Horace's reprise of Melpomene's wreath amounts to a declaration that he will add no new flowers to his original "garland" of lyric poems.[38] It looks as if the fourth book of odes will end before it can really begin.

As in the *Epodes*, here too silence bespeaks potency. It figures as a testament to the aging poet's self-mastery, his willed and reasoned submission to the rules and regulations of decorum. But Horace once again fails to curb his tongue. The circle does not hold; the poet will not be

---

[36] See Habinek (1986).

[37] This "Ich-Schluß" (so Esser [1976] 118) would yield a poem of eight four-line "stanzas" – a good Horatian total, as Mark Griffith points out to me.

[38] For the lyric collection or "anthology" as a garland, cf. the "Garland" of Meleager. Horace may also be alluding, here as at the end of *C.* 1.38 and 3.30, to the closural punctuation mark known as the *coronis* (also meaning "wreath"). On the *coronis*-poems of Meleager and Philodemus, see Bing (1988) 33–5.

permitted to rest on his laurels. In a beautifully scripted outbreak of spontaneous desire, Horace simulates the tones of an authentic lyric voice (*C.* 4.1.33–40):[39]

> sed cur heu, Ligurine, cur
> manat rara meas lacrima per genas?
>   cur facunda parum decoro
>   inter verba cadit lingua silentio?
>   nocturnis ego somniis
> iam captum teneo, iam volucrem sequor
>   te per gramina Martii
>   campi, te per aquas, dure, volubilis.

> But why, why, Ligurinus, does an occasional tear slide down my cheeks? Why does my eloquent tongue fall indecorously silent in the midst of speech? In my dreams at night now I hold you caught, now follow you as you fly across the grass of the Campus Martius, cruel boy, follow you through the voluble waves.

The relation between these couplets and the body of the poem depicts in little the relation between the fourth book of odes and *Odes* 1–3: a coda is appended to something complete in itself.[40] Within these supplementary couplets, moreover, the overarching opposition between self-control and loss of control, decorous enclosure and indecorous effusion, is transcribed in erotic terms as an oscillation between possession and pursuit (*iam captum teneo, iam volucrem sequor*). In this recurrent dream, which suggests the nightmare race of Achilles and Hector around the walls of Troy, closure figures as one phase of an endlessly repeating erotic cycle – Ligurinus always enters and always eludes Horace's enclosing embrace.

The dynamic of the ode is encapsulated in the elision, across the line-break, of the final hypermetric *o* of *decoro*: *cur facunda parum decor(o)* | *inter verba cadit lingua silentio?* ("Why does my eloquent tongue fall indecorously silent in the midst of speech?" *C.* 4.1.35–6). Flowing over the boundary of the verse, the metrical irregularity is not only an emblem of

---

[39] The strategy goes back to Catullus 8; see Fowler (1989) 98–9. Cf. Sonnet 71 of Sidney's *Astrophil and Stella*, which follows thirteen lines of reasoned discourse on virtuous love with a very Horatian "but," venting the "authentic" voice of animal appetite: "'But ah,' Desire still cries, 'give me some food.'"

[40] Cf. the structure of the epode book (a seven-poem extension appended to a seemingly complete ten-poem collection), a structure likewise determined by an eruption of desire; see above, 92–4.

Horace's irregular and excessive desire[41] but also a token of the very fluency he here claims to lack. After all, desire does not silence Horace but keeps him from keeping quiet; the elusive Ligurinus elicits his tear (*lacrima*) and loosens his tongue (*lingua*).[42] And yet the elision that blurs the boundary also underscores it, prolonging the silence at the end of the line that articulates Horace's flow of words into a metrical form. What Horace is offering here is in effect an aetiology of lyric versification. If it is desire that creates the abrupt stops and starts that distinguish poetry from prose and lyric from more expansive verse-forms such as the hexameter, these interruptive silences express not only erotic vulnerability but also poetic power.

A similar interplay of continence and disclosure structures Horace's invitation to Tyndaris, *Odes* 1.17. For its first five stanzas, the poem presents itself as a refuge from the blazing heat, at once environmental and sexual, of the Dog Star (*Caniculae* | . . . *aestus, C.* 1.17.17–18).[43] At the start of the ode, the Greek god Pan is domesticated – translated into the Latin language and into an Italian landscape, and purged of his traditionally rapacious sexuality, which he leaves behind him, as it were, at the ode's door. Unlike the Faunus Horace addresses in *Odes* 3.18, this "fleet-footed Faunus" (*velox* . . . | . . . *Faunus, C.* 1.17.1–2) does not, it seems, exploit his speed to pursue fugitive nymphs. Exchanging wolf-haunted Mount Lycaeus for "lovely Lucretilis" (*amoenum* . . . *Lucretilem*, 1), this Faunus weaves a protective spell around Horace's property, enabling his flocks to graze in safety, without fear of snakes or wolves (5–9). It is within the magic circle of Faunus' music that Horace sets, in the third stanza, the name of Tyndaris (*utcumque dulci, Tyndari, fistula*, 10), as if miming the security she will find within his enchanted valley.[44] Horace's words, Faunus' music, and the landscape harmonize to master what they encircle.

Whereas the failure to master desire produced the intemperate landscape and overheated language characteristic of the *Epodes*, the mastery of desire produces charming music and refreshing shade. The gods reward Horace's "piety and Muse" (*dis pietas mea* | *et musa cordi est, C.*

---

[41] See Commager (1980) 65–6.

[42] This poetic logic depends in part on the liquid interplay (aided by the recurrent *cur*) of *Ligurine*, *lacrima*, and *lingua*. On the punning de*cor*o, see Reckford (1969) 125; on *volubilis*, Putnam (1986) 38 n. 5.

[43] On the "ambience of continence" in this ode, see Minadeo (1982) 58.

[44] So Putnam (1994) 362.

1.17.13–14)[45] by ensuring that his country cornucopia is always full to overflowing: "Here for you plenty will pour forth to the full, rich with the country's glories, from the generous horn" (*hic tibi copia | manabit ad plenum benigno | ruris honorum opulenta cornu*, 14–16). Semantic redundancy and sonic opulence collaborate to produce an extraordinary sense of liquid plenitude. There is no trace of "dry old age" here (cf. *arida | ... | ... canitie, C.* 2.11.6–8). Horace's rustic abundance sublimates sexual resources into an inexhaustible material and poetic *potentia*. The song Horace proposes to Tyndaris in the next stanza involves a similar translation (17–20):

> hic in reducta valle Caniculae
> vitabis aestus et fide Teia
> dices laborantis in uno
> Penelopen vitreamque Circen.

> Here in a protected valley you will avoid the blaze of Canicula and, on Anacreon's lyre, you'll tell of Penelope and glassy Circe, suffering over the same man.

The overheated femininity associated with the rule of Canicula (an excess represented in this case by simple multiplication: two women in love with one man) is cooled and processed into its poetic representation. Tyndaris will fill her leisure with a song of love's labor, singing dispassionately of passion.

With this summative stanza – gathering up the heat of stanza 1, the security of stanza 2, the valley of stanza 3, and the music of stanza 4 – *Odes* 1.17 might well have concluded.[46] Tyndaris would then be named, fittingly enough, at the ode's precise center, while "Circe" would coincide with the closing of the lyric circle. Such an ending, projecting the pangs of desire onto the characters of epic, would confirm the godlike ease of the blessed goatherd and his musical guest.[47] We might compare the end of Horace's ode to Quinctius, where Horace orders a slave to

---

[45] No single word suffices to translate the Latin *pietas*, which denotes what the *Oxford Latin Dictionary* terms "an attitude of dutiful respect" in all relations involving reciprocal obligation. To signal the presence of this concept I will either retain the Latin or use the English cognates "piety" and "pious," even though their religious connotations are often absent from the Latin.

[46] Cf. *Caniculae | ... aestus* (17–18) / *igneam ... aestatem* (2–3); *reducta* (17) / *tutum* (5); *valle* (17) / *valles* (11); *fide Teia* (17) / *fistula* (10).

[47] Note that when the poem does end, it imitates the pattern of line 20: noun, adjective + *que*, noun.

summon Lyde to their party: "Run and tell her to hurry here with her ivory lyre, just tying back her hair, Spartan-style, in a neat knot" (*eburna dic age cum lyra | maturet in comptum Lacaenae | more comas religata nodum*, C. 2.11.22–4).[48] If Lyde introduces the specter of erotic conflict (between, say, the two male friends she is invited to entertain), the danger is defused by this perfectly self-reflexive ending, which assimilates Lyde to the Horatian lyre and gathers her straying tresses into a neat knot, emblem at once of poetic closure and of moral restraint. Here as elsewhere in Horace's poetry, the desire diverted away from the woman's body and toward her song ultimately fuels the desire of the reader or listener for Horace's braided odes, of which the song is the synecdochal representation.

But *Odes* 1.17 continues past Tyndaris' song. Horace attaches, with another anaphoric "here" (*hic*, C. 1.17.21, completing a tricolon with *hic* at lines 14 and 17), another stanza, promising Tyndaris that the harmless wine he has to offer will stir up no battles. And this stanza overflows into another (24–8):

> nec metues protervum
> suspecta Cyrum, ne male dispari
> incontinentis iniciat manus
> et scindat haerentem coronam
> crinibus immeritamque vestem.

> nor will you have to worry about that hothead Cyrus and his suspicions, for fear he might lay unrestrained hands on you, unequal as you are, and tear the garland clinging to your curls, and your undeserving dress.

Cyrus is a perfect foil for the peaceable poet; his hands are "incontinent," his intentions violently sexual, his actions disruptive of the trappings and mood of the projected picnic.[49] And yet it remains the case that, in Pietro Pucci's words, "the poet performs, at the figurative level, the violence that Cyrus is prevented from enacting."[50] It is as if the very perfection of Horace's control, the very fullness of his contentment, could not but generate a violent return of everything he has labored to repress. Poetic, moral, and territorial forms of mastery are all simultaneously compro-

---

[48] See Reckford (1969) 97 on this tempered "carousal."

[49] See Putnam (1994) 363–5; Davis (1991) 204.

[50] Pucci (1975) 275; my reading of the ode follows in the wake of Pucci's cogent deconstruction of the Cyrus/Horace polarity.

mised as Horace cedes control at once of his poem, of himself, and of the borders of the *locus amoenus*. The disruption of the boundary between inside and outside, self and other, shapes the ode's final image. If Lyde's "knot" (*nodum*, C. 2.11.24) represents the well-closed poem, Tyndaris' torn dress and shattered garland figure an irreparably torn text. While Horace's *ne*-clause brackets this image, the vivid description, which is left to stand as the poem's conclusion, keeps it before our eyes. The intertwined failure of *pietas*, potency, and closure that stamps the *Epodes* is rewritten here in the form of an erotic farce.[51]

The complications of closure in the grand Alcaic sequence that launches Horace's third book of odes have more ominous implications.[52] Like the ode to Tyndaris, this sequence of six odes, commonly known as the "Roman odes," centers on a declaration of *pietas*. I am referring to the unexpected second condition Juno attaches to her prophecy of interminable imperial expansion in the third Roman ode. For Rome's citizens, according to Juno, must bridle not only their greed for gold but also the excessive *pietas* that might spur them to rebuild their ancestral Troy (*ne nimium pii* | . . . *avitae* | *tecta velint reparare Troiae*, C. 3.3.58–60). This condition is consistent with the end of Virgil's *Aeneid*, where Juno likewise links the future of Rome to the irretrievable pastness of Troy (*Aen.* 12.821–8). But Horace's phrasing is a little unsettling. Juno's "excessively pious" Romans seem quite unrelated to the "impious generation" (*impia* . . . *aetas*, I. 16.9) whose despair is vented in Horace's sixteenth epode. Perhaps the gap between *nimium pii* and *impii* is historical, a measure of the distance between these early Romans and their decadent descendants. But in the context of this ode, where Romulus, whose apotheosis provides the occasion for Juno's speech, figures as a precursor of the *princeps* (who contemplated but decided against the honorific "Romulus" in favor of the less regal "Augustus"), Juno's warning cannot but read as a didactic message aimed at the present. While the precise significance of her warning may be obscure (perhaps intentionally so), the hypercorrective effect remains sufficiently clear. What threatens Roman dominion is no longer impiety, as in Epode 16, but, perhaps less plausibly, a superabundance of piety.

The erasure of the *impietas* of civil war reaches its pinnacle here, but it

---

[51] Cf. the interrupted sex scene (likewise framed within a *ne*-clause: *nec vereor ne dum futuo vir rure recurrat*, etc.) at the end of *S.* 1.2 (127–32).

[52] Tracing the broad outlines of this drama means neglecting its innumerable local ups and downs; I hope my reader will forgive the consequent simplification of the story.

is at work throughout the sequence. In *Odes* 3.1, Horace reduces the competition for political honors to a trivial exercise while deploying a generalizing present tense that (as in *Odes* 1.1) implicitly affirms the stability of the status quo. In *Odes* 3.2, no trace of civil bloodshed stains the young Roman who is training to do battle with the Parthian. In *Odes* 3.4, which glances at the civil war under the cover of myth, the *impietas* is all on the other, defeated side, with the "impious Titans" (*impios* | *Titanas*, C. 3.4.42–3) – overreachers, as their name suggests – and the monstrous Aloidae, "stretching" (*tendentes*, 51; the verb translates the Greek τιταίνω, the Aloidae are also "Titanic") to reach the sky by piling Pelion on Olympus (*Pelion imposuisse Olympo*, 52). The problem that engages Horace in *Odes* 3.5 is located not at home but abroad, where the tough soldiers of rustic Italy have been corrupted by their subjection to foreign kings and foreign wives – Italy itself remaining, by implication, a relative bastion of moral strength. Horace begins *Odes* 3.6 in a similarly grim but nonetheless hopeful mood (1–4):

> Delicta maiorum immeritus lues,
> Romane, donec templa refeceris
> aedesque labentis deorum et
> foeda nigro simulacra fumo.

> You will atone, Roman, though blameless, for the sins of your
> ancestors, until you have rebuilt the temples and decaying shrines of
> the gods, and their images grimed with black smoke.

Horace's "blameless" whitewashes the present generation almost as thoroughly as Juno's *nimium pii* (C. 3.3.58). Augustus' Romans are after all not at fault, it is their ancestors who are to blame for the horrors of civil war. Rome will confirm her renewed moral luster by repairing the temples and restoring the statues of the gods to their original brilliance, thereby offering a practical demonstration of the *pietas* which is, as Horace reminds her (*dis te minorem quod geris, imperas*, "you rule because you hold yourself subject to the gods," C. 3.6.5), the ultimate source of her imperial power.

But the discourse of civil war *impietas*, so carefully repressed, so heedfully circumscribed, up to this point in the sequence, makes in the end a quite spectacular return. It is as if the position of the present generation, below the gods (*dis minorem*, C. 3.6.5), but morally above their *maiores*, were ideologically untenable. Horace barely makes it through his second stanza before the rush of bad memories takes over. The corruption externalized in *Odes* 3.5 is now relocated at the very heart of the empire. The maternal fecundity of a "generation fertile in crime" (*fecunda culpae saecula*, C. 3.6.17), Horace laments, has flooded the fatherland with disaster, contaminating the Roman home with whorish wives and pimping husbands. The Romans who defeated Hannibal were not born of such parents; they were the "masculine offspring of farmer soldiers" (*rusticorum mascula militum* | *proles*, 37–8 – the emphasis falls on the adjectives: masculine, not effeminate; farmers, not decadent city-dwellers). The corrupt wife of the present forms a stark contrast to the "stern mother" (*severae* | *matris*, 39–40) of the past, a good housekeeper who oversees the labors of her obedient son.

Horace's nostalgic vignette of this exemplary son carrying logs home while the setting sun lengthens the shadows on the mountains, unyokes the weary oxen, and brings on the "friendly hour" of night (*amicum* | *tempus*, C. 3.6.43–4), would have made a beautifully muted close, completing the circle of the sequence with a return to the temperate rusticity and tough militarism celebrated in the first and second Roman odes – virtues located here within an ideal past, but not beyond recall. But Horace chooses to end instead with a vision of unstoppable moral devolution (45–9):

> damnosa quid non imminuit dies?
> aetas parentum peior avis tulit
>   nos nequiores, mox daturos
>   progeniem vitiosiorem.

> What does the ruinous day not diminish? Our parents' generation,
> inferior to their parents, bore our more worthless selves, destined
> soon to produce children more vicious still.

The static, conventional, generalized, repeatable vignette of sunset on the farm yields to a grim narrative of inexorable descent. Time is not "friendly" to Horace's Rome; like a profligate son, the ruinous day diminishes Rome's moral capital. It would be difficult to imagine a more radical inversion of the ode's opening assertion (*Delicta maiorum immeritus lues*, 1). The comparison is now all in favor of the *maiores*.[53] If the begrimed images of the gods can be scrubbed clean, the children of

---

[53] See Williams (1969) 64–5. The ode is laden with comparatives: *maiorum*, 1; *minorem*, 5; *melior*, 16; *iuniores*, 25; *peior*, 46; *nequiores*, 47; *vitiosiorem*, 48. On the relation of the final stanzas to the *Epodes*, see Fraenkel (1957) 285–6.

a progressively deteriorating race cannot be restored to the pristine virtue of their ancestors. The image has devolved too far from the original.[54] The result is that the sequence as a whole enacts a tragic version of the disclosure staged in *Odes* 1.17, this time with the virile community, not the individual poet, in the starring, faltering role. Arresting this headlong descent is a task for Augustus, the individual behind the blameless temple-restoring *Romanus* addressed in the opening stanza of the ode.

The poet and the emperor

What happens, how does Horace's face change, when Augustus enters his lyric domain? What difference does Augustus' name make to a Horatian ode? Let me begin by remarking that while the lyric domain of *Odes* 3.18 and the pacified empire of *Odes* 4.5 have much in common, they diverge in one obvious but crucial respect – the hymn to Faunus has no space within it for Augustus, and the hymn to Augustus, contrariwise, has no space within it for Horace. By "Horace" I mean here Horace's authorial persona – the more or less elaborately individuated character we encounter in the *Satires*, *Epodes*, and some of the odes: son of a virtuous freedman, friend of Maecenas, owner of a Sabine villa, and, increasingly, the publicly recognized author of artfully polished verse.[55] It is one thing for the farmer, "on his own hills" (*collibus in suis*, C. 4.5.29), to pay homage to Augustus; it is quite another for the poet to do the same from within his own domain (*meos finis*, C. 3.18.2). The presence of Faunus, a fictive and relatively plastic addressee, may motivate Horace's demonstration of lyric mastery. But Augustus is too strong a center of gravity. Once introduced into a poem, he will tend to warp it into a shape that represents his own supreme authority.[56]

Both the problem and the solution are already sketched out in the twofold introduction to the collected odes. For if *Odes* 1.1 and 1.2, taken together, reveal the complicity of aesthetic with political power, they also suggest ways in which these forms of power are incompatible. Whereas *Odes* 1.1 showcases the first person singular, *Odes* 1.2 shuns the privileged "I" for a communal "we," saving the spotlight for Augustus. As *Odes* 1.2 opens, Rome (*urbem*, C. 1.2.4) – and indeed, by a kind of ripple effect, the

---

[54] Cf. Schenker (1993) 164; contrast the more hopeful assessment of Witke (1983) 72–7.

[55] On Horace's nonidentification with the speaker of *C.* 4.5, see DuQuesnay (1995) 149–50.

[56] On the problem Augustus poses for Horace's poetry, cf. Feeney (1993) 54–5; Lyne (1995) 196.

whole world (*gentis*, 5)[57] – is united by a common terror. What this undifferentiated community fears, moreover, is the image of itself: the eradication of difference in a second flood, a second civil war involving the world in a chaos of indistinction (*grave ne rediret | saeculum Pyrrhae nova monstra questae*, 5–6). This danger is averted by the emergence of Caesar, whose name supplies the ode's last word, at the head of what is now redefined as an imperial army (*neu sinas Medos equitare inultos | te duce, Caesar*, 51–2). But while Caesar regrounds certain differences, he eclipses others – those detailed in *Odes* 1.1, for example. In *Odes* 1.2, Horace cannot raise his singular head above the crowd. The starry heavens are only large enough to accommodate one garlanded man-god at a time.

Odes 1.1 and 1.2 operate within a rhetorical economy that obeys a kind of "exclusionary rule": Horace asserts his authority in the absence of Augustus and effaces his authorial persona in the imperial presence. The operation of this rule is well illustrated by *Odes* 3.24 and 3.25. These poems, which are coupled by their common meter, divide the contents and form of an "Augustan" poetry between them.[58] In *Odes* 3.24, Horace issues a diatribe against the moral corruption embodied by avaricious men, promiscuous women, and effeminate boys.[59] Opening with a rebuke aimed at a representative rich "you" (*C*. 3.24.1–8), Horace eventually turns partway around (this nascent apostrophe combines the vocative *o* with not the second but the third person) toward another unspecified individual (25–9):

> o quisquis volet impias
> caedis et rabiem tollere civicam,
>   si quaeret PATER URBIUM
> subscribi statuis, indomitam audeat
>   refrenare licentiam.

> O whoever wishes to put an end to impious bloodshed and intes-
> tine frenzy, if he seeks to be labeled "father of cities" on his statues,
> let him dare to curb untamed license.

If Horace does not exhort Augustus himself (for example, "Augustus, if you would win our lasting reverence, be bold, check the immorality of

---

[57] The ideological work involved in the inclusion of the *gentes* becomes clear when in the sixth stanza *Persae* emerge as the appropriate target of Roman swords.

[58] Cf. Santirocco (1986) 140–2, reading *C*. 3.25 as a "retrospective commentary" on *C*. 3.24.

[59] Women are targeted only by implication, via Horace's praise of the nomadic Scythians, who hold (for the purposes of Horace's argument) their land but not their women in common.

your people"), one reason is that the exhortation would be redundant; preaching to the converted, when the converted in question is the *princeps*, readily reduces to flattery. Such an exhortation would also be presumptuous – Horace can hardly represent himself as the *auctor* of Augustus' moral platform. Either way, Horace would forfeit some measure of his poetic authority. But even this appeal to a quasi-anonymous "whoever" suffices to trigger the exclusionary rule. Immediately after invoking the profile of Augustus, the moralizing speaker descends from his pedestal and joins the corrupt audience he began by addressing, delivering a communal self-reproach in the first person plural (*odimus*, 31; *quaerimus*, 32; *nos*, 45, etc.). Still, in the absence of the name of Augustus, the ode resists choralization, and the poet stays at a certain satiric distance from the mob (from, for example, the indefatigable merchant of lines 36–40). But the point I wish to stress is that Horace retains his own singular authority to the degree that he excludes Augustus from his Augustan discourse.

The brilliantly blank encomium Horace offers the *princeps* in *Odes* 3.25 is the other side of this Augustan coin. The ode begins as the reverse of a *recusatio* – not a self-depreciating refusal, but a declaration of the irresistible force of the inspiration driving Horace to celebrate the majesty of Augustus (*C.* 3.25.1–8):

> Quo me, Bacche, rapis tui
> plenum? quae nemora aut quos agor in specus
>   velox mente nova? quibus
> antris egregii Caesaris audiar
>   aeternum meditans decus
> stellis inserere et consilio Iovis?
>   dicam insigne recens adhuc
> indictum ore alio.

Where, Bacchus, are you carrying me off, full of you? To what groves, what caves am I being driven racing in my strange new frame of mind? In what grottoes will I be heard practicing to set the deathless glory of outstanding Caesar in Jove's starry council? I will say something remarkable, fresh, until now unspoken by any other voice.

While there is a strong element of compulsion here, it does not derive from Augustus. In the rhetorical economy of this ode, Bacchus steps in between the poet and the emperor, relieving them both of the responsibility for Horace's "deviation" into encomium, and enabling Horace to represent himself as the passive vehicle of praise, not its agent. To celebrate Augustus is indeed to speak with another's mouth (*ore alio*, 8).

But if Horace is evacuated by Dionysiac inspiration, the vacuum thus created is not filled by Augustus. Although Horace begins by associating his glory with Caesar's, the exclusionary rule soon renews its force. What follows Horace's boast is truly "something remarkable," *insigne*, but it is not the deification of the *princeps* (C. 3.25.8–14):

> non secus in iugis
> exsomnis stupet Euhias
> Hebrum prospiciens et nive candidam
> Thracen ac pede barbaro
> lustratam Rhodopen, ut mihi devio
> ripas et vacuum nemus
> mirari libet.

> Not otherwise on the mountain ridge does the sleepless Bacchant stare dumbfounded, gazing out at the river Hebrus, and snow-bright Thrace, and Mount Rhodope tracked by barbarian foot – so it pleases me to wander and marvel at the riverbanks and the empty grove.

This simile is in all senses the high point of the poem. Passing through the secluded, enclosing groves and caves of the first stanza, the poem opens out on a vast and exotic landscape. The thick sonic texture (the consonantal clusters, the sibilance of lines 8 and 9, the clattering rhyme of *Thr<u>ac</u>en <u>ac</u>)* lends the passage a foreign flavor, as if to suggest that Augustus can only properly be celebrated in a foreign idiom – in the metrical "feet" of the unRoman, emperor-worshipping east. But Augustus is nowhere in sight. As the contrast between *dicam* and *stupet* emphasizes, the poem in his praise remains a sublime blank. Although Caesar is destined to be the subject of Horace's inspired verse, it is the poet who is imaged in the poem's central simile. The mountaintop displaces the starry *consilium*, and Horace – himself destined for stardom, as he ventures to hope elsewhere (*sublimi feriam sidera vertice*, C. 1.1.36) – deposes Caesar. If Horace returns to the domesticated imagery of Alexandrian deviance (C. 3.25.12–13), renews his apostrophe to Bacchus (14–16), and reiterates his promise of great poetry to come (17–18), these repetitions serve chiefly to lock the ode's central, enormous image into place.[60] The

---

[60] On the ode's shift from wild to tame, see Troxler-Keller (1964) 55–6.

renewal of Horace's promise seems, indeed, both redundant and anti-climactic. His inspiration has already peaked in the mountains of Thrace.

While odes such as these tend to segregate the poet and the *princeps*, Horace's sequence of Roman odes brings the two together, elevating both. The poet's eminence is clear from the opening stanzas of the sequence, where he announces his aversion to the mob (*Odi profanum vulgus et arceo*, C. 3.1.1) and adopts the lofty perspective of Jupiter himself (*cuncta supercilio moventis*, 8), looking down, as if from a great height, upon the petty kingdoms far below.[61] For most of the sequence, accordingly, Horace shuns not only the *vulgus* but the choral, communal first person plural. Moreover, the singular poetic *ego* of the Roman odes is not merely the inspired mouthpiece of the Muses but Horace's individuated author-ial persona – the contented owner of a modest Sabine property (*C.* 3.1.47), a native of Apulia (*C.* 3.4.9), a veteran of Philippi (*C.* 3.4.26). The result is that a kind of autobiographical static complicates the delivery of the Muses' message by the "Muses' priest" (*Musarum sacerdos*, 3).

In the event, however, the sequence does not so much suspend as bend the exclusionary rule governing poet–emperor relations. The poet of the Roman odes never comes face to face with Caesar. While he mentions Caesar in three of the six odes, Horace scrupulously avoids addressing him directly. In two of these three odes, the emperor's name occurs in the vicinity of the first person plural, a rare form within this ego-centered sequence – the elusive *scimus*, "we know" (*C.* 3.4.42), that introduces Horace's account of Olympian warfare, and the doxic *credidimus*, "we have [always] believed" (*C.* 3.5.1), that conveys a communal faith in the omnipotence of Jupiter in the sky and (one day) Augustus on earth. Horace puts other safeguards in place. Whereas the odes that do not mention Augustus focus on the Roman present, the odes that include the emperor's name retreat into the legendary past – the apotheosis of Romulus in *Odes* 3.3, the war between Olympian Jupiter and his chthonic opponents in *Odes* 3.4, the martyrdom of Regulus in *Odes* 3.5.[62] And in each case, as he shifts from the present to the past, Horace yields the podium to another authoritative speaker: to Juno, who offers a capsule history of the origins of Rome in *Odes* 3.3; to Regulus, who delivers his empassioned plea for pitilessness in *Odes* 3.5; and, more nebu-lously, to the authority of tradition, signaled by the plural "we know,"

---

[61] On the Jovian perspective, see Witke (1983) 20; on *odi* and *arceo*, Fraenkel (1957) 263–4.
[62] On this evasive tendency, see Williams (1969) 42, 51–2.

which introduces Horace's account of Jupiter's victories in *Odes* 3.4. If Horace is presuming to advise Augustus in these odes, the space that opens up between the Augustan present and the exemplary past and between the poet and his persona is wide enough to render the content of his exhortation untranslatable. What precisely does Juno's reiterated prohibition against rebuilding Troy signify for Augustus' Rome? Does the myth of *Odes* 3.4 constitute a call for clemency, or is Augustus already a shining example of Jovian "tempered force" (*vim temperatam*, C. 3.4.66)? Should Augustus steel his heart against Crassus' soldiers, as Regulus against his own men in *Odes* 3.5, or is Regulus rather a generic emblem of moral determination in the face of popular opposition? While Horace makes the duty of Augustan boys (as warriors) and girls (as wives and mothers) clear enough, the responsibilities of Augustus himself remain carefully unspecified.

In writing before the emperor, Horace uses various devices not only of tactful evasion but also of self-restraint. The very design of the sequence offers an exemplary demonstration of deferential authority. As if to counter the poetic ambition of the sequential form, which overrides the boundaries between odes and expands lyric in the direction of epic, Horace emphasizes the boundaries of individual odes, repeatedly pulling the sequence up short: curbing his tongue at the end of *Odes* 3.2, rebuking his Muse at the end of *Odes* 3.3, arresting the representative sinner Pirithous at the end of *Odes* 3.4. The closing polysyllabic comparatives that elongate rather than punctuate the first and last poems of the sequence (*operosiores*, "more laborious," C. 3.1.48; *vitiosiorem*, "more corrupt," C. 3.6.48) encapsulate the formal excessiveness of the sequence, but they also sum up its ethos of restraint ("more" is "worse"). The message is underscored by the deployment of odes within the sequence: four extroverted, imperial odes framed by two odes focusing on domestic, moral issues.[63]

The sequence is characterized, moreover, by a prevailing downwardness. While some of the odes begin by ascending, all of them end by returning to earth. When *Odes* 3.1 opens, Horace already occupies the Olympian heights, whence he enjoys an eagle's-eye view of the world below. He has nowhere to go but down, and down he goes, trading this eminence at the end of the poem for the depths of a lowly valley (*valle . . . Sabina*, C. 3.1.47). Although he begins by promising to be original (cf.

---

[63] This is but one of many patterns; for an overview, see Santirocco (1986) 113–18.

carmina non prius | audita, 2–3), he ends by decrying the pursuit of novelty: "why should I toil to heap my hall high, with envy-inspiring pillars, in a newfangled style?" (*cur invidendis postibus et novo | sublime ritu moliar atrium?* 45–6).[64] In *Odes* 3.2, *Virtus* ascends to heaven (*caelum, C.* 3.2.22) on "fugitive wing" (*fugiente pinna*, 24), but the ode returns to earth, ending not (as we might have expected) with this exaltation, but with the "limping foot" (*pede . . . claudo*, 32) of Punishment, a humbler and more mundane means of poetic locomotion. In *Odes* 3.3, Horace describes how heroes have successfully attained the "fiery citadels" of heaven (*arces . . . igneas, C.* 3.3.10), but ends by reining in his over-ambitious Muse – Olympus is home to the gods but too exalted for this humble poet. At the start of *Odes* 3.4, and thus at the center of the sequence, Horace bids his Muse "descend from heaven" (*Descende caelo, C.* 3.4.1); the ode ends by "descending" all the way down to the under-world. The first word of *Odes* 3.5 returns to "the heavens" (*Caelo, C.* 3.5.1), but its last image presents a self-humbled Regulus (*ut capitis minor*, 42), departing Rome as if to go down to the seaside (56).[65] And *Odes* 3.6 provides its equivalent of a final descent in the catalogue of ever more depraved "descendants" with which the sequence achieves its troubled ending. While the sequence expresses the poet's ambition and confirms his authority, this deferential downwardness repeatedly cedes the heights to the emperor.

Odes 3.4 illustrates the combination of authority and deference which the poet deploys in hosting the emperor. Before turning to Caesar and launching into the cosmic battles which occupy the second half of the poem, Horace devotes nine stanzas to his own mythologized poetic autobiography. The theme throughout is the divine protection the poet enjoys. In his infancy, having wandered "across the threshold" (*extra limen, C.* 3.4.10), Horace was miraculously protected by doves (12–13), who cloaked him in myrtle and laurel leaves (19) – rough drafts of the enclosing garlands (myrtle in *Odes* 1.38, laurels in *Odes* 3.30) that will crown the mature poet. In later years, the Muses themselves pre-

---

[64] Cf. Pearcy (1977) 778–9. The contrast between the opening and close is underscored by the echo of Pind. *Ol.* 6.1–4: "As if raising on golden pillars a fair-walled porch, building a mar-vellous palace, we must give the work that is begun a front that gleams afar." If any Horatian poem sports a πρόσωπον τηλαυγές, it is *C.* 3.1. It would have been easy for Horace to stop short of these puzzling personalized stanzas, ending instead with the powerful image *post equitem sedet atra Cura* (40;cf. the personification that closes the next ode: *raro antecedentem scelestum | deseruit pede Poena claudo, C.* 3.2.31–2).

[65] So Horace writes at *E.* 1.7.11 of "going down to the sea," *ad mare descendet.*

served their poet from harm, watching over him at Philippi, shielding him from the infamous falling tree, and saving him from shipwreck (25–8). So long as the Muses are with him, Horace concludes, he will gladly travel to the ends of the world (29–36). We have encountered another such venturesome bard in the "Lalage" ode, where poetry likewise enables the poet to traverse perilous thresholds in perfect safety. But what I would like to underscore here is how strange this passage is (a mythologized biography of the poet not the emperor) as a prologue to an encomium of Augustus – the Roman "Jupiter" who has successfully crushed his titanic opponents and restored order to the world. In *Odes* 4.5, Horace claims that Rome can scoff at the Spaniard in the west and the Scythian in the east "so long as Caesar is unharmed" (*incolumi Caesare, C.* 4.5.27), and we might have expected him to follow the same script here, attributing his sense of security not to the Muses but to the emperor.

Gregson Davis has treated these stanzas under the rubric of "authentication," arguing that Horace is displaying the poetic qualifications that fit him for the grand encomiastic project he undertakes in the rest of the ode.[66] I would add that Horace's rhetoric here is also defensive. From the ode's sixth through its eleventh stanza, Horace addresses himself with a certain emphasis to his Muses, the Italic Camenae (*vester, Camenae, vester, C.* 3.4.21; *vestris*, 25; *vos*, 29; *vos*, 37; *vos*, 41). This anaphoric address hinges the poet's autobiography to his encomium of Caesar – the "you" who protect Horace is identical to the "you" who "refresh great Caesar in a Pierian grotto" (*vos Caesarem altum . . . Pierio recreatis antro*, 37, 40). The Muses thus form a kind of communicating wall, enabling Horace to address Caesar without directly confronting him. Horace says *vos Caesarem* (37) so as not to say *tu Caesar*.

But Horace's autobiography also serves as a declaration of poetic autonomy. The threefold *vester . . . vester . . . vestris* that declares Horace's devotion to the Muses shields him from another, equally plausible declaration: Horace says "I belong to the Muses" in order to prove that he doesn't belong to Caesar.[67] The poet is not only independent of Caesar, he has also traded places with him, traveling to the edges of Caesar's world while Caesar rests within the "Pierian grotto" at the ode's

---

[66] Davis (1991) 101–7.

[67] Cf. *I.* 1.11–14, where Horace makes a similar pledge to Maecenas. On the discourse of *amicitia* here, see Davis (1991) 105.

secluded center. It is significant that Horace lists, among the perils from which the Muses rescued him, the "battle line routed at Philippi" (*Philippis versa acies retro*, C. 3.4.26) – the battle Horace fought, under Brutus' command, against Caesar. It is true that Horace often refers to this battle, a paradigmatic event within his poetic autobiography, and that the reference may be taken, here as in *Odes* 2.7 (addressed to a former comrade-in-arms newly released from exile), simply as an index of Augustus' clemency. But the reference also works to seal off the first from the second half of the poem. In this case at least, the Muses favored an enemy of what would one day be reconceived as an Augustan, "Olympian" order.

I do not mean to imply that the fourth Roman ode should be read as a document of anti-Augustan sentiment. Rather, I am trying to show the rhetorical dangers that haunt any ode that addresses Augustus, however obliquely, in the authorial singular (as opposed to the generic, vatic singular or the choral, communal plural). In fact there are signs within the ode that Horace recognizes that his self-promotion pushes the limits of decorum. Soon after Caesar enters the poem, everything changes (*C.* 3.4.42–8):

> scimus ut impios
> Titanas immanemque turbam
> fulmine sustulerit caduco,
> qui terram inertem, qui mare temperat
> ventosum, et urbes regnaque tristia
> divosque mortalisque turmas
> imperio regit unus aequo.

We know how the impious Titans with their monstrous mob were dispatched by the plummeting thunderbolt of the god who tames the inert earth, the windy sea, who rules alone, with impartial power, cities and the grim kingdoms and gods and the ranks of men.

I have already called attention to the shift from the authorial singular of the opening stanzas to the first person plural "we know" with which Horace submits himself to the authority of tradition. But the impact of Caesar's entrance on Horace is also registered in this titanic story – a story about the punishment inflicted on overweening ambition by the king of the gods. Horace collaborates in this punishment in the final stanza of the ode, where he achieves closure by imposing it violently on those who transgress moral limits (77–80):

> incontinentis nec Tityi iecur
> reliquit ales, nequitiae additus
> custos; amatorem trecentae
> Perithoum cohibent catenae.

> nor has the liver of unrestrained Tityus been released by the bird assigned to watch over his vice; the lover Pirithous is held in check by three hundred chains.

And yet the contrast between the poet of Muse-sanctioned extravagance whom we met in the ode's opening stanzas and the irregulated sinners who decorate its close is not absolutely clearcut. Earlier, Horace registers a modest doubt: "does a fond madness delude me?" (*an me ludit amabilis | insania?* 5–6). Although he feels himself to be "hearing" music and "wandering through pious groves" (*audire et videor pios | errare per lucos*, 6–7), perhaps he is to be classed rather among the "impious Titans" (*impios | Titanas*, 42–3; like *pios* earlier, the adjective closes its stanza's second line) whose pretensions are punctured by Jove's thunderbolt. It is as if Horace's poetic ascent up the steep Sabine mountains (*in arduos | tollor Sabinos*, 21–2) risked being mistaken for a variation on the piling of Pelion on Olympus by Jove's would-be usurpers.[68] If so, Horace's ringing declaration of the supreme god's unique power (*imperio regit unus aequo*, 48) effectively demonstrates to Augustus and to the world that the poet recognizes and accepts his subordinate place within the Augustan order.

A less comfortable confrontation of poetic with imperial power is staged in *Odes* 1.37, familiarly known as the "Cleopatra" ode. Like *Odes* 3.4, this ode commemorates Caesar's victory over a "monstrous" opposition, and here again Caesar occupies the center of the ode and changes its course. But the "Cleopatra" ode begins where *Odes* 3.4 leaves off and ends where *Odes* 3.4 begins, proceeding from communal celebration to a displaced but nonetheless recognizably Horatian affirmation of poetic authority. At the outset, the poet's identity merges with that of the "comrades" he addresses (*C.* 1.37.1–6):

---

[68] As Davis (1991) 104–5 remarks, the fourth and sixth stanzas both proceed from high to low – "to schematize" the Muse's "all-inclusive range," according to Davis, but also perhaps to temper ascent with descent.

Nunc est bibendum, nunc pede libero
pulsanda tellus, nunc Saliaribus
   ornare pulvinar deorum
    tempus erat dapibus, sodales.
antehac nefas depromere Caecubum
cellis avitis . . .

Now we must drink, now beat the earth with liberated feet, now is
it high time to thank the reclining gods with splendid banquets,
comrades. Before now it would have been wickedness to bring the
Caecuban out of the ancestral cellars . . .

The contrast with the opening of the ninth epode is illuminating (*I.*
9.1–4):

    Quando repostum Caecubum ad festas dapes
      victore laetus Caesare
    tecum sub alta – sic Iovi gratum – domo,
      beate Maecenas, bibam?

When will I, rejoicing in Caesar's victory, drink the Caecuban wine
saved for holiday feasts, under a high roof again (such is Jove's pleasure), in your company, blessed Maecenas?

Unlike the celebration envisioned in the epode, Horace's new party is
located in no particular house and remains generally and representatively
Roman. And whereas in the epode the identity of the poet is reciprocally
specified by his address to "blessed Maecenas," the speaker of *Odes* 1.37
remains a cipher devoid of particular social associations and obligations
(except, of course, the widely-shared attribute of Caesarian partisanship).
Horace underscores the representative character of this celebration by
setting it next to an ode calling for a party in honor of Numida's safe
return from Spain (*C.* 1.36). That party also features a plurality of anonymous "comrades" (*sodalibus*, *C.* 1.36.5). But by singling out Lamia (a
friend to whom Horace dedicated an earlier ode, *C.* 1.26) as Numida's
closest friend and a deep-drinking woman he calls Damalis as Numida's
doting lover, Horace creates the impression of a particular social circle.[69]
In the "Cleopatra" ode, by contrast, the speaker is purely a jubilant
comrade among comrades.

Not only the speaker but the argument of these opening stanzas has a

---

[69] On the links between *C.* 1.36 and 37, cf. Santirocco (1986) 78–9.

generic quality. Horace musters against the defeated queen the standard themes of contemporary propaganda, recasting the final episode in Rome's civil wars as a battle between the central Roman self and its marginalized "other" – between West and East, man and woman, *virtus* and *impotentia*, reason and passion, Republican liberty and monarchical enslavement.[70] The partisans of Caesar, so the argument runs, are the true descendants of the ancestors whose wine and whose *mores* they have carefully preserved. By capping their celebration with a thanksgiving to the gods, moreover, they demonstrate the *pietas* on which Rome's global *imperium* is founded. On the other side is the Egyptian queen, drunk with "sweet good fortune" and with "Mareotic wine" (*fortuna ... dulci | ebria*, 11–12; *mentem ... lymphatam Mareotico*, 14) and surrounded by a "tainted herd of men befouled by vice" (*contaminato cum grege turpium | morbo virorum*, 9–10). The Roman general who reduces this male impersonator to the status of a properly feminine "soft dove" or fugitive "hare" (*mollis columbas aut leporem*, 18) figures, accordingly, as the champion of both sexual and political decorum.[71] If the drunken queen embodies *impotentia*, Caesar is the very incarnation of Roman power.

Horace reaches a climax of oppositional invective when he labels Cleopatra with the famous and untranslatable phrase *fatale monstrum* (*C.* 1.37.21; the phrase combines "fateful portent," "deadly monster," and *femme fatale*).[72] Both ideologically and rhetorically, the image supplies a plausible ending for the ode. We might compare another sympotic lyric, *Odes* 1.27, the last word of which is *Chimaera*.[73] Like its more famous counterpart, for which it provides a kind of ideological map, this ode is addressed to Horace's comrades (*sodales*, *C.* 1.27.7 – this is the only other example in Horace's poetry of this particular corporate addressee). At the outset, Horace represents himself as intervening to restore order at a party. Having rebuked the troublemakers for their "impious uproar" (*impium | ... clamorem*, 6–7), he masterfully defuses any remaining tension by focusing attention on one of their number, demanding as the price of his participation in the drinking the name of a fellow-drinker's beloved (9–14). After the bashful lover has been prevailed upon to deposit the name in Horace's trusty ears, the poet breaks out in exclamations of mock-horror: the poor boy has fallen victim to a veritable "Charybdis" (*quanta laborabas Charybdi*, 19), a "triform Chimaera," from whose toils

---

[70] See most recently Wyke (1992).

[71] On the "sweetly indiscreet allusion" embedded in the erotically colored second simile (hunter pursuing hare, cf. *S.* 1.2.105–6), see Lyne (1995) 182–3.   [72] See Luce (1963).

[73] Cf. Luce (1963) 254–5, identifying the Caesar of *C.* 1.37 as a kind of Bellerophon.

even a monster-slayer such as Pegasus will hardly extricate him (*vix illigatum te triformi | Pegasus expediet Chimaera*, 23–4).

The opposition between literal and figurative battles that structures *Odes* 1.27 has been well discussed by Steele Commager.[74] But we should also note the historical resonance of Horace's displacement of violence from the center of the male community onto a marginal and unnameable woman (Rome declared war on the queen of Egypt, not Antony). If the disrupted symposium encapsulates the chaos of Rome's civil wars, by the poem's end a woman has come to embody all the monstrous *furor* these wars unleash.[75] The "Cleopatra" ode operates within the same logic and might have reached a similar conclusion, albeit with Caesar not ensnared by but snaring his own monster (*daret ut catenis | fatale monstrum*, *C.* 1.37.20–1; compare the "three hundred chains" binding Pirithous at the end of *C.* 3.4). But Cleopatra would not be displayed in chains at her conqueror's triumph. The closural image of the monster is invoked, in this case, only so as to be pointedly revoked. The false climax generates a sudden revolution, and the poem veers from its expected course.

While the poem as it stands may seem inevitably and brilliantly "right," it is crucial to recognize that Horace might well have completed the ode in the same impersonal and quasi-official tone in which he began it. That would, indeed, have been the path of least resistance. It is easy enough to trace the basic plotline of the ode that Horace chose not to write. He could have gone on to describe the retreat of the defeated and disempowered queen as forcefully as Propertius, whose Cleopatra flees homeward "with an empty faith in her boat, achieving only this, not to die on the appointed day" (4.6.63–4), or as gently as Virgil, whose doomed queen is enfolded within the embrace of the Nile (*Aen.* 8.709–13). Returning to his convivial theme, he might have discovered a kind of poetic justice in Cleopatra's suicidal drink: the wine-loving queen enjoys one last drink, yes, but a bitter one. Insofar as the ode is constructed as the fulfillment of Epode 9, we might also have expected some description of Caesar's triumph – the triumph that Horace impatiently anticipated, along with the consumption of celebratory Caecuban, in the prior poem.[76] "And so let us drink, friends," he might

---

[74] Commager (1962) 72–5.

[75] This Girardian dynamic is familiar from the *Epodes*; see above, chap. 2. On scapegoating and civil war, cf. Barton (1993) 145–7.

[76] "Io Triumphus, are you delaying the golden chariots and untouched heifers?" (*io Triumphe, tu moraris aureos | currus et intactas boves?* I.9.21–2).

have concluded, closing the ode with a reprise of its opening,[77] "now that Caesar has banished our cares!"

But the ode does not, of course, continue in this vein. At its center, Caesar drives Cleopatra in flight from Italy, and instead of accompanying the triumphant Caesar back to the Capitol, the ode follows the defeated queen to Egypt, where it and she together end. The ode is thus both spatially and discursively centrifugal, returning neither to Rome nor to the "comrades" Horace began by addressing. What these final stanzas give us, moreover, is a radically transformed Cleopatra, not a monster of vicious depravity but an emblem of virtuous nobility, who "witnesses her defeat with stoic fortitude," in Steele Commager's words, "and then embraces a death worthy of Cato himself."[78] In the midline gap between the objectified dehumanized neuter *monstrum* and the subjective feminine *quae* (*C.* 1.37.21), Cleopatra's transgression of natural categories is rearticulated as a form of transcendence. Instead of ruling a herd of unmanly men, Cleopatra – or rather the "man" in Cleopatra (cf. *nec muliebriter*, 22) – now rules herself. By committing suicide, by exercising unwomanly force upon her woman's body, the once-impotent queen succeeds in ending her life in perfect self-possession.

Much scholarly energy has been invested, quite properly and profitably, in making sense of this representational turn.[79] And yet however hard we labor to enlist Horace's Cleopatra in the service of Caesar, the fact remains that she has displaced Caesar within Horace's poem. Horace's syntax may assign the "proud triumph" of the closing lines to Caesar, but his rhetoric assigns it to Cleopatra, who thus acquires a glorious epitaph: *superbo* | *non humilis mulier triumpho*, "in proud triumph, no humble woman" (*C.* 1.37.31–2). Caesar may have appreciated the obliquity of this poetic tribute, which lets him participate in an act of exemplary magnanimity while shielding him from the *invidia* to which the *triumphator* is especially vulnerable. But the obliquity serves the poet's interests as well. Horace uses Cleopatra, as he uses the Muses in *Odes* 3.4, to fend the emperor off; he celebrates her triumph so as to avoid celebrating Caesar's.

It is instructive to compare the "Cleopatra" ode with the "Regulus"

---

[77] On the absence of such a reprise, cf. Syndikus (1972) 335.

[78] Commager (1962) 92.

[79] For antithetical arguments along these lines, see Davis (1991) 233–42 (Cleopatra's elevation redounds to the credit of her conqueror); Johnson (1967) (the poem exemplifies Horace's "ironic detachment" [388] from the propaganda he here rehearses).

ode, *Odes* 3.5, where Caesar is likewise eclipsed by another commanding individual. Horace opens with an encomiastic analogy – Augustus will be reckoned a god on earth, as Jupiter is in the heavens, "once the Britons and dangerous Persians have been added to the empire" (*C.* 3.5.3–4) – which sounds like a preamble to praise of Augustus' imperial accomplishments to date, combined perhaps with an exhortation to further conquests. But the mention of the Persians derails that encomium, conjuring up in its place Horace's lament for the scandalous surrender of Crassus' army to the Parthians in 53 BCE.[80] And instead of urging Caesar to avenge this disgrace, Horace turns his gaze toward the Republican past, devoting the rest of the ode to the heroic figure of Regulus, who advised the Senate against bargaining for the return of the soldiers (himself among them) taken by the Carthaginians in 255 BCE. The solution offered by Horace's ode is thus less practical than rhetorical. The ode that begins by decrying, in a series of pointed juxtapositions, the *inversi mores* (7) of Crassus' captured soldier, who has settled down with an anomalously "barbarian wife" (*coniuge barbara*, 5) and submitted his Italian self to the rule of a Median king (*sub rege Medo Marsus et Apulus*, 9), ends with a display of similarly inverted *mores* on the part of Regulus, who puts aside his "chaste wife" (*pudicae coniugis*, 41) and willingly exchanges Rome for barbarian Carthage (cf. *barbarus*, 49), not because he has forgotten what it means to be Roman, but because he remembers. As the vicious failure of *Romanitas* in Crassus' conquered soldier is figuratively cured by the virtuous abdication of *Romanitas* by Regulus, so Cleopatra's monstrous *impotentia* is countered by an equally "monstrous" (unnatural, memorable, portentous) display of *potentia* – the chief difference being that in the "Cleopatra" ode one individual takes on both roles.

Like Cleopatra, Regulus triumphs by embracing his defeat.[81] In direct contrast to the quasi-deified Augustus invoked at the start of the ode, Horace's Regulus wins his glory by performing and enforcing his own humiliation, keeping his "virile countenance" trained not on the heavens but on the earth (*virilem | torvus humi posuisse vultum*, *C.* 3.5.43–4), veiling the noble image that might sway the Senate to pity. Whereas Augustus is destined to be a "present god" (*praesens divus*, 2), Regulus preserves Rome by permanently absenting himself. And yet Augustus' brilliant

---

[80] For *Persae* representing *Parthi*, see *C.* 1.2.22 (with Nisbet and Hubbard [1970] 28); *C.* 1.21.15; *C.* 4.15.23.　　[81] So Porter (1987) 166.

presence is finally eclipsed by Regulus' sublime self-effacement. By the time we reach the magnificently litotic final simile (Regulus exits in the most ordinary way possible, as if merely withdrawing from public life for a well-deserved holiday),[82] the opening Augustan hyperbole has been long forgotten. Once again, this shift may be Horace's way of shading the emperor from envy. But it is a shift that not only protects the emperor's but promotes the poet's face. If Regulus is a model for Augustus, who will one day "defeat" the Parthians by negotiating the return of Crassus' captured battle standards (hence the prominence accorded to "battle standards," *signa*, at the very start of Regulus' speech, 18), he is also a model for the poet in his role of heroic adviser. As well as underscoring the validity of his eyewitness account, Regulus' reiterated *ego* (18, 21 – the only first person singular of the ode; cf. also *auctor*, 46) bespeaks the poet's authority.

Like the "Regulus" ode, the "Cleopatra" ode is energized by the friction between Republican and Augustan modes of representation. In the opening stanzas of the ode, everything conspires to depict the conflict as one between slaves and free peers, between a mad queen and the Roman Republic, represented here by the corporate body of Horace's comrades, who, in contradistinction to Cleopatra's "herd," acknowledge no master. The depiction is thus underwritten by Caesar's absence, which enables Horace to match Cleopatra at first not with an individual head of state but with the Capitol, the site and symbol of Rome's (not just Caesar's) *imperium* (*Capitolio* | *regina*, C. 1.37.6–7). This rhetoric accords well with that deployed by Augustus, who will open his *Res gestae* with the claim "I liberated the Republic, oppressed by the tyranny of a faction" (*rem publicam a dominatione factionis oppressam in libertatem vindicavi, RG* 1), and it is not only Augustus' defeat of Cleopatra but this "liberation" – the long-awaited restoration of the Republic – that Horace is inviting his comrades to celebrate. The "Cleopatra" ode thus participates in what Duncan Kennedy has described as the "progressive reorganization of a fragmented discourse, whose previous center was provided by the institutions of the Republic, around the *princeps*"[83] – a reorganization iconically represented in the ode's design, which puts the name of Caesar at the head of its central line.

And yet, as Kennedy remarks in the course of the same essay, any such

---

[82] On the philosophical resonance of the simile, see Harrison (1986).

[83] Kennedy (1992) 35.

"establishment discourse is shaped by and contains traces of its opposition."[84] We can bring these traces into focus by remarking just how appropriate the first stanza of the "Cleopatra" ode would have sounded on the lips of the tyrannicide Brutus, who "liberated" Rome from a homebred despot in the hope of restoring the traditional aristocratic prerogatives of the old Republic. When Horace opens his ode with an allusion to Alcaeus' jubilant poem on the death of the tyrant Myrsilus (*Nunc est bibendum* translates Alcaeus' νῦν χρῆ μεθύσθην, fr. 332 LP), it is evident that he is casting Cleopatra in the dead tyrant's role. But it might also be argued that the battle of Actium did not so much destroy a tyrant as create one. From the perspective of a Brutus, the victory celebrated in the "Cleopatra" ode would signal not the resumption but the definitive end of aristocratic *libertas*. The fact that a staunchly Republican rhetoric was deployed by all the parties to the civil war does not vitiate Caesar's ability to wield it. Still, by segregating his comrades from the singular figure of Caesar, Horace registers his residual sense of their incompatibility. The queen of Egypt may have threatened to absorb these representative Romans into her abject herd of unmanly men, but so, in a different fashion, does Caesar. If Horace's comrades do not reappear as expected at the end of the poem, it is perhaps because they no longer exist.

Horace's "Romanization" of Cleopatra has been remarked by Viktor Poeschl, who points out that Horace's characterization of the suicide of the Egyptian queen resituates her within the thoroughly Roman tradition of the honorable death, a tradition that includes not only Cato but Cicero, Brutus, Cassius, and of course Antony as well.[85] Perhaps we should refer the metamorphosis of Cleopatra to the pressure of her absent consort. This pressure has already left its mark on the ode, which almost releases the unspeakable name at the start of its second stanza (*antehac*, C. 1.37.5) and perhaps registers Antony's infatuated presence at Cleopatra's side in the plural "soft doves" (*mollis columbas*, 18) that flee before the Caesarian hawk. At any rate, we should note that "national" attributes are not only transferred here but interchanged. As Cleopatra is Romanized, the comrades whom Horace invites to drink to her defeat are Egyptianized. Horace confounds the oppositions that underlie his opening stanzas by adding the temporal difference between "now" and "then." "Now" it is time to drink, to relax, to luxuriate – "now" is, in other words, the time for lyric and for Egypt. "Before," such indulgence

---

[84] Kennedy (1992) 40.   [85] Poeschl (1991) 113–16.

would have been a sin – not only because it would have shown a lack of concern for the imperiled Republic, but because it would have blurred the distinction between sober Rome and inebriated Egypt. But in the new lyric era, such distinctions no longer need to be so zealously guarded. Horace's Roman comrades can enter the Egyptian present because Cleopatra has disappeared into the Roman past. The ode which takes as its subject the victory that marked the effective end of Republican competition also registers the transvaluation that accompanied this historical shift, whereby the virile hardness that was once the signature of Rome's imperial identity comes to signify subjection, while effeminate softness – as embodied, to take one well-known example, in a figure such as Maecenas – functions as an index of power.[86]

But Horace does not end his ode with a carousal of relaxed Egyptianized victors. Instead, he focuses on the glamorous virility his comrades have not just temporarily doffed but effectively forfeited. We can clarify what is at stake in Horace's turn from drunken invective to sober praise by comparing the progress of a later poem, to Lyce (*C.* 4.13). Horace opens the ode with an almost comically gleeful taunt: "The gods have heeded my prayers, Lyce" (*Audivere, Lyce, di mea vota, C.* 4.13.1) – Lyce is growing old, but she still wants to play the part of a girl. Unlike *Odes* 4.1, where Horace rebukes his own indecorous resistance to old age, this ode is initially innocent of any self-knowledge; Lyce may have aged, but there is no suggestion that Horace has. It is the substitution of "the gods" for the natural agency of time that makes this double standard possible, and it is the return of time, in the poem's central stanza, that disables Horace's fantasy of omnipotent immortality. Winged Cupid (cf. *transvolat*, 9) may be Horace's ally, but the "winged day" (*volucris dies*, 16) flies by all mortals at the same rate. The shock of this recognition generates a sudden turn, from the young man's invective to the old man's nostalgic laudation: "where has that charm fled, alas, that complexion?" (*quo fugit Venus, heu, quove color?* 17). Horace is remembering Lyce as she once was, which means remembering himself as he once was.[87] Both Lyce and Horace are survivors, who lacked the grace to follow the example of the beautiful Cinara (cf. *Cinarae brevis | annos fata dederunt*, 22–3) by dying young. Within the "Cleopatra" ode, it is the Egyptian queen who fills the place of Cinara – the one who died early enough to avoid the humiliations of survival. Like Lyce, Horace chose instead to survive. Years before,

---

[86] See Barton (1994).
[87] On this dynamic, see Putnam (1986) 224–8; Ancona (1994) 95–100.

he had another option; he could have imitated Brutus and fallen on his sword after the battle of Philippi. And in this sense, Cleopatra's suicide represents to Horace the path he did not follow.

But the poem itself serves as some compensation. Horace's shift from invective to praise is an essentially willful act that remains in an important respect beyond explication, by which I mean that there is no way we could have predicted that the poem would take this particular turn. That this swerve happens just after Caesar has routed his last significant competitor may express Horace's impulse to create a space, over against the space now occupied by Caesar, for the exercise of his own power, his own lyric fortitude. Giving the verb *deducere* some of the aesthetic freight it elsewhere carries, we could say that while Cleopatra avoids being displayed at Caesar's triumph, she cannot avoid being made the subject of Horace's song. *Odes* 1.37 is thus a rehearsal for *Odes* 3.30. The *princeps* of poets here fashions his own triumph at the expense of Caesar's and in the image of Cleopatra's.[88]

The rhetorical strategies with which Horace confronts Augustus are visible in all their disparateness in *Odes* 3.14, Horace's notoriously eccentric celebration of the emperor's victorious return home from Spain.[89] As in the "Cleopatra" ode, but more pointedly, Horace here exploits the potential of the false ending. Where Horace's *fatale monstrum* eludes the ending designed by Augustus, in *Odes* 3.14 it is Horace himself who slips out of the Augustan enclosure. Casting himself in the role of a poetic "master of ceremonies," Horace first announces the safe return of Caesar – mistakenly believed, like the hero Hercules, "to have sought laurels that cost his death" (*morte venalem petiisse laurum | Caesar, C.* 3.14.2–3) – and then calls for public celebration: Augustus' wife (*mulier,* 5) and sister (*soror,* 7), matrons garlanded with suppliant ribbons (*decorae | supplice vitta | … matres,* 7–9), well-behaved boys and girls (*pueri et puellae,* 10) – all are bidden to welcome the victor home.[90] In the fourth stanza, Horace turns to his own representative case. The lyric functionary not only orchestrates but participates in the communal sigh of relief (13–16):

> hic dies vere mihi festus atras
> eximet curas; ego nec tumultum
> nec mori per vim metuam tenente
> Caesare terras.

---

[88] On the links between *C.* 1.37 and 3.30, cf. Putnam (1982) 138.
[89] For an instructive attempt to smooth away this ode's wrinkles, see Syndikus (1973) 145–53.
[90] On the textual problems in these lines, see Nisbet (1983).

This day, to me truly a holiday, will banish black cares; I will fear neither civil uproar nor violent death so long as Caesar controls the world.

This stanza, which sports a superabundance of closural features, would have made a plausible ending. The echoes of *morte* (2) and *Caesar* (3) in *mori* (15) and *Caesare* (16) fashion a poetic ring, while the final syllables of the stanza, *Caesare terras*, form a miniature aural figure of closure as chiastic enclosure. These effects are buttressed by two other characteristically Horatian closural features: the contrastive self-reference (*mihi, ego*) and the "neither . . . nor" construction. "No doubt this would have been a sonorous and dignified close,"[91] with Horace's *ego* figuring not a poet but a representative rejoicing Roman.

But it seems that the communal rejoicing described in the first half of the poem will not suffice. In an outburst of enthusiasm, Horace decides to throw his own party. The centripetal movement of the first stanza (Caesar is done seeking laurels, *petiisse laurum*, C. 3.14.2, and is now returning home, *repetit penatis*, 4) is countered by a renewal of centrifugal energy (17–22):

> i pete unguentum, puer, et coronas
> et cadum Marsi memorem duelli,
> · Spartacum si qua potuit vagantem
>   fallere testa.
> dic et argutae properet Neaerae
> murreum nodo cohibere crinem.

Go fetch perfume, boy, and garlands, and a cask that remembers the Social War, if any bottle managed to cheat the roving Spartacus. And tell clear-voiced Neaera to hurry up and bind up her chestnut hair in a knot.

The closural potential of this image is reinforced by the echo of the close of Horace's ode to Quinctius, where another anonymous slave-boy is sent in quest of one Lyde, who is to hurry up and join Horace's party, with her hair tied back in a simple knot (*C.* 2.11.21–4). Horace could easily have filled out the stanza to make *Odes* 3.14 end on this note, with his personalized celebration complementing the formal ceremony decreed in the first half of the poem.

---

[91] Fraenkel (1957) 290. Fraenkel, followed by Dyson (1973) 174, identifies the *ego* of the fourth stanza with the distinctive "person of the poet"; but this is to read a contrast back into this stanza from the stanzas which follow.

And yet the more Horace expresses his delight at Caesar's return, the more problematic his relation to Caesar appears. Caesar may be a conquering general, the lord of the world, but within the poem it is Horace who gives the orders. This implicit rivalry would have gone unnoticed if Horace had remained in the role of "master of ceremonies," ending *Odes* 3.14 with stanza 4. It is the similarity of the speech acts in the two parts of the poem that gives one pause (*prodeat*, 6; *parcite*, 12; *pete*, 17; *dic*, 21; *properet*, 21). This congruity (underscored by the echo of *prodeat* in *properet* and of *parcite* in *pete*) disregards the differences between Horace's addressees – citizens and members of the imperial family on the one hand, slaves or ex-slaves on the other. Indeed the two groups are oddly similar. Horace's slave-boy, like Caesar, seeks garlands; and Neaera, like the beribboned matrons, is neatly coiffed.[92] The point is that, within the compass of the poem, all of these characters are equally subordinate to the designs of the poet, whose absolute power finds expression in the imperative with which the master addresses his slave: *i pete . . . puer*. Horace's party in Caesar's honor finally serves to bring to the surface the latent rivalry between the master of the world and the master of the poem.

Horace has good reasons, then, to break the parallelism he has taken such care to establish. And so he goes on to qualify his ambition and to check his desire. Horace is, after all, no match for Caesar. Caesar's Spanish campaign was successful, but Horace's fighting days are over. Neaera's luxuriant locks are displaced by the poet's whitening hair, and competitive desire subsides into a mellower emotion (*C.* 3.14.23–8):[93]

> si per invisum mora ianitorem
> fiet, abito.
> lenit albescens animos capillus
> litium et rixae cupidos protervae;
> non ego hoc ferrem calidus iuventa
> consule Planco.

> But if the hateful doorkeeper causes a delay, come away. Whitening hair calms spirits that long for disputes and love-quarrels; I wouldn't have stood for it in my youth's heat, when Plancus was consul.

[92] See Dyson (1973) 169.

[93] While it is generally assumed that the Herculean exploit to which the first stanza alludes is the defeat of Geryon, the closing allusion to the "hateful doorkeeper" also suggests Hercules' triumph over Cerberus, the doorkeeper of Hades (cf. *C.* 2.11.15; *invisus* perhaps plays on Ἀίδης, cf. *invisi. . . Taenari* at *C.* 1.34.10, the *invisos cupressos* of *C.* 2.14.23). For Horace as a burlesque Hercules, see Scholz (1971) 136.

Once again, however, Horace has succeeded in saying a little too much. As is often remarked, the phrase "when Plancus was consul" dates Horace's hot-blooded youth to the year of the battle of Philippi, where Horace served under Brutus against the young Caesar. At this point the formal conflict between two discrete kinds of power – the poet's over his poem, the emperor's over his empire – is given a specific historical content. The poem moves into allegory, with sexual heat standing in for the political fervor of republicanism. Ostensibly, this is an allegory of political submission: Horace closes by circumscribing belligerent passion within a certain phase of his own life-story.[94] But Horace's backward glance at his fiery youth is tinged with nostalgia.[95] In the ode's central stanza, Horace claims not to fear a violent death so long as Caesar controls the world. Here, he looks back fondly on the days when he risked just such a death confronting Caesar's army. If Horace has to remind himself that his passion has cooled, the reason may be that he feels its lingering warmth. The self-restraining final gesture retroactively refigures his party as the locus of a resurgent competitive hostility that must be quelled. Horace thus reenacts in the present of the poem the very rebellion he claims to have outgrown.

In fact the battle of Philippi is the third in a series of bloody conflicts, all fought against not external but Italian enemies, recollected in passing within this poem. When wine crowns a celebration, it is usually described in terms that suit the occasion.[96] But the wine for which Horace calls in *Odes* 3.14, stained as it is by both the Social War and the rising of Spartacus, seems peculiarly ill-chosen. The phrase that dates this wine, a wine "that remembers the Marsian war" (*Marsi memorem duelli*, C. 3.14.18), is especially striking; elsewhere in Horace wine is an aid to forgetfulness, not memory. One pertinent example is *Odes* 2.7, where Horace welcomes home a former comrade-in-arms, the beneficiary of an Augustan amnesty (an official act of "forgetting"), with cups full of "forgetful Massic" (*oblivioso . . . Massico*, C. 2.7.21), a vintage inducing oblivion of the troubled days of, precisely, Philippi. While the lyric drinking party often figures as a moment of careless pleasure stolen from a care-burdened time,[97] in *Odes* 3.14 these roles are reversed. It is the day of Caesar's return which will "banish black cares"

---

[94] So, e.g., Wickham (1877) 214; Griffin (1993) 18.
[95] Cf. La Penna (1963) 71–2; Connor (1987) 86.   [96] See Nisbet and Hubbard (1970) 245–6.
[97] For the conventional theme of "wine routing cares" see *I*. 9.37–8, *C*. 1.7.31, *C*. 2.11.17–18, *C*. 4.12.17–20.

(*atras | eximet curas*, C. 3.14.13–14) and Horace's wine which brings care back into the picture.

One might argue that the benefits of the Augustan principate stand out all the more vividly against the bloody backdrop of wars here recollected.[98] Perhaps Horace is offering an oblique argument in favor of Caesar's unrivaled supremacy not only abroad but (a more delicate issue) at home. These two spheres intersect in the slightly illogical central stanza of the poem, where Horace announces that he will not fear a renewal of civil war so long as Caesar controls the world – a world that includes, evidently, not just Spain but Italy.[99] But this Augustan argument does not explain why Horace's reminders of civil war surface right after the resounding, closural "while Caesar controls the world" (*tenente | Caesare terras*, C. 3.14.15–16), simultaneously reopening the poem and the troubled case of Italy. At the same time, the poet's *ego* slips past the encompassing wall of Caesar's name, countering the universalizing "world" and the unique "Caesar" with a barrage of specifications and proper names. Resistance to closure here enacts a resistance to Caesar's authority, and the conciliatory gesture with which Horace does finally conclude only serves to identify the historical dimensions of this resistance.[100]

In offering these readings of *Odes* 1.37 and 3.14, I do not mean to suggest that Horace was an unreconstructed Republican who resented Augustus' rise to power and vented his subversive beliefs, more or less covertly, in poems such as these. Horace's poems support Augustus,[101] and in this sense Horace was in effect a supporter of Augustus. How wholehearted a supporter is a question Horace himself might not have been able to answer. Thoroughly implicated as he was in the Augustan regime, there was nowhere outside it for him to sit and think. On the

---

[98] So, e.g., Williams (1969) 94.

[99] Scholz (1971) 129–30 suggests that Horace means "hurry home and save Italy from the new civil war that is brewing," Williams (1969) 93 that he is expressing his relief that Augustus, "the one guarantee against a recurrence of civil war," did not die in Spain. But *tenente | Caesare terras* does not quite constitute the expected qualification for either interpretation. It is true, however, that so long as Caesar controls the world, no one will have a base from which to contest his supremacy at Rome. On the way Augustan poets mark the difference between Caesar's status abroad and at home, see White (1993) 167 with n. 31.

[100] Hence the unease provoked by this poem in many readers; see, e.g., Fraenkel (1957) 291; Murray (1993) 99.

[101] I do not mean that Horace's poems are not open to "resistant" readings but that such readings must be undertaken against the grain – whether at Horace's express invitation or not is a question I am willing to leave open.

other hand, I do not believe that every reference to the civil war under-scores the preferability of the present, that every reference to Horace's presence at Philippi is designed to illustrate the clemency of Augustus. Such references also have a rhetorical function within Horace's poetry. By including this alternative allegiance, by forestalling the historical closure of Actium, Horace opens up a space for his own authorial asser-tion. Horace's political resistance may be nothing more than an after-effect or a side-effect of his poetic resistance. It may be, that is, not the cause but one consequence of his need to assert his poetic authority. But this assertion does count for something. However complicit Horace was in whatever good or evil deeds Augustus perpetrated, he has succeeded in affording his poems their measure of autonomy.[102]

It is in his fourth book of odes, and more particularly in the paired odes that close the collection – in the odes, that is, that constitute his last words as a lyric poet – that Horace exposes himself most directly to the full glare of Augustus' authority. At the start of *Odes* 4.14, Horace asks what honors proposed by the Senate and citizens of Rome (*Quae cura patrum quaeve Quiritium, C.* 4.14.1) could suffice to eternize "your virtues, Augustus" (*tuas, | Auguste, virtutes,* 2–3) – a rhetorical question which implies that nothing they can propose will measure up to their leader's extraordinary merits and that it is left to Horace to settle the account by offering Augustus the honorific gift of this ode. This opening implicitly distinguishes the poet Horace, purveyor of immortal and immortalizing poems, from the rest of the Augustan public – distinguishes him in a way that the choral, childlike opening of *Odes* 4.5, for example, does not. Accordingly, when Horace elaborates his apostrophe, "O greatest of leaders, wherever the sun shines upon populated shores," *o, qua sol habit-abilis | illustrat oras, maxime principum* (5–6), it is, so far as we know, the authorial persona who is speaking. It is the individual poet, not some slavish easterner, who is one *qua* away here from a quite unRoman and unRepublican identification of Augustus with the sun.[103] True, Horace is careful to pair only subject peoples and lands with the reiterated hymnic "you" that studs the closing stanzas of the ode (appearing at lines

---

[102] Cf. Dunn (1995) 176, locating "the rhetoric of lyric" at "the intersection of literary and social discourse, where neither can fully exclude or control the other."

[103] The third in a series (following *C.* 4.2.46–7 and 4.5.5–7) of close calls or near misses; con-trast *S.* 1.7.24, where the easterner Persius flatters Brutus without subterfuge as *sol Asiae*. On this figuration, see Doblhofer (1966) 86–90; Fowler (1995) 249.

41, 42, 45, 47, 49, and 51). The Sygambri worship Caesar, but among his own people Augustus has the status not (quite) of a god but of the "present guardian of Italy and masterful Rome" (*tutela praesens* | *Italiae dominaeque Romae*, 43–4; *praesens* is often used of a god "present" to help, cf. *praesens divus* at *C.* 3.5.2). Rome is the *domina* of the world, but Augustus is not the *dominus* of Rome. Still, while foreigners supply the subjects of Horace's verbs, it is the poet who reverentially intones the Augustan *te* within this ode.

The confrontation between the poet's *ego* and the emperor's *tu* is even more immediate in the opening lines of *Odes* 4.15 (1–5):

> Phoebus volentem proelia me loqui
> victas et urbis increpuit lyra,
> ne parva Tyrrhenum per aequor
> vela darem. tua, Caesar, aetas
> fruges et agris rettulit uberes …

> When I wanted to talk of battles and conquered cities, Phoebus gave a warning on his lyre to keep me from setting my little sails toward the Etruscan sea. Your era, Caesar, has restored rich crops to the fields…

After the Apollonian interruption, we expect a turn to slighter and more personal themes, a turn from military to sexual "conquest," for example, on the pattern of "refusal" poems such as *Odes* 1.6 and 2.12. The apostrophe to Caesar might have been integrated into this refusal ("other poets, Caesar, will celebrate your greatness …"). We also expect some elaboration of the poet's self-definition, along the lines laid down by Callimachus, Virgil, and Horace himself in *Satires* 1.10. Such an elaboration might, indeed, have served to bridge the gap between the opening declaration of poetic principle and the celebration of the fruits of the Augustan peace that occupies the rest of the poem. Horace could have written (for example) "others may sing of wars, I will sing of peace" or "not for me the broad sweep of epic, I will cultivate a lyric garden in honor of Augustus." Instead, this poetics is oddly abridged. The authorial persona is interrupted not once but twice: first by Apollo, who warns him off epic, and then by Caesar, who puts a sudden period to his self-reflexive meditation.

But Caesar also has a role to play within Horace's *recusatio*. The pointed contrast between *me* at line 1 and *tua* at line 4 effectively casts the emperor himself as the alternative poet (the variable in the formula "not me but x") to whose superior merits the poet here modestly defers. The fourth book of odes concludes, accordingly, with Caesar's accomplishments, not Horace's – with the *edicta . . . Iulia* (*C.* 4.15.22), not Horace's poetic *dicta*. What is completed here is the labor of the imperial artist, who has closed his text (*clausit*, 9), curbed its excesses (*frena licentiae | iniecit*, 10–11), and edited out its faults (*emovitque culpas*, 11).[104] The contrast with *Odes* 1–3, which closes with Horace's proud recital of his own poetic achievements, is astonishing. Whereas the poet gains autonomous poetic authority in the course of the earlier collection, graduating from the patronage of Maecenas in *Odes* 1.1 to the protection of the immortal Muse in *Odes* 3.30, he seems to forfeit this authority in the course of *Odes* 4.[105] True, Horace opens his final lyric collection by addressing not a mortal but the goddess Venus, whom he casts as the instigator of his belated return to lyric – a displacement that gains piquancy in light of Suetonius' assertion, exaggerated but probably not groundless, that it was Augustus himself who elicited a fourth book of odes from the reluctant poet. And yet if Horace begins by representing the collection as a spontaneous and purely personal production, a response to an inner rather than an external compulsion, he ends with an act of self-obliteration that leaves Caesar in sole possession of the poem.[106]

As in *Odes* 1.37 and 3.14, Caesar occupies the center of *Odes* 4.15 (*custode rerum Caesare*, 17). But this time no alternative individual authority emerges in the ode's second half. Horace concludes instead with an image of communal song: on holidays, in the company of "our children and wives" (*cum prole matronisque nostris*, 27 – the detail confirms the gap between the poet's bachelor persona and the generic *nos*), "we will sing of Troy and Anchises and the offspring of nurturing Venus" (*Troiamque et Anchisen et almae | progeniem Veneris canemus*, 31–2). Horace's last word is *canemus*, "we will sing." It is a brilliant choice to end thus, in the stopless future tense. And yet as Horace braves time, he erases himself. Horace writes *we* will sing – not *I* will sing.[107] If Horace's final lyric collection performs a "major *revocatio*" of Augustus,[108] the fulfillment of this speech

---

[104] Cf. *S.* 2.1.28 for versification as "enclosure" (*claudere*); *Ars* 51, 211, 265 on the limits of poetic "license" (*licentia*); *Ars* 267 on the aesthetic "fault" (*culpa*).

[105] On the "paradigm of the displaced patron" in *C.* 1–3, see Zetzel (1982).

[106] On the relation between *C.* 4.1 and 4.15 see further Putnam (1986) 296–9.

[107] Fraenkel, who ends his book on Horace with a discussion of this ode, rewrites Horace's last words in a moving last effort to revive the poet's "own true self" (Fraenkel [1957] 453).

[108] Putnam (1986) 241.

act determines not only the emperor's entrance but the author's exit. The "present guardian" saluted in the previous ode (*tutela praesens*, C. 4.14.43, where *tutela* functions almost as a noun-equivalent of the intensive pronoun *tute*) leaves no space, rhetorically speaking, for the activity of the poet. At the last frontier of Horace's last collection, the emperor usurps the place of the poet, and the empire overwhelms the poem.

It is difficult to know what happened, in the decade that intervened between *Odes* 1–3 and *Odes* 4, to motivate this ultimate extinction of authorial identity. Perhaps Horace felt unwilling, at this late stage in his career, to compromise his accumulated authority by putting it on the line. The disappearing act of *Odes* 4.15 may indeed represent not a failure of authority but a retreat from the Augustan challenge – Horace's exit from a game that he has ceased to enjoy. Such a reading would align the end of *Odes* 4 with the end of the *Epodes*, where Horace likewise abdicates his poetic power in favor of another's purported omnipotence. Perhaps the silence that follows *Odes* 4.15 marks the poet's disappearance from, rather than into, the choral plural of *canemus*. And yet there is something magnificent and sublimely seductive in the swelling of this final communal voice.

4

Overreading the Epistles

In the opening speech act of *Epistles* 1, Horace responds to his patron's request for a poetic encore with a polite refusal, citing a prior commitment to the study of philosophy. I will return to this initial gesture shortly. For now, it suffices to point out that this portrait of studious retirement effectively keeps its author in the world's eye. Horace's epistles are characterized throughout by the doubleness implicit in the very form of the letter, a kind of writing that at once assumes and crosses the distance between letter-writer and addressee. The epistles are, accordingly, not only detached or "philosophical" meditations on society but also strings of attachment that maintain and in some cases modify social connections. Chief among these connections is Horace's friendship with Maecenas,[1] and my aim in the first section of this chapter is to read *Epistles* 1 from the perspective of Horace's overreading patron. Another important overreader is the emperor Augustus, and in the second section of this chapter I will consider a few poems of *Epistles* 1 with the emperor in mind. I will conclude with a look at how Horace preserves his own face in *Epistles* 2.1, where he finally turns to face Augustus directly.

(No) strings attached: epistles for Maecenas

What was expected of Horace, what benefits was he to receive, what services if any was he to perform, after Maecenas "enrolled" him in his circle of friends (*iubesque* | *esse in amicorum numero, S.* 1.6.61–2)? The rights and duties of superior and subordinate *amici* – to whom I will often refer, for simplicity's sake, as "patron" and "client," although these are not the terms a Roman would have used – are nowhere legally specified, and what passes between the two is reciprocal *beneficia, officia,* or *merita,* good turns that deserve but cannot compel other good turns.

---

[1] Cf. Johnson (1993) 33 on Maecenas' "ubiquity" in *E.* 1.

Given the indeterminate nature of many *beneficia*, moreover, a friend can never be sure that he has paid off his debt. Such a calculation is in any event just what the ideology of *amicitia* cannot admit. While every gift may in fact come with strings attached, those strings exert their proper force only when obligation is transformed, through the mutual (tacit) understanding of donor and recipient, into unconstrained compliance.[2] What makes Horace's epistolary exploration of these issues exciting, even nerve-racking at times, is that it is conducted in full view of his patron. Horace's meditations on "what is right and proper" (*quid verum atque decens*, *E.* 1.1.11) are thus fraught with potential consequences.

This is nowhere more obvious than in the first and seventh epistles of the collection, poems that effectively test the elasticity of the strings attaching Horace to Maecenas. As I began by remarking, Horace's first epistle is at once a dedication and a *recusatio* (*E.* 1.1.1–4):

> Prima dicte mihi, summa dicende Camena,
> spectatum satis et donatum iam rude quaeris,
> Maecenas, iterum antiquo me includere ludo?
> non eadem est aetas, non mens.

> You, the theme of my first Muse, and destined to be the theme of my last: now that I've performed to satisfaction and been presented with my wooden sword, are you wanting, Maecenas, to lock me up again in the old gladiatorial school? I'm not the same age I was then, nor of the same mind.

Only an established author could use this negative face, a bid not for intimacy but for privacy, as the frontispiece of a new collection. The contrast with Horace's previous dedicatory poems is striking. In his first epode, Horace stressed his contentment and Maecenas' more-than-adequate generosity (*satis superque me benignitas tua | ditavit, I.* 1.31–2). But in *Epistles* 1.1 it is Horace who has done "enough" (*spectatum satis, E.* 1.1.2). Far from obliging Horace further, the "gift" featured in these lines (*donatum iam rude*, 2; the image is of a gladiator presented with a wooden

---

[2] Cf. Bourdieu (1977) 171 on the "misrecognition" essential to gift exchange. On the paradoxical combination of disinterestedness and instrumentality in the ideology of Roman *amicitia*, see Saller (1982) 12–15. This chapter is in part an exploration of what Konstan (1995) calls the "tense dialectic between *amicitia* and clientship" (341), forms of relation which, as Konstan stresses, are potentially coexistent but nonetheless distinct. The one time Horace identifies himself as a "client," it is not as Maecenas' (cf. *cliens Bacchi, E.* 2.2.78, of the "chorus of writers," including Horace).

sword on the occasion of his retirement from the arena) signals the end of all obligations. The poet who opened *Odes* 1–3 by placing himself and his poetry under Maecenas' protection seems to have grown weary of his patron's interest.

If anyone is the benefactor here, it is Horace. While the formula that fills the epistle's opening line reaffirms Horace's overarching commitment to Maecenas, soothing in advance the mild sting of his refusal to comply with what he represents as his patron's latest request, it also serves as a reflexive advertisement of the value of Horace's poetry. Whereas Maecenas is identified at the start of the *Epodes* as the devoted friend of Caesar and at the start of the *Odes* as the "offspring of royal forefathers" (*atavis edite regibus*, C. 1.1.1), his claim to fame here is his status as privileged Horatian dedicatee. The first name we encounter within the *Epistles* is thus not "Maecenas" (the name that heads both the *Satires* and the *Odes*)[3] but "Camena" – Horace's Muse. Horace's poetry no longer seems to need either the protection or the reflected luster of his patron's name. If Horace was a "somebody" in the satires to the degree that he was, and was recognized as, Maecenas' friend, his celebrity is no longer as dependent on his patron's. The poet of *Odes* 3.30 has glory enough and to spare.

Whereas the satirist studied to please his friends (*sic dulcis amicis* | *occurram*, S. 1.4.135–6), the epistolary poet will labor first and foremost to be a friend to himself (cf. *quid te tibi reddat amicum*, E. 1.18.101). This inward turn is supported in Horace's first epistle by an insistent rhetoric of self-reliance and self-sufficiency. If Horace was once a pleasure-loving grasshopper, he has matured into an industrious ant, putting up a supply of wisdom for his wintry age (*condo et compono quae mox depromere possim*, E. 1.1.12). This philosopher is quick to assert that he is not affiliated with any particular school (13–15):

> ac ne forte roges quo me duce, quo lare tuter,
> nullius addictus iurare in verba magistri,
> quo me cumque rapit tempestas, deferor hospes.

> If you're wondering under whose leadership, in whose household I look after myself: compelled to follow no teacher's dictation, wherever the storm carries me, I come to shore a guest.

---

[3] Cf. *Qui fit, Maecenas* (S. 1.1.1), *Maecenas atavis edite regibus* (C. 1.1.1); in *I*. 1, "Maecenas" (4) follows hard upon "Caesar" (3).

In his first epode, Horace declared his readiness to follow Maecenas to the ends of the world (*forti sequemur pectore*, I. 1.14); in *Satires* 1.9, he defended the purity of his patron's *domus*. Here, Horace's stance of philosophical noncommitment constitutes an implicit rejection of his patron's "leadership and household." Horace will take care of himself by himself: "what's left is for me to guide and comfort myself with these ABCs" (*restat ut his ego me ipse regam solerque elementis, E.* 1.1.27). Horace is indeed returning to the *ludus* – not Maecenas' gladiatorial school, but the *ludus litterarum* or "elementary school" of his own verse letters.

And yet the verse epistles that follow must have gone a long way toward satisfying Maecenas' desire (or the desire Horace ascribes to him) for more Horatian poetry. In the event Maecenas will receive two more epistles from Horace, the last occupying the privileged penultimate position that Horace also reserves for his patron in *Odes* 1–3. Before the first epistle ends, moreover, Horace will have readmitted Maecenas into his epistolary *ludus* and resubmitted himself to his patron's authority. It is characteristic of the poet of the epistles that this final tribute takes the form of a complaint.[4] Maecenas is quick to scold him, Horace points out, when he is improperly groomed (*E.* 1.1.94–7). But when it is not his clothes but his ideas and behavior that are in disarray, Maecenas thinks nothing of it; "and yet," Horace reproachfully adds, "you are the guardian of my affairs and are annoyed by a badly trimmed nail in the friend who depends on you, who looks to you" (*rerum tutela mearum | cum sis et prave sectum stomacheris ob unguem | de te pendentis, te respicientis amici*, 103–5). The philosopher who earlier claimed to be his own guardian (*me . . . tuter*, 13) here acknowledges, albeit with a certain face-saving petulance, that he does after all need his patron's protection (*tutela*, 103). Horace closes by smiling at his own philosophical aspirations: "to sum up: the wise man is second only to Jove" (*ad summam, sapiens uno minor est Iove*, 106), endowed with all worldly blessings, and, "above all, sound – except when he's bothered by a cold" (*praecipue sanus, nisi cum pituita molesta est*, 108). With this play on the double meaning of *sanus* ("sound" in both mind and body), Horace gets off his high-minded hobby-horse and acknowledges the force of his friend's body-oriented perspective.

If Horace stretches the ties of friendship in *Epistles* 1.1, in *Epistles* 1.7 he pulls away with more force – hard enough, indeed, to risk snapping the connection. An exercise in polite rudeness or amicable hostility, the

---

[4] Cf. Lyne (1995) 145.

poem at once (re)creates and averts a crisis by renegotiating a contract that Horace can no longer honor in its original form. Here again Horace represents himself in the act of declining Maecenas' request, in this case not for poems but for a speedy return to Rome. He commences by representing Maecenas' complaint in free indirect discourse: "I promised you I'd be in the country for five days, and here I've been missing, liar that I am, for the whole of August" (*Quinque dies tibi pollicitus me rure futurum,* | *Sextilem totum mendax desideror, E.* 1.7.1–2; the lines purport to render Maecenas' "You promised me, you liar," etc.). Now it is the health not of his soul but of his body that prevents his compliance. If Maecenas cares about his friend's well-being, he will indulge his fears of illness and forgive him for prolonging his absence (*dabis aegrotare timenti,* | *Maecenas, veniam,* 4–5). Horace will stay away not only for the fever-laden month of September but also, as he goes on blithely to announce, through the winter months, months "your bard" (*vates tuus,* 11) – the expression assures Maecenas of his friend's fidelity – is planning to spend at the seaside, resting and reading. "He'll come back to see you, my indulgent friend," Horace concludes, "with the spring winds, if you'll allow it, and the first swallow" (*te, dulcis amice, reviset* | *cum Zephyris, si concedes, et hirundine prima,* 12–13). It is true that Horace has carefully sweetened his refusal with tokens of deference and affection.[5] Still, as in *Epistles* 1.1, the only "gift" he asks of his patron (*dabis . . .* | *. . . veniam,* 4–5) is leave to stay away.

The rest of the epistle will explore the question of the gift through a series of exemplary tales – several very brief, the last expanding to fill the second half of the poem. What is most striking about these tales, and about the personal reflections with which Horace intersperses them, is that they serve for the most part less to illustrate than to obscure a point. To track Horace's twists and turns, it is necessary to keep close to the ground, and I will accordingly read this epistle in some detail. The first of Horace's tales is contrastive and is prefaced by a strongly marked *non*: "Not the way a Calabrian host presses his guest to eat pears did you make me rich" (*non quo more piris vesci Calaber iubet hospes* | *tu me fecisti locupletem, E.* 1.7.14–15). The inept Calabrian, who refuses to take his guest's politely reiterated "no" for an answer, ends by informing him that the pears he leaves behind will be fed to the pigs (15–19); "a good and wise man," by contrast, "says that he's available for the deserving, and yet he

---

[5] See Drexler (1963) 28; Kilpatrick (1986) 9.

isn't ignorant of the difference between real and play money" (*vir bonus et sapiens dignis ait esse paratus,* | *nec tamen ignorat quid distent aera lupinis,* 22–3). Maecenas too, we presume, knows how to tell deserving from undeserving recipients and valuable from valueless gifts. But the persuasive import of this characterization remains unclear. In this context, just after Horace's refusal to return to Rome, we might have expected a different kind of story – one involving a contrast between two ways of giving gifts (with or without strings visibly attached: "*you* would never call in your debts so ungraciously") or between two ways of dealing with a friend's refusal (petulantly or graciously: "*you* would never berate a friend so uncomprehendingly"). That Horace goes on to stress that he is himself deserving (*dignum praestabo me etiam pro laude merentis,* 24) may betray his residual anxiety over the unspoken accusation of ingratitude. But what perhaps resonates most here is the guest's final refusal of his host's unwelcome offer: "I am as obliged by your gift as if I were departing weighed down with pears" (*tam teneor dono, quam si dimittar onustus,* 18). It is Horace who is feeling obliged, Horace who is feeling "weighed down," not by Maecenas' gift but by the continuing obligations it carries with it.

That weight leaves its impression on the two apparently disconnected passages that immediately follow. (1) If it is the case that Maecenas wants Horace never to leave his side (*quodsi me noles usquam discedere, E.* 1.7.25), he will need to give him back (*reddes,* 25) the youthful attributes that enabled him to play the subordinate friend's role gracefully and well – his strength, his curls, his lyric eloquence (26–8). (2) A vixen once crept through a crack into a bin of grain, ate her fill, and then found herself unable to squeeze back out again, provoking an onlooking weasel's sage remark: "If you want to get out of there, look for the chink when you're as skinny as you were when you slipped in" ("*si vis*" *ait* "*effugere istinc,* | *macra cavum repetes artum, quem macra subisti,*" 32–3). Despite their surface resemblances – both passages have to do with going back to an earlier state of being: Horace to his youth, the vixen to her former skinny self[6] – the "restorations" in question are in fact antithetical, the first involving a return to service, the second an escape from confinement. It is Horace's conclusion to the vixen's tale – "If I'm pressed with this image, I turn everything over" (*hac ego si compellor imagine, cuncta resigno,* 34) – that allows us to piece together the unspeakable condition that he is at once

---

[6] Cf. also the instructively false parallelism of *forte . . . angusta* (26) and *forte . . . angustam* (29).

delivering and suppressing: *quodsi me noles discedere, cuncta resigno.* "If you insist on my staying at your side, then I'll give you back everything that makes you feel you can make such a demand."

As Colin Burrow has pointed out, this lightly veiled subtext is laid bare by the poet Ludovico Ariosto, who borrowed Horace's fable to illustrate his own troubled dependence on Ippolito d'Este, concluding boldly (albeit not to his patron's face; the poem is addressed to Ariosto's brother): "If the reverend Cardinal thinks he has bought me with his gifts, it's not hard or bitter for me to give them him back, and take my original liberty."[7] If some other readers of Horace's epistle have labored to bury this subtext by devising an alternative interpretation of the flow of these lines, their labor may be understood as a response to, and an index of, the indecorous boldness, even violence, of Horace's gesture (Horace cannot be doing what he seems to be doing – therefore he must be doing something else).[8] The critical denial serves as evidence of Horace's success in achieving a certain level of "plausible deniability" – or rather, in this case, implausible but still possible deniability; it is Horace's crisscrossing of his argument that enables these variant inter- pretations. What is amplified by Ariosto remains muted within Horace's epistle, which retains what Burrow aptly terms a "quality of imminent offense."[9] The offense is also carefully mitigated. As it stands, Horace's fable saves Maecenas' face – the greedy vixen is responsible for her own entrapment.[10] And the very hyperbole of Horace's condition – "if you want me *never* to go away from you" (*noles usquam,* E. 1.7.25) – suggests that Maecenas is entitled to, Horace ready to supply, some measure of friendly attendance; it is not the existence but the tightness of the strings binding Horace to Maecenas that is in question here. It is only if Maecenas believes that he has effectively purchased his friend's continual attendance that Horace undertakes to return the purchase price in full.[11] Horace is staking everything on his faith that Maecenas does not in fact view their friendship in terms of a strict quid pro quo.

---

[7] Burrow (1993) 31–3 (the translation of Ariosto is Burrow's). Cf. Berres (1992), who notes the "delicacy of feeling" (237) shown by Horace's disjunction of his potentially offensive condition.

[8] See, e.g., Becker (1963) 33–4; Kilpatrick (1986) 11–12. Most recently Horsfall (1993) 54–5 supplies the fable with the decorously generalized moral "Don't change your ways when your circumstances change," omitting the troublesomely specific narrative of fattening and entrapment. For full bibliography and detailed refutation of such interpretations see Berres (1992).   [9] Burrow (1993) 36.   [10] So Johnson (1993) 44–5.

[11] Cf. Lyne (1995) 153.

That the stakes are high here is clear from Horace's continued attempts to hedge his rhetorical bets. "I don't praise the sleep of the commoner while stuffed with pheasant," he goes on to proclaim, "and I don't trade my free untrammeled leisure for the wealth of Arabia" (*nec somnum plebis laudo satur altilium nec | otia divitiis Arabum liberrima muto, E.* 1.7.35–6). The phrase "stuffed with pheasant" recalls the fable of the fat-bellied vixen. But is Horace fat or thin, in or out of Maecenas' granary? In, according to the logic of the fable; out, according to the next line, where "free untrammeled leisure" is Horace's to trade. More significantly, the very formulation of the couplet points away from such context-bound, historicizing interpretations, toward the safer realm of philosophical generalities. The lines that follow likewise muffle the indecorous force of Horace's proposition, in this instance by reframing his pledge to "turn everything over," somewhat unconvincingly, not as a movement toward independence but as further evidence of his clientary deference (37–9):[12]

> saepe verecundum laudasti, rexque paterque
> audisti coram, nec verbo parcius absens:
> inspice, si possum donata reponere laetus.

> You've often praised my modesty, you've been called "king" and
> "father" to your face, and no less often in your absence: look and see
> if I can return your gifts with a light heart.

Horace closes the epistle's first half by invoking the example of Telemachus, who declined King Menelaus' proffered gift of horses as ill-suited to the terrain of rocky Ithaca. Likewise Horace: "small things befit a small man: not regal Rome pleases me now, but empty Tibur or unwarlike Tarentum" (*parvum parva decent: mihi iam non regia Roma, | sed vacuum Tibur placet aut imbelle Tarentum,* 44–5).

"Not regal Rome, but –." The expected alternative is surely Horace's Sabine farm, the ideal negative space for Horace's negative face, the rustic domain where he rather than his patronal *rex* is king. And yet, were the Sabine farm named here, Horace would find himself in the uncomfortable position of at once refusing Maecenas' request and clinging wholeheartedly to Maecenas' most famous and eminently suitable gift.[13] By substituting Tibur and Tarentum, Horace reminds his patron that he does, after all, have other retreats available to him. But he goes further

---

[12] This sequence also arouses the suspicions of Drexler (1963) 33.
[13] Similarly McGann (1969) 52.

still, not only erasing his own Sabine farm but introducing another, in the next and final tale of the epistle, in the startling role of a paradigmatically "unsuitable gift." Once upon a time, an overworked senator named Philippus caught sight of a smooth-shaven individual contentedly cleaning his nails in the quasi-pastoral "deserted shade of a barber shop" (*vacua tonsoris in umbra, E.* 1.7.50).[14] His attendant, dispatched to investigate, returns with a favorable report. The man is a small-time auctioneer of blameless character (*praeconem, tenui censu, sine crimine,* 56) named Vulteius Mena (56–9):

> notum
> et properare loco et cessare et quaerere et uti,
> gaudentem parvisque sodalibus et lare certo
> et ludis et post decisa negotia Campo.

> a man known, as the occasion warrants, to bustle, to relax, to go after money and to spend it, a man who enjoys his humble circle, his own secure home, the games, and (after his business is done) the Campus.

As if seduced by this portrait of humble contentment, the great man invites the little man to dinner, but the astonished auctioneer declines. Undeterred, the senator seeks him out the next day and traps him into apologies (convention assigns the role of suitor to the subordinate, not the superior), a dinner engagement, and the role of client. The independent man who once delighted in the company of men like himself and in the stable possession of his own home is thus drawn into the orbit of another and greater man's household. One day, on a trip to Philippus' country estates, he launches into endless praises of the "Sabine fields and climate" (*arvum caelumque Sabinum,* 77). Anticipating amusement, Philippus helps Mena buy a little farm. But the farmer's life does not agree with the former city-dweller, and Mena finally jumps on a horse, races to Philippus' house, and begs him to "return me to my former way of life" (*vitae me redde priori,* 95). Horace concludes the epistle by drawing the moral. A man who finds he's made a mistake should make haste and return to his former ways; each man should measure himself by his own yardstick (96–8).

Like the tales that precede it, this culminating exemplum sheds more

---

[14] On Mena as a version of Virgil's Tityrus, *lentus in umbra,* see Stégen (1963) 50. The echo may underscore the difference between Philippus and Octavian – the one abusing his power to deprive his client of ease, the other standing surety for that ease.

darkness than light on Horace's immediate situation. While it is evident that Mena in some way stands for Horace, Philippus for Maecenas, Horace has taken care to complicate the analogy. As M. J. McGann has pointed out, the behavior of the freedman and the senator is designed to contrast point for point with that of Horace and Maecenas as depicted in *Satires* 1.6 (Horace and Maecenas can pride themselves on not having acted "like that").[15] It is not by chance, moreover, that when we first meet the dapper Mena, he is taking his time cleaning his nails in the shade of a barber shop where he has just had a shave (*adrasum*, E. 1.7.50); it is in just these matters that Maecenas was famously fastidious and Horace notoriously lax (cf. E. 1.1.94, 104).[16] It is suggestive, in this connection, that "Mena" distantly echoes "Maecenas," "Philippus" "Flaccus." Lest any one should make the mistake of identifying Mena too closely with Horace, Horace issues a further corrective in the form of *Epistles* 1.14, a letter purportedly addressed to the steward of his Sabine farm, a slave who once longed for the country but has since grown eager for a return to city service (E. 1.14.14–15). In this variation on *Epistles* 1.7, Horace plays Philippus to his slave's Mena.[17] I do not mean to suggest that the Horace of *Epistles* 1.7 shares Mena's urgent desire to resume his old way of life in the city. Indeed, the most obvious difference between Horace and Mena is that Horace loves his Sabine farm while Mena comes to hate his.

And yet the tale cannot be read strictly *e contrario* as a model of bad patron–client relations and unhappy gifts designed to bring the right-eousness of Maecenas and Horace and the rightness of Maecenas' gift into sharper relief. The unambitious Mena, content with his modest live-lihood and simple pleasures, is less the antithesis than a caricature of the virtuous Horace portrayed in *Satires* 1.6.[18] Like the satirist, Mena is

---

[15] McGann (1969) 54–5; cf. Gold (1987) 128.

[16] Maecenas is held to have written a pamphlet *de cultu suo*; see André (1983) 1768.

[17] Cf. McGann (1969) 56. Two stray details reinforce the link: the prominence of the number five in their opening lines (*Quinque dies*, E. 1.7.1; *quinque focis et | quinque bonos . . . patres*, E. 1.14.2–3), and their references (the only references within E. 1) to Cinara (E. 1.7.28, E. 1.14.33). As in S. 2, Horace here transfers elements of his autobiography onto a lower-status surrogate: the slave's former prayers for the country (*tacita prece rure petebas*, E. 1.1.14) echo Horace's (cf. *Hoc erat in votis*, S. 2.6.1), while the company of urban slaves he is now eager to join (*horum tu in numerum voto ruis*, E. 1.14.41) is reminiscent of the company of *amici* in which Maecenas enrolled Horace (*in amicorum numero*, S. 1.6.62; *suorum | in numero*, S. 2.6.41–2).

[18] On the strategic irony involved in the coupling of this portrait with Horace's account of the origins of his friendship with Maecenas, see above, 30–6.

entirely passive – far from seeking to better himself by making up to the great man, Mena is the befuddled object of Philippus' verbal solicitations. This is not the distribution of roles we might have expected. As a man who lives off the powers of his wit and his voice, the auctioneer has a natural affinity to the *scurra* or "satirical wit" from whom Horace struggles to distinguish himself in *Satires* 1.4. Some men played both roles – for example Lucilius' Granius, an auctioneer whose witticisms earn the praise of Cicero (*De or.* 2.244, 254, 281–3), and the ne'er-do-well Sextus Naevius, whom Cicero attacks for pursuing the same (double) line of work (*Quinct.* 3.11–12). In *Satires* 1.6, Horace claims that he himself might well have been a *praeco*, following more or less in the footsteps of his father the *coactor* (the middleman who handled the money for the buyer and seller at an auction), had his life taken a less fortunate turn (*S.* 1.6.86–7). Juvenal will likewise write of poets, disappointed in their hopes for patronage, who have taken up the more lucrative career of auctioneering (7.5–12). When Horace represents Mena as being "hooked" (*occultum visus decurrere piscis ad hamum*, 74) by the persistent senator's flattering attentions, he is working against the grain of a more conventional story, in which it would be the auctioneer who "hooked" himself a patron by displaying the kind of uninhibited verbal fluency that he would use elsewhere to bring in custom. And when he describes Philippus as "prevailing upon" Mena to accept his help and purchase a farm (*persuadet uti mercetur agellum*, 81), he is quietly revising the image of the client as angling and eager for gifts. The auctioneer thus has a role to play in the poet's ongoing defense.

But Mena's assumption of the key Horatian trait of unambitious passivity does not explain and indeed does not affect the puzzling essence of Horace's final tale – the distress a Sabine farm causes its owner. Perhaps Horace is suggesting that his desire to preserve his autonomy outweighs his attachment to his villa and that he is ready, accordingly, not only to imitate but to outdo Mena by giving up a way of life he finds deeply congenial. But however we interpret this tale – and critics have tied themselves into knots attempting to unsnarl its complications[19] – we cannot

---

[19] So, e.g., Becker (1963) 36 submerges the troublesome details into the overarching lesson of decorum (which I would term Horace's philosophical cover story), while at the other extreme Desch (1981) 43 argues for a sustained parallel between Horace and Mena (both embarked on careers which were beyond their powers – farming in the one case, lyric poetry in the other; hence Horace's readiness to return the Sabine farm, "which had brought him so much unhappiness"). For more nuanced discussions, see Drexler (1963) 34–6; Reckford (1959) 204–6; Johnson (1993) 43–4.

get away, any more than Horace can, from the essential problem of this epistle. The Sabine farm is at once the clearest reminder of Horace's dependence and the site and figure of his independence.[20] It is this paradox that produces the peculiarly uncommunicative communication of *Epistles* 1.7. If Mena is wont to say either too little or too much – the auctioneer responds to Philippus' overtures first with a dumbfounded silence (*mirari secum tacitus, E.* 1.7.62) and then, at the dinner table, with an indiscriminate stream of speech (*dicenda tacenda locutus*, 72) – Horace presents his patron with a tacit discourse that succeeds in conveying significantly less than it says.

One of Horace's most pointed commentaries on this stifled communication is the expansive garrulousness of *Epistles* 1.15. This letter finds Horace busy planning the winter excursion to the seaside that he mentioned to Maecenas at the outset of *Epistles* 1.7 (*E.* 1.15.1–3, 25):

> Quae sit hiems Veliae, quod caelum, Vala, Salerni,
> quorum hominum regio et qualis via (nam mihi Baias
> Musa supervacuas Antonius [facit] . . .)
> scribere te nobis, tibi nos adcredere par est.

> What kind of winters they have at Velia, what kind of climate at Salernum, Vala, what sort of people live there, what the road there is like – for Baiae is judged useless for what ails me by Antonius Musa . . . it's right for you to write me, and for me to heed what you say.

The doctor, Antonius "Musa" (the cognomen is displaced prominently forward), who warns Horace away from a resort once listed among the Muses' favorites (*seu liquidae placuere Baiae, C.* 3.4.24), is an apt embodiment of Horace's new Muse. As in the first epistle, so here Horace would seem to be turning away, for the sake of his health, from the frivolities of lyric toward philosophical severity. Such a turn would also accord with the staid and solitary hibernation Horace envisioned in the seventh epistle (*ad mare descendet vates tuus et sibi parcet | contractusque leget, E.* 1.7.11–12). And yet the enormously overstuffed, continually interrupted

---

[20] Similarly Miller (1994) 152, 160. True, in *E.* 1.11 Horace asserts that place should be a matter of indifference – compare his assertion of undifferentiated discontent at *E.* 1.8.12 (*Romae Tibur amem ventosus, Tibure Romam*). But critics are not in error when they slight the "lesson" of *E.* 1.11. If Horace wanted to equalize country and city, he should have written a discontented letter *from the country* praising the pleasures of city living. That such a letter is unimaginable (the closest Horace comes, and it is not very close, is *E.* 1.15) is a sign of the "ruricentric" perspective of the epistles, against which *E.* 1.11 strikes, in the interests of independence, only a feeble blow.

first sentence of *Epistles* 1.15, which stretches to fill twenty-five lines (the citation above pares this sentence down to its barest essentials), bespeaks excess and extravagance, not simplicity. If Horace's aim is to live aright (*recte vivere*, a phrase that appears in various forms throughout the collection), this long and winding sentence signally fails to travel *recta via*.[21]

And in fact the excursion Horace is contemplating is not a peaceful retreat but a hedonistic debauch. In *Epistles* 1.7 he claimed to have lost forever the youthful vigor that fitted him for life with Maecenas. But in *Epistles* 1.15 he is eagerly anticipating a magical rejuvenation – the reconstruction, however temporary, of his late-lamented lyric persona, with the help of a bottle of excellent wine, "the kind that will supply me with a stock of words and recommend me, a young man again, to a Lucanian girlfriend" (*quod verba ministret,* | *quod me Lucanae iuvenem commendet amicae, E.* 1.15.20–1).[22] Horace's use of the verb *commendare* here is slightly and wittily improper; "recommendations" are usually delivered by men, not bottles of wine, and they typically target VIPs. But in this holiday epistle social jockeying yields to amorous intrigue, and Horace's friend makes way for his girlfriend, an object of desire who poses a less powerful threat to her suitor's virile autonomy. A similar trend shapes the second half of the epistle, where Horace likens himself to one Maenius, "a roving parasite, not the sort who has an established manger" (*scurra vagus, non qui certum praesepe teneret,* 28). If the auctioneer who delights in "his own secure home" (*lare certo, E.* 1.7.58) resembles the Horace of *Satires* 1.6, Maenius recalls the wandering Horace of *Epistles* 1.1, a man who claims to have no fixed (philosophical) abode (*quo me cumque rapit tempestas, deferor hospes, E.* 1.1.15).[23] The parasite of every man is under no particular obligation to any man.

The discourse on obligation that is splendidly evaded in *Epistles* 1.15 surfaces in *Epistles* 1.10, a letter addressed to Horace's old friend Aristius Fuscus. In the rhetorical economy of the epistles, Fuscus is both a foil and a cover reader for the overreading Maecenas (*E.* 1.10.1–5):

---

[21] On the various forms of "pilgrimage" in *E.* 1, see Johnson (1993) 129 n. 12.

[22] A similar undercutting of *E.* 1.7 is perhaps implicit in *E.* 1.5, where Horace invites a friend to a dinner to be held that same day, which Horace specifies as the day before Caesar's (presumably Augustus') birthday, i.e. 22 Sept. If we ask ourselves where we are to imagine the dinner as taking place (a question that the poem does not, of course, require us either to ask or to answer), we are likely, in view of the short notice Horace gives his guest, to answer "at Rome" (so, e.g., Mayer [1994] 137). So much, then, for the dangers of Rome in autumn (*E.* 1.7.3–9). On *E.* 1.5, see further below, 182–4.

[23] Mena and Maenius are contrasted by Kiessling and Heinze (1959) 79.

Urbis amatorem Fuscum salvere iubemus
ruris amatores, hac in re scilicet una
multum dissimiles, at cetera paene gemelli
fraternis animis – quidquid negat alter et alter –
adnuimus pariter vetuli notique columbi.

To Fuscus, lover of the city, greetings from the lover of the country –
in this one matter we are certainly much unlike, we are in everything else almost twins, with kindred spirits. Whatever the one says
"no" to, so does the other; we nod approval in unison, old familiar
doves.

The emphatic rhetoric of twinship (the matching tags for sender and
addressee, the doubled *quid* and *alter* of line 4) underscores Horace's assertion of amicable parity. Where Maecenas is Horace's "king and father"
(*rexque paterque, E.* 1.7.37), Fuscus is a kind of brother or double. When
Horace asks "What do you want?" or (more idiomatically) "What more
can I say? I'm really alive and my own master as soon as I've left behind
everything that you and your sort praise to the heavens" (*quid quaeris?*
vivo et regno simul ista reliqui | quae vos ad caelum fertis, 8–9), his question
remains strictly rhetorical. Although Fuscus, like Maecenas in *Epistles* 1.1
(compare *quaeris, E.* 1.1.2), champions the claims of the city, he cannot
and would not compel his friend to return to Rome.

The enabling exclusion of Maecenas is registered in both the style and
the content of the argument which exfoliates from this opening salutation. As he extols the virtues of country living, Horace assumes the
clipped tones of didactic authority – tones he will never use to
Maecenas: "What you admire you will be reluctant to give up. Shun
grandeur: one may live better under a pauper's roof than do kings and the
friends of kings" (*si quid mirabere, pones | invitus. fuge magna: licet sub*
paupere tecto | reges et regum vita praecurrere amicos, E. 1.10.31–3).[24] Beneath
the familiar opposition between careworn wealth and carefree poverty,
moreover, we glimpse a more pertinent contrast between rustic self-

[24] Horace is no doubt parodying the tone of Fuscus, himself a schoolmaster; see Mayer (1994)
186. Although Horace often slips into the didactic mode in poems to Maecenas, his words
of wisdom are usually not directed at his patron but at an unspecified "you." The chief
exception is *C.* 3.29.9–16 – an unusually and pointedly self-assertive poem (see Santirocco
[1986] 163–5). But even here Horace tempers his didactic authority with a subordinate's
deference, favoring politely impersonal formulations (e.g., "country simplicity is often a
pleasant change for the careworn rich," *plerumque gratae divitibus vices*, etc., *C.* 3.29.13) over
direct imperatives.

sufficiency (compare *vivo et regno*, 8) and urban enslavement to (otherwise known as friendship with) a "king" or patron in the city. Horace reinforces this lesson with the fable of the horse who sought man's help in defeating the stag, only to find, after vanquishing his rival, that he couldn't "shake the rider from his back or the bit from his mouth" (*non equitem dorso, non frenum depulit ore*, 38). So too with the man who "forfeits his freedom out of fear of poverty" (*pauperiem veritus . . . | libertate caret*, 39–40): "he'll carry a master, the wretch, and be his slave forever, because he will not learn how to make do with little" (*dominum vehet improbus atque | serviet aeternum, quia parvo nesciet uti*, 40–1). Although the fable ostensibly bears on the rich man's enslavement to his own greed, the figuration of the horse saddled with a masterful rider suits the subordinate *amicus* uncomfortably well.[25] The subtext here – and it is not very far below the surface – is that the material rewards of befriending a "king" are outweighed by the loss of freedom such a friendship entails. Within a letter to Maecenas, the bearing of this fable on the relation between the letter's sender and its receiver could hardly pass unnoticed. Within a letter to Horace's "twin," the fable may bear the same meaning without having the same sting.

Two epistles Maecenas would be likely to overread with particular interest are *Epistles* 1.17 and 1.18, paired poems in which Horace offers instruction in the art of winning and keeping a patron to two young men who are about to embark on their clientary careers. These epistles open onto what Erving Goffman has termed the "backstage": the place where social impressions are "painstakingly fabricated" and "the impression fostered by the performance is contradicted as a matter of course." "In general, of course," as Goffman remarks, "the back region will be the place where the performer can reliably expect that no member of the audience will intrude."[26] As we will see, however, it is not through negligence that Horace has left the door to the clients' dressing-room ajar.

The first of these epistles forges a bond between author and overreader over the head of its blinkered addressee, a man with the suggestive name of "Scaeva" ("Mr. Inept"). The epistle thus generates two readings – one (that of Scaeva) that takes the poem at face value, and another (that of the overreader, for example Maecenas) that takes it as a satiric portrayal

[25] On the horse and rider in Horace as "an allegory of power," see Ahl (1984) 53. By contrast, the "aging horse" (*senescentem . . . equum*, 8) of *E*. 1.1, a poem addressed to Maecenas, is kept relatively clear of social content (sanctioned, and thus distanced, by Ennian precedent, and with no rider in sight).   [26] Goffman (1959) 112, 113.

of both the unscrupulous teacher and his crassly ambitious student.[27] For Scaeva's teacher has in effect internalized the perspective and the rhetoric of the social climber with whom Horace contended in *Satires* 1.9. In the satire, Horace's ironic encouragement – "your valor is such that you'll take [Maecenas] by storm" (*quae tua virtus | expugnabis, S.* 1.9.54–5) – elicited from his interlocutor a hilarious expression of heroic determination, capped by a lofty motto: "life gives us mortals nothing unless we labor greatly for it" (*nil sine magno | vita labore dedit mortalibus,* 59–60). In the epistle, Horace uses a similarly overinflated rhetoric of manly valor to spur a purportedly hesitant Scaeva into action. The greatest glory may go, Horace concedes, to those who "perform great deeds and display the enemy in chains to the populace" (*res gerere et captos ostendere civibus hostis, E.* 1.17.33), but there is glory too for those who succeed in trapping a patron: "it is not the least of glories to have found favor with leading men" (*principibus placuisse viris non ultima laus est,* 35). "Either manliness is an empty word," Horace concludes, "or the man of enterprise does right to seek renown and rewards" (*aut virtus nomen inane est, | aut decus et pretium recte petit experiens vir,* 41–2).

Some readers have been inclined to take this rhetoric at face value, urging that the distaste Horace's advice arouses in others is entirely anachronistic – in Horace's Rome, social ambition was acceptable, association with the great a source of distinction – and pointing out that Horace boasts elsewhere in the collection (albeit without laying claim to quasi-military glory) of his own success at pleasing the leading men of his day (*me primis Urbis belli placuisse domique, E.* 1.20.23).[28] But what is troubling about the epistle to Scaeva is less the recommendation of social ambition in itself than the discrepancy between Horace's stance here and in his satires. Horace may take pride in his connection with Maecenas, but he never represents himself as endeavoring (whether heroically or otherwise) to forge that connection. If Horace's satires aim to demonstrate anything, it is that a truly virtuous friend such as Horace does not actively "seek renown and rewards" (a highly dubious pair in any case). For the man who sets out in pursuit of them (the social climber of *Satires*

---

[27] See Perret (1964) 104, reading *E.* 1.17 as "a true satire" and aptly comparing Horace's role here with Tiresias' in *S.* 2.5. If, as argued by Williams (1968) 14–17, "Scaeva" is a real person, not just an aptly named fall guy, he must be very far from the vice of parasitism – far enough to be able to function not only as the poem's addressee but as its knowing overreader; otherwise Horace's joke will not amuse him.

[28] See Moles (1985) 43–8; Mayer (1995) 287–9, 292; contrast Seager (1993) 34–5.

1.9, for example), "manliness" is indeed nothing more than the word with which he covers his unmanly self-abasement. The satirical argument of the epistle is clinched by the juncture between Horace's pseudo-elevated reflections and the practical advice that immediately ·follows: "Those who keep quiet in their king's [i.e. patron's] presence about their poverty will carry away more than will a man who duns him" (*coram rege suo de paupertate tacentes | plus poscente ferent,* E. 1.17.43–4). The first rule for the client who actively "seeks rewards," it emerges, is to keep his goal under wraps. What Scaeva's unscrupulous teacher offers here is a Machiavellian reformulation of the admirable principle Horace espoused in the satires: it is crucial for a client (not to be but) to appear uninterested in gifts if he is (not to be but) to appear worthy of them.

As usual, however, Horace's irony is double-edged. A client's silence can always be (mis)read as a tactical maneuver in an overarching campaign to extract gifts from his patron, and there is thus no absolutely reliable way to distinguish strategic from actual disinterestedness, the detachable mask from the inalienable face. If Horace makes a point throughout his poetry of never asking Maecenas for any material thing, he succeeded nonetheless, as everyone knew, in profiting from Maecenas' patronage. An invidious overreader might suppose, accordingly, that Horace himself practiced the hypocrisy he here purports (not) to preach. It is perhaps to disarm such readers that Horace, instead of "keeping quiet about his poverty," regularly proclaims that he is blissfully content to be "poor" ("poor" meaning here, naturally, comfortably well off rather than extravagantly wealthy) and that he neither needs nor wants any (further) gifts from his patron.[29] Those who are so inclined, however, will have no difficulty puncturing this "pretense" (as they will term it) as well.

In his epistle to Scaeva, Horace shares a slightly strained smile with Maecenas over Scaeva's head. In his next epistle, to Lollius, Horace reverts to his authorial persona, offering sage advice – passing the clientary baton, as it were – to a young friend who is almost a mirror image of his own youthful self. But this epistle too is directed to the overreading Maecenas, who might be expected to notice that Horace instructs Lollius to do just what Horace himself declines to do in *Epistles* 1.1 and 1.7. If he wants to succeed in his chosen career of "friendship" (*professus amicum,* E. 1.18.2), Horace advises, Lollius will have to be ready to "yield to the gentle orders of [his] powerful friend" and to "put off the severity

---

[29] See, e.g., *I.* 1.23–34 and *C.* 2.18.10–14.

of the unsociable Muse" (*tu cede potentis amici | lenibus imperiis*, 44; *inhumanae senium depone Camenae*, 47) when his patron decides, for example, to go hunting. The conflict between writing poems and gratifying one's "powerful friend" may be less clear-cut when the friend in question is Maecenas. Still, by characterizing Lollius' poetry as "severe" and "unsociable," Horace brings it into relation with the kind of writing – suited to old age, independent, introverted – that he espouses in his first epistle. On the other hand, whereas Horace can claim to be too old for the "sporting life" of Rome and lyric, Lollius has no comparable pretext for refusing to comply with his patron's demands. If Horace is an aging horse (*E.* 1.1.8–9), Lollius is as swift as a hunting-dog and as tough as a boar (*vel cursu superare canem vel viribus aprum | possis, E.* 1.18.51–2); if Horace is a retired gladiator (*E.* 1.1.2), Lollius is an able performer whose mock-battles earn the applause of the spectators (*adde virilia quod speciosius arma | non est qui tractet, E.* 1.18.52–3). The epistle thus helps Horace formulate his excuses to Maecenas, completing his earlier *recusationes*, as it were, by proposing a more suitable candidate (not Lollius himself, but a Lollius: a younger, more energetic man) in his stead.

This strategy is inoffensive enough. But the epistle does not turn simply on the contrast between youth and age. There is much in Horace's advice to Lollius that might distress Maecenas, if he took it seriously – and there is nothing to prevent him from taking it seriously; by comparison with the satirical letter to Scaeva, this letter is more difficult to disavow.[30] The harshest lines for Maecenas to overread are probably those in which Horace issues a general warning against Lollius' chosen career: "the cultivation of a powerful friend is sweet to those who haven't tried it; a man who has is wary of it" (*dulcis inexpertis cultura potentis amici; | expertus metuit, E.* 1.18.86–7) – where the shift from plural to singular singles out Horace as the man who has tried this kind of "friendship" and found it wanting. Whereas Horace elsewhere depicts his relations with Maecenas as essentially harmonious, his emphasis here on the clientary virtue of "compliance," *obsequium*, suggests that patron–client relations are typically characterized by a divergence of desires. It is thus open to us and to Maecenas to read this letter as retroactively revealing the internal

---

[30] On the problematic character of Horace's instruction here, see Hunter (1985); Seager (1993) 35; Konstan (1995) 340. Contrast *E.* 1.2, also addressed to Lollius, where Horace paints patronage in the rosiest of moral hues (*nunc adbibe puro | pectore verba puer, nunc te melioribus offer, E.* 1.2.67–8). In *E.* 1.18 Lollius' attendance on his "betters" has less pure aims and new kinds of disadvantages.

resistance Horace himself had to overcome when complying with his patron's demands, not only for poetry – in this sphere Horace always retains a certain independence – but for the more mundane services Horace occasionally describes himself as providing, for example the escort duty commemorated in *Satires* 1.5. As regards Maecenas, the letter to Lollius is guilty of an ungraciousness that Horace allows himself nowhere else in his poetry.

The sting may be soothed, however, by the oblique but overwhelming expression of gratitude that fills the end of the epistle. Here Horace turns from Lollius' relations with his "powerful friend" to the friendship that binds him to Horace. Lollius will oblige this genial patron not by setting his own interests aside but by "reading and inquiring of learned men" – Horace included – "what can make you a friend to yourself" (*inter cuncta leges et percontabere doctos . . . quid te tibi reddat amicum, E.* 1.18.96, 101). Horace's own answer to this question takes the form of a description of his Sabine countryside, the place he elsewhere describes as "restoring me to myself" (*mihi me reddentis agelli, E.* 1.14.1) (*E.* 1.18.104–6):

> me quotiens reficit gelidus Digentia rivus,
> quem Mandela bibit, rugosus frigore pagus,
> quid sentire putas? quid credis, amice, precari?

> As often as I'm made new by the cold stream of Digentia, the stream
> that quenches the thirst of Mandela, a district wrinkled with cold,
> what do you suppose I feel? What, my friend, do you think I pray for?

It is not by chance that it is in this setting that Horace finally, for the first time, calls Lollius "friend." It is as if, under the influence of this landscape, the very word "friend," which Horace uses through most of the epistle to mean essentially "a party (client or patron) to an asymmetrical social relationship," were refreshed and restored to its affective roots. Chilled and wrinkled, emblematic of old age and ill-suited to Lollius' green youth, Horace's Sabine landscape is the ideal setting for the aging poet, who is rejuvenated here by his own philosophically inflected version of Antonius Musa's cold-water cure. Maecenas' name may be missing from this passage.[31] But we can hear, and Maecenas would have heard, the thanks Horace can best express thus indirectly. It is Horace's gratitude to Maecenas that lends the vocative *amice* (used only once elsewhere in the collection, at *Epistles* 1.7.12, to Maecenas) its emotional force.

---

[31] Cf. the opening of *S.* 2.6 and the comments of McGann (1969) 81.

When he returns to Maecenas in the penultimate epistle of the collection, Horace has nothing to say about his own (in)dependence or his patron's demands. With the exception of Horace's initial salutation of "cultivated Maecenas" (*Maecenas docte*, E. 1.19.1), nothing specifies his patron as the addressee of this epistle, which could be addressed to any number of Horace's friends with equal propriety. Horace writes to Maecenas here as a famous poet to a learned friend, a friend who can be expected to appreciate both his achievements and his wit. The epistle treats the perils of Horace's literary eminence – on the one side, the "servile herd" (*servum pecus*, 19) of Horace's imitators; on the other, the "ungrateful reader" (*ingratus . . . lector*, 35) who, though privately enjoying Horace's work, plays the severe critic in public. The intersection of aesthetic and ethical issues in this epistle has been demonstrated in detail by Colin Macleod, who is concerned to show that the epistle is not out of place in a book explicitly committed to ethics.[32] From my perspective, however, what is striking is that Horace figures here not as a client but as a disgruntled patron surrounded by inept clients.

The reversal is complete, and pointed. Once upon a time Damasippus accused Horace of a similarly botched imitation of his own patron (*longos imitari*, S. 2.3.308), embroidering his attack with the fable of the mother frog who puffs herself up in emulation of a calf, only to be informed that she won't equal him even if she bursts trying (*non si te ruperis . . .* | *par eris*, 319–20). In *Epistles* 1.19, it is Horace who is the object of imitation, and when he glances back at Damasippus' fable ("striving to emulate Timagenes, Iarbitas' tongue blew Iarbitas up," *rupit Iarbitam Timagenis aemula lingua*, E. 1.19.15), it is clear that he is now aligned not with the frog but with the calf.[33] If Horace cuts a risible figure in *Epistles* 1.1 (*ridendus*, 9; *rides*, 95, 97), *Epistles* 1.19 awards him the last laugh, at the expense of his own hangers-on: "Imitators, you servile herd, how often your uproar has moved me to irritation, how often to laughter!" (*o imitatores, servum pecus, ut mihi saepe* | *bilem, saepe iocum vestri movere tumultus! E.* 1.19.19–20). In contrast to this herd of followers, Horace is an autonomous leader: "I stepped freely where no one had ever stepped before; my foot pressed no other man's prints. Who trusts in himself will lead and govern the swarm" (*libera per vacuum posui vestigia princeps,* | *non aliena meo pressi pede. qui sibi fidet* | *dux reget examen*, 21–3).

Horace is, then, a patron, like Maecenas. And like Maecenas, who was

---

[32] Macleod (1983) 266–79.   [33] See Préaux (1968) 206.

famous for remaining a knight, Horace disdains (*non . . . dignor, E.* 1.19.39–40) the traditional path to "public" poetic honors, neither courting the votes of the fickle *plebs* (*non ego ventosae plebis suffragia venor,* 37), nor entering into competition with the literary *nobiles* (*nobilium scriptorum auditor et ultor,* 39), nor soliciting the support of the "tribes" of scholars (*grammaticas ambire tribus,* 40). This refusal begets resentment which is not allayed by his token protestations of poetic inadequacy. As his critics recognize, if Horace declines to read his work to the theater audience (*spissis indigna theatris | scripta pudet recitare et nugis addere pondus,* 41–2), it is not because he doubts its value but because he is sure of it: "you're laughing at us – you're keeping that stuff of yours for Jupiter's ears – you're perfectly certain that you alone exude poetic honey, you self-admirer" (*rides . . . et Iovis auribus ista | servas: fidis enim manare poetica mella | te solum, tibi pulcher,* 43–5). The accusation recalls the irritated remark of the passer-by who is quoted in *Satires* 2.6: "would you shove everything out of your way when you're racing to Maecenas' side, your mind only on him?" (*tu pulses omne quod obstat, | ad Maecenatem memori si mente recurras?* 30–1). As they complain of his lack of respect for the larger world, these critics enable Horace to pay deference to the great man whose connection with Horace they inadvertently advertise. But in *Epistles* 1.19 the "great man" in question is not Maecenas but Augustus – a significant displacement, to which I will return shortly.

One of the crowning ironies of *Epistles* 1 is that Horace proceeds immediately from this proclamation of elitism to an envoi which sends his epistolary collection forth into the world. The poet who earlier likened himself to a peacefully retired gladiator (*E.* 1.1.4–6) and praised the "hidden path, the side-alley of a life that passes unremarked" (*secretum iter et fallentis semita vitae, E.* 1.18.103) now sallies forth and effectively plunges into the crowded streets of Rome. The contradiction suits the liminal position of the envoi, which takes its stand on the threshold between the authorial home and the public square. A similar contradiction lends piquancy to the finale of *Satires* 1, where Horace first advises aspiring authors to shun the crowd and "be satisfied with just a few readers" (*neque te ut miretur turba labores, | contentus paucis lectoribus, S.* 1.10.73–4) and then, in a closing authorial aside, reveals that his own book is on the point of being released to the general public: "off with you, boy, on the double, and add these verses to my little book!" (*i, puer, atque meo citus haec subscribe libello,* 92). In this miniature envoi, *i, puer,* the slave is an instrument or extension of the master's conflicting impulses toward elitism and popularization. *Epistles* 1.20 distributes these conflicting impulses between the master and the slave, here identified with the book.[34]

The "transparent fiction"[35] elaborated in the first half of the poem is that Horace's foolish book is responsible for its own publication (*E.* 1.20.1–16):

> Vertumnum Ianumque, liber, spectare videris,
> scilicet ut prostes Sosiorum pumice mundus.
> odisti clavis et grata sigilla pudico;
> paucis ostendi gemis et communia laudas,
> non ita nutritus. fuge quo descendere gestis.
> non erit emisso reditus tibi. "quid miser egi?
> quid volui?" dices, ubi quid te laeserit, et scis
> in breve te cogi cum plenus languet amator.
> quodsi non odio peccantis desipit augur,
> carus eris Romae donec te deserat aetas;
> contrectatus ubi manibus sordescere vulgi
> coeperis, aut tineas pasces taciturnus inertis,
> aut fugies Uticam aut vinctus mitteris Ilerdam.
> ridebit monitor non exauditus, ut ille
> qui male parentem in rupes protrusit asellum
> iratus: quis enim invitum servare laboret?

You seem, book, to have your eye on the marketplace; you're eager (it's obvious) to take your stand on the street corner, prettied up by the pumice of Sosius and Co. You hate the lock and seal that modest books are grateful for, you groan at being displayed to a few, you praise publicity, though you weren't brought up that way. Run away down where you're so eager to go. Once you're let out, there won't be any way to come back. "What have I done, wretch that I am? What did I want?" you'll say, when something has hurt you, and you feel the pinch, when your sated lover flags. If my prophetic powers aren't diminished by my disgust at your misconduct, you'll be treasured in Rome until your youthful bloom deserts you; once you start to show signs of wear, fingered by vulgar hands, you'll feed lazy booklice, or run off to Utica, or be tied up and shipped to Ilerda. The adviser you ignored will have the last laugh, like the man who pushed his disobedient donkey onto the rocks in anger – why struggle to save someone who doesn't want to be saved?

[34] On the details of the personification, see Fraenkel (1957) 356–9; West (1967) 17–19.
[35] Macleod (1983) 288.

The looks that crisscross the poem's opening lines convey desires at cross-purposes. The author's possessive gaze renders his desire to keep his book out of general circulation, while the extroverted gaze of his book renders its (his) desire to be more widely seen and admired.[36] If Horace elsewhere construes himself as a public figure and his poems as public (and thus inherently publishable) productions, the perspective of the opening lines of the envoi is strictly domestic. As the verb *descendere* (5) suggests, once the book leaves the guarded seclusion of Horace's household, it is on its way down. The message of the first full-fledged envoi of the European tradition is thus not "Go little book" but "Stay little book." Or rather, Horace manages to avoid saying either "stay" or "go" – an equivocation encapsulated in the one direct order the master issues within the poem, an imperative of insurrection: "run away" (*fuge*, 5).[37]

But the imperative has the tone less of a master's order than of a challenge issued by an injured lover – this master–slave relation is complicated by desire. With its dire prophecy of future misfortunes, the poem represents the lover's attempt to frighten his restless beloved into giving up the idea of marketing its charms to a wider public.[38] The wittily sustained identification of publication with prostitution that underpins the poem may be traced back through Theocritus and Callimachus to the famous passage in Plato's *Phaedrus* in which Socrates describes the manhandling suffered by a piece of writing in promiscuous circulation.[39] If Horace's desire for sexual and literary "exclusivity" is frustrated by his errant book of epistles, it is perfectly satisfied in the anti-envoi, as it might be termed, that closes his first book of odes (*C.* 1.38):[40]

> Persicos odi, puer, apparatus,
> displicent nexae philyra coronae;
> mitte sectari, rosa quo locorum
> sera moretur.

---

[36] On these conflicting impulses, cf. Citroni (1986) 117–18.

[37] Astonishingly, Mayer (1994) 270 renders *fuge quo* as "avoid the place to which . . .," completely missing the discursive flavor of the passage.

[38] On the poem as a piece of "lover's discourse," see Kilpatrick (1986) 154 n. 10; Harrison (1988) 473. A good parallel is furnished by *C.* 4.10, likewise addressed to a heartless male beloved (one closely associated, moreover, with the book in which he appears) who will live (Horace promises) to regret his coldness.

[39] Theoc. *Id.* 16; Callim. *Epigr.* 28 (Pfeiffer); Pl. *Phdr.* 275d–e. On the Callimachean connection, see Bramble (1974) 59–60; for a Callimachean reading of *E.* 1.20, see Pearcy (1994).

[40] For the comparison, cf. Ferri (1993) 79. On the links connecting *E.* 1.20 to *S.* 1.10, *S.* 2.7, *C.* 1.38, and *E.* 1.14, see McGann (1969) 85–6.

> simplici myrto nihil allabores
> sedulus curo: neque te ministrum
> dedecet myrtus neque me sub arta
> vite bibentem.

I detest Persian trappings, boy; no pleasure for me in garlands woven with bast; stop looking for where a late rose lingers. You'll please me with plain unlabored myrtle, no call for extra effort: myrtle disgraces neither you as you pour nor me as I drink under the thick-clustering vine.

Within the minimal lyric space of two Sapphic stanzas, Horace has constructed an image of ideal closure and self-sufficiency: the drinker under the vine, enjoying the product of culture under the aegis of nature. This naturalized culture or cultured nature includes, naturally, the hierarchical relation between master and slave, *magister* and *minister*, each crowned with the artless ornament of "plain myrtle."[41] The reward of self-restraint, for both master and servant, is the suspension of time. Where the end of the first stanza suggests death (*moretur*, 4, cf. *mors*), the end of the second resonates life (*vite bibentem*, 8, cf. *vita*, *viventem*); if death waits outside, within the artful shelter of his stanzas Horace manages to stop the clock. As the abundance of negations suggests, however, this lyric perfection depends on nonfruition. The garlanded pair, caught in the lyric moment as if in amber, resembles the immortal lovers on Keats's urn, forever suspended within their parallel enclosing clauses: "Forever wilt thou love, and she be fair!"

Horace's much-handled and much-traveled book of epistles may lose its pristine bloom, but it will gain another kind of (after)life, in the form of a readership that will carry it onward both in space and in time. This side of the story is also told in Horace's epistolary envoi. When read as a piece not of lover's but of author's discourse, Horace's rehearsal of the humiliations to which his errant book will succumb takes on a different appearance. As many readers have remarked, the begrimed book is a popular success, its journey to the provinces a variation on the grand tour of the proud swan-poet of *Odes* 2.20. The book will also come to serve as its author's *monumentum*, albeit one very definitely not impervious to the onrush of time. In a final twist, one that is marked as an addition to the story, Horace envisions the eventual degradation of the contents of the bookroll: "This too awaits you: stammering old age will overtake you in

---

[41] On pleasure, labor, and the master–slave relation in this poem, see Fitzgerald (1989) 85–92.

some remote corner teaching boys their ABCs" (*hoc quoque te manet, ut pueros elementa docentem | occupet extremis in vicis balba senectus*, *E.* 1.20.17–18). Horace here acknowledges, as if incidentally, the public, didactic dimension of his "private" correspondence. But the book will not be teaching the elementary philosophical lessons that Horace rehearsed in his first epistle (*elementis*, *E.* 1.1.27).[42] In its "old age," the book will be nothing more than a collection of alphabetical stumbling-blocks. Horace captures this reduction of the signified to its constituent material signifiers in the onomatopoetic adjective *balba*, "stammering," with its repeating *a* and *b*.[43] The book of letters, *litterae*, will finally be nothing more than a series of letters, *litterae*.

But something else has happened in these lines. The everturning wheel of erotic fortunes is displaced here by the cycle of generations, as Horace passes away and the book takes his place in the *ludus litterarum*, among boys as young and fresh as it once was. And with this indirect admission of the mortality of both author and book, the erotic tension animating the poem dissipates. After this, there are no more recriminations or accusations. Instead, Horace foretells a happier day when the book will speak its piece before an appreciative audience. The envoi thus contains not one but two biographies – the book's, as foretold by the author, and the author's, as recollected by the book. The book leaves home, but its words faithfully recollect their source (*E.* 1.20.19–25):

> cum tibi sol tepidus plures admoverit auris,
> me libertino natum patre et in tenui re
> maiores pennas nido extendisse loqueris,
> ut quantum generi demas virtutibus addas;
> me primis Urbis belli placuisse domique;
> corporis exigui, praecanum, solibus aptum,
> irasci celerem, tamen ut placabilis essem.

When the afternoon sun turns more ears your way, you'll tell them that I, born of a freedman father and of slender means, spread my wings wide beyond my nest – thus crediting to my character what you subtract from my birth; that I found favor with the first men of the city in war and at home, that I was short, that my hair whitened early, that I was suited to sunshine, quick to anger, but readily appeased.

---

[42] The echo is noted by Préaux (1968) 216.

[43] The lines thus not only allude to but partially transcribe the Aratean epigram on the fate of Diotimus, now reduced to teaching boys their ABCs (παισὶν βῆτα καὶ ἄλφα λέγων, *Anth. Pal.* 11.437).

As in *Odes* 3.30, part of Horace escapes death, keeping his memory fresh for posterity. But the differences between Horace's lyric and epistolary *monumenta* are at least as striking as their resemblances.[44] While Horace's self-effacing and self-defacing representation of his slave-book may indicate the supreme confidence of an established author, there are other gestures of deference here that are less easily recuperated as gestures of authority. Most obvious perhaps is the way Horace's soaring ascent peaks in a gesture of deference to the leading men of his day – a relatively modest boast, when measured against the proud pronouncements of *Odes* 3.30. But the most significant form of deference here is Horace's acknowledgment of the power of time. This acknowledgment is implicit in his description of his body, a Horatian "corpus" made up not of immortal poems but of mortal flesh. But it is also written into the very fabric of the envoi, which begins under the sign of Janus and ends in December, completing its year as the author completes his years (*E.* 1.20.26–8):

> forte meum si quis te percontabitur aevum,
> me quater undenos sciat implevisse Decembris
> collegam Lepidum quo duxit Lollius anno.

> If someone should happen to ask you my age, let him know that I completed forty-four Decembers the year that Lepidus was brought in to be consul along with Lollius.

Unimaginable at the end of Horace's "timeless" lyric collection, this dating suits a collection comprised of epistles, inherently topical and transient documents which customarily record the circumstances of their composition with some degree of specificity. How long will the book survive its own circumstances? How long will it survive its author? If Lepidus and Lollius may be taken to qualify the year of publication (the book postdates their consulship, presumably not by long), Vertumnus and Janus, the matching pair of proper names in the opening line of the poem, evoke temporality itself. But shape-shifting Vertumnus (god of the *vertens annus*, the "revolving year," according to one popular etymology) and two-faced Janus are figures not of monumental permanence but of mutability.[45] Nor are the individual names of Lollius and Lepidus tokens

---

[44] See Harrison (1988); Ferri (1993) 131–7.

[45] See Hardie (1992) 72–5 (discussing Janus in Ov. *Fast.* 1 and Vertumnus in Prop. 4.2). In the *Ars*, Horace similarly associates mortal *sermo* with mutable Roman public works (*mortalia facta peribunt, | nedum sermonum stet honos et gratia vivax, Ars* 68–9). The words of the Roman poet are no more eternal than the works of his purportedly "eternal city."

of immortality but mortal, passing occupants of an institution that will long outlast them. They will last in Horace's poem, if Horace's poem lasts.

Looking back at the collection as a whole, we can see that it repeats the pattern of *Odes* 1–3.[46] Whereas Horace's first epistle, like his first ode, announces his dependence on his patron, his penultimate epistle, like his penultimate ode, effectively casts him as a patron in his own right. The climax of this ascent in both collections is a meditation on poetic immortality that looks past Maecenas to a figure that embodies Horace's poetry – the Muse in *Odes* 3.30, the poetry book itself in *Epistles* 1.20. And yet, as befits a collection as insistently social as the epistles, Horace's epistolary envoi is shaped, in a way that *Odes* 3.30 is not, by the pressure of Maecenas' overreading gaze. Granted the license of a Horatian hyperbole, we could say that the book now is what Horace once was: a creature who uses his (poetic, erotic) charms to win favor.[47] The poetic and the erotic are, moreover, less easy to disentangle than one might suppose. Consider the portrait of his youthful self that Horace paints for Maecenas in *Epistles* 1.7 (25–8):

> quodsi me noles usquam discedere, reddes
> forte latus, nigros angusta fronte capillos,
> reddes dulce loqui, reddes ridere decorum et
> inter vina fugam Cinarae maerere protervae.

> But if you want me never to go away, give me back my strong chest,
> the black curls that narrowed my brow, give me back my powers of
> sweet speech and graceful laughter, give me back the tears I shed
> amid the winecups over the flight of wanton Cinara.

What Horace has sketched here is not only an idealized lyric symposiast but a champion of desire. And while the framing allusions to his stamina and his laments for Cinara may cast Horace in the lover's role, the other details – the black curls, the sweet speech, the graceful laughter – align him rather with the beloved. We might compare his description of Alcaeus' beloved Lycus, who is likewise distinguished by black curls (*nigroque* | *crine decorum*, *C.* 1.32.11–12), and his praise of his own Lalage, she of the "sweet laughter and sweet speech" (*dulce ridentem . . .* | *dulce loquentem*, *C.* 1.22.23–4). Like the various women Horace invites to sing

---

[46] On this pattern in *Odes* 1–3 see Zetzel (1982); Santirocco (1986) 153–68.

[47] Cf. the self-depreciating opening simile at *E.* 2.2.2–22, where Horace compares himself to an attractive and talented but unreliable slave; see above, 8–10.

at his lyric parties (Lyde in *Odes* 2.11 and 3.28, for example), this youthful Horace holds out the promise at once of poetic and of sexual pleasure – the same double promise Horace ultimately transfers to his self-prostituting book.

But the transfer is incomplete. If Horace poses as the lover of his book, he does not altogether shun the mask of the beloved. In his epistolary relations with Maecenas, Horace proves to be as elusive as the Cinara over whom he once shed tears – as fugitive, indeed, as his own beloved book. The culminating irony of *Epistles* 1.20 is that Horace's book does to Horace just what Horace does to Maecenas.[48] As Horace resists the desire of his patron, so the book disobeys its master; as Horace gently extricates himself from Maecenas' possessive clutches, so the book declares its independence of its doting author. Still, it may be that the patron has to be left behind if he is to be remembered. The dutiful slave of *Odes* 1.38 will never represent his master to the world. But Maecenas will survive through Horace, as Horace through his book.

Epistles for Augustus

Horace's penultimate epistle ends, as we have seen, with a self-congratulatory bow to Augustus, the "Jupiter" for whom Horace is accused of reserving his poetic honey. When Horace's book advertises the favor its author found with the "first men of the city" (*primis Urbis*, *E.* 1.20.23), the name it will report with the most pride is perhaps that of the *princeps*, the first among the first. Within the rhetorical economy of *Epistles* 1, Horace's drift away from Maecenas' *domus* is balanced by his progress toward the imperial center.[49] I will return to this rapprochement shortly. I begin, however, with the other side or negative face of this Horatian coin, and with an episode from Horace's biography that brings that face into high relief. In a letter reproduced in Suetonius' life of the poet, Augustus informs Maecenas that he can no longer cope with his personal correspondence (*scribendis epistulis amicorum*) and that he wants "our Horace" (*Horatium nostrum*) to come help him write his letters (*nos in epistulis scribendis adiuvabit*). According to Suetonius, when Horace declined the request, pleading ill health, Augustus not only took the refusal in stride but continued to shower Horace with tokens of his favor

---

[48] On the parallel demands for freedom made by author and book, see Johnson (1993) 69–70. Horace's self-depiction in *E.* 1.7 is part of an overarching eroticization of patron–client relations; see further Oliensis (1997).

[49] On the "centripetal social structure" implied by *E.* 1, see Mayer (1985) 44.

(*ne recusanti quidem aut succensuit quicquam aut amicitiam suam ingerere desiit*). But what interests me here is the fact that Augustus wanted Horace to help him with his personal correspondence. If, as the generally accepted chronology holds, Augustus made this proposal before Horace published his own collection of *epistulae amicorum*, then the collection will have shown Horace to be an originating sender and not a mere transcriber of letters – as who should say, "much obliged, but I have my own epistles to write." But whatever the chronology, it remains the case that Horace chose to write letters on his own account and not on the emperor's. "Our Horace" thus belongs no more to Augustus than to Maecenas.

As in the odes, so in the epistles Horace endeavors to carve out his own negative space within what he represents as an encompassing Augustan discourse. This is the burden of *Epistles* 1.5, a dinner invitation addressed to Horace's friend Torquatus. With its promise of plain fare but ample conversation, the invitation is reminiscent of those Horace extends to Maecenas in *Odes* 1.20 and 3.29, and one point of the epistle to Torquatus is that it is not addressed to Maecenas (such a gesture would not square well with the distancing *Epistles* 1.1 and 1.7). But the epistle also circulates in another economy. Horace's party is scheduled for the night before "Caesar's birthday" (*E.* 1.5.8–11):

> mitte levis spes et certamina divitiarum
> et Moschi causam: cras nato Caesare festus
> dat veniam somnumque dies; impune licebit
> aestivam sermone benigno tendere noctem.

> Let go of your fickle hopes and the struggle for wealth and the trial
> of Moschus. Tomorrow is Caesar's birthday – the holiday lets us off,
> and lets us sleep; we can stretch out the summer night with genial
> conversation without worrying about the consequences.

The lawyer Torquatus can stay up late because he can sleep late; Augustus' birthday is a public holiday, and the courts will not be in session. By specifying the holiday as Augustus' birthday, Horace helps rewrite Roman time as Augustan time.[50] Indeed the passing allusion makes it seem as if the emperor's extraordinary status is something to be taken for granted, part of the fabric of ordinary life.

It is upon this fabric that Horace, the jocular *imperator* of this dinner party (cf. *imperium fer*, *E.* 1.5.6; *imperor*, 21) proceeds to weave the pattern

[50] See Wallace-Hadrill (1987) 223–5.

of his own authority.[51] While Caesar's birthday marks one kind of boundary, Horace himself carefully constructs others. More than any other Horatian invitation, this one harps on the theme of cleanliness.[52] The hearth is sparkling, the furniture has been dusted (*splendet focus et tibi munda supellex*, 7) – the whole house, it seems, has been washed and polished to a condition of pristine brilliance. Not only inappropriate matter but inappropriate persons are scrubbed out by Horace's *ne*-clauses (22–6):

> ne turpe toral, ne sordida mappa
> corruget naris, ne non et cantharus et lanx
> ostendat tibi te, ne fidos inter amicos
> sit qui dicta foras eliminet, ut coeat par
> iungaturque pari.

> [I'm seeing to it] that no soiled coverlet or dirty napkin wrinkle your nose, that both jug and platter show you to yourself, that there be no one to carry outdoors what is said between trusted friends, that like come together and be joined with like.

By sweeping dirt and tale-tellers out of the house, Horace ensures that the *dicta* of his guests will remain safely within doors. In this company, Torquatus will see nothing but faithful friends, candid second selves who reflect his self, like the polished jug and platter.[53]

It is Horace's scrupulous precautions that make possible the moment of openness, the inebriated revelation of secrets, that is celebrated in the poem's central line: "What does drunkenness not unseal? It uncovers what is hidden" (*quid non ebrietas dissignat? operta recludit*, E. 1.5.16). Hedged about and protected by its encircling verses, the line provides an image of its circumscribed occasion.[54] Moreover, unlike Horace's discreet satiric account of his journey to Brundisium (a poem which likewise stands fifth in its collection), this invitation to Torquatus is positioned to one side of "official" Rome and does not flaunt its discre-

[51] Horace's addressee may himself harbor delusions of imperial grandeur, being descended, as the provenance of Horace's proposed wine confirms, from the Republican hero Torquatus, surnamed Imperiosius; see Nisbet (1959) 73–4.

[52] Contrast, e.g., the late invitation to Phyllis (C. 4.11), on which see Owen (1989) 26–31.

[53] Cf. Putnam (1995) 205.

[54] I owe this description of the poem's central moment to Stephen Owen (unpublished lecture). Contrast E. 1.18, which dedicates its midpoint to a description of Augustus' universal mastery (E. 1.18.54–7) – a reminder to Lollius, who is perhaps prone to the vice of emulation (28–31), to keep his own athletic "victories" (53–4, 61–4) in perspective. On E. 1.18, see Ahl (1984) 52; Bowditch (1994).

tion on behalf of Augustus. And whereas *Satires* 1.5 practiced discretion without preaching it, this epistle draws attention to what it will not report. What liberties, we might wonder, will be taken by these tongues loosened by the wine-god Liber? Will the night preceding Augustus' birthday provide an occasion for an expression of resentment at Augustus' preeminence? Perhaps the language of "pardon" and "impunity" (*veniam . . . impune*, 10) applies not only to the prolongation of the summer night but also to the content of the conversation that prolongs it. That these speculations are unverifiable is part of the point. The poem remains nonactionable because it is uninformative.[55] In contrast to *Satires* 2.6, which reports the exemplary conversation at Horace's rustic *cena* at some length, this epistle is not the loquacious equivalent of the party; it is not a sample of private discourse but a public description of the conditions of its possibility. Horace's invitation builds a wall between a world suffused by Augustus' eyes and ears and a private enclave of *libertas* from which he is (as we are) effectively excluded.

If Horace keeps his back to Augustus in *Epistles* 1.5, he turns around toward him in *Epistles* 1.9, the first of two poems to present Horace's positive face (his desire for recognition and approbation) to the imperial household. It may be significant that this poem, a "letter of recommendation" addressed to the emperor's stepson Tiberius on behalf of a friend named Septimius, stands ninth in the collection. In the ninth poem of *Satires* 1, Horace declined to perform a similar service for an unnamed interlocutor seeking an entree into the *domus* of Maecenas. While the social situation – a status squeeze to which Horace's middling position is always vulnerable – is essentially the same, Horace's shift from a defense of Maecenas' *domus* to a mild-mannered assault on Tiberius' marks his advance in the social hierarchy. Whereas Horace is recognized as an intimate of Maecenas' in the satire, in the epistle he is at pains to stress that he is not, with respect to the household of Tiberius, quite an insider (*E.* 1.9.1–6):

> Septimius, Claudi, nimirum intellegit unus
> quanti me facias. nam cum rogat et prece cogit
> scilicet ut tibi se laudare et tradere coner,
> dignum mente domoque legentis honesta Neronis,
> munere cum fungi propioris censet amici,
> quid possim videt ac novit me valdius ipso.

---

[55] Within *E.* 1, Horace comes closest to voicing resistance to Augustus in *E.* 1.16, on which see Armstrong (1989) 128–31.

Septimius, Claudius, is obviously the only man who understands
how highly you value me. When he asks me – when he compels me
with entreaties – to exert myself to commend him to you and to
introduce him as a man worthy of the mind and household of Nero,
who favors all things honorable; when he judges that I enjoy the
privileges of quite a close friend – he sees and knows what I can do
better than I do myself.

Not only the "incidental" praise (so much more effective than the
declarative "you know how to choose deserving men") but the very hes-
itancy of Horace's approach pays homage to the emperor's stepson.
While Septimius thinks Horace enjoys the privileges of "quite a close
friend," perhaps a "closer friend" (*propioris*, 5) than he really is, Horace
capitulates because he fears Septimius will otherwise think he is pre-
tending that his social capital is "less" than it really is (*timui mea ne finxisse
minora putarer*, 8). The unspecific, negatively polite comparatives leave it
up to Tiberius to determine the precise degree of the *amicitia*.[56]

Still, the burden of the poem is to convince Tiberius to act as if he
agreed with Septimius' overestimation of Horace's social value. Horace's
first words – "Septimius, Claudius" (*Septimius, Claudi*, where *Claudi*
looks like a possessive genitive) – iconically perform the act of bringing
the two men in question together, and his closing line formulates an
admirably concise recommendation. But the felicity of this final speech
act hinges on Tiberius' "commendation" of the recommender: "if you
commend my setting aside all modesty in compliance with a friend's
orders, enroll this man in your set and account him a fine and brave
fellow" (*quodsi | depositum laudas ob amici iussa pudorem, | scribe tui gregis
hunc et fortem crede bonumque*, E. 1.9.11–13). This letter is itself, moreover, a
specimen of the kind of service the poet is capable of rendering Tiberius.
Relaxed but respectful, deferential but not insultingly flattering, the
letter projects an addressee to match, an imperial grandee who radiates
an envy-disarming blend of eminence and affability.

Horace comes close to addressing the emperor himself in *Epistles* 1.13,
a letter addressed to the emissary he has entrusted with the weighty
responsibility of delivering his poems to Augustus. Although the epistle
opens onto a scene of what looks like philosophical instruction, with
Horace "teaching" a Stoic wayfarer (a *proficiens*, cf. *Ut profici[sc]entem docui
te*, E. 1.13.1), philosophy is immediately superseded by etiquette. The

---

[56] See Mayer (1985) 42.

central question here is, it emerges, not how to live but how to behave (1–5):

> Ut proficiscentem docui te saepe diuque,
> Augusto reddes signata volumina, Vinni,
> si validus, si laetus erit, si denique poscet;
> ne studio nostri pecces odiumque libellis
> sedulus importes opera vehemente minister.

As I instructed you repeatedly and at length when you were setting out, Vinnius, you will hand over my sealed bookrolls to Augustus [only] if he is well, if he is in a good mood, and finally if he asks for them; see that you don't stumble in your enthusiasm on our behalf, that your zealous service and vehement efforts don't make my little books hateful.

Twelve more lines of sedulous instructions follow. Don't oafishly throw down your load of books when you reach your destination (6–9); use all your strength on the road, muster all your grace in the imperial presence (10–15); and keep discreetly quiet about the nature of your mission (16–18). "Off with you, and fare well" (*vade, vale*, 19), Horace winds up, and then adds one final warning: "take care you don't stumble and shatter what's been entrusted to you" (*cave ne titubes mandataque frangas*, 19).

The epistle, which shows Horace adjusting his face for public viewing, is located in the backstage, and it is this location that produces its witty contradictions. The explicit speech act of the represented private letter and the implicit speech act of the published poem are hilariously at odds: the letter displays the very overzealousness against which it warns and broadcasts the very information it purports to censor. Although Horace concedes that he has already dinned his instructions into Vinnius "often and at length" (*saepe diuque*, E. 1.13.1), he is incapable of refraining from repeating them yet once more. And as he lectures Vinnius on the importance of discretion, he spells out, in a self-violating prohibition, precisely what Vinnius is not to say: "don't tell the world that you sweated carrying poems such as might engage the eyes and ears of Caesar" (*ne vulgo narres te sudavisse ferendo | carmina, quae possint oculos aurisque morari | Caesaris*, 16–18). The overall effect is not unlike that of *Satires* 2.7, where Horace's slave Davus, exploiting his access to the domestic backstage, describes the indecent haste with which his master speeds off in response to a belated dinner invitation from Maecenas (*S.* 2.7.32–5) – a description that functions as a compliment to Maecenas, one more gracefully paid this way than directly. Horace's instructions to Vinnius likewise convey a flattering message to Augustus about just how eager the poet is to please and just how proud he is that his poems are such as to interest his imperial reader.[57] Were this message expressed directly, it might wear the appearance of ingratiation or mockery. What renders it palatable, even delightful, is the high humor, the self-consciously bumbling profundity, of Horace's bow ("see, if you please, how I'm falling all over myself in my desire to please you").

Horace is represented, before Augustus, both by his representative (the emissary Vinnius) and by his representations, including not only the unspecified poems with which Vinnius has been entrusted but also and perhaps especially the poem that does the entrusting. The sender will be judged, that is, by the deportment of his messenger and by the character of his message. Indeed sender, messenger, and message are in this case but three facets of a single person; when Horace writes of Vinnius' enthusiastic efforts on behalf of "us" (*nostri*, E. 1.13.4), he may be using a true plural. Vinnius is thus not only a "personified letter," as Rolando Ferri has suggested,[58] but a carnival-mirror image of the letter-writer. Horace's instructions comprise, accordingly, a kind of *ars poetica* tailored to the epistolary form. With its warning against overzealousness, the epistle recalls in particular *Odes* 1.38, where a fastidious drinker declares his distaste for Persian luxuries (*odi*, C. 1.38.1; cf. *odium*, E. 1.13.4) and instructs his attendant (*sedulus . . . ministrum*, C. 1.38.6; cf. *sedulus . . . minister*, E. 1.13.5) not to belabor their garlands.[59] In the epistle as in the ode, Horace's aesthetic labor is at once represented and displaced by the physical labor of his servile double. If Vinnius "sweats carrying" Horace's poems (*sudavisse ferendo*, E. 1.13.16), it is Horace who sweated to produce them; if Vinnius runs a risk of tripping over his own feet (*pecces*, 4, reinforced by *titubes*, 19), so does the poet every time he launches into verse.[60] Horace's worry that Vinnius will find his load too heavy and will dash it down unceremoniously at his journey's end (6–9) finds a parallel in the *Ars poetica*, where Horace advises aspiring poets to "choose a subject that matches your strength and consider well what your shoulders cannot

[57] On the effect of Horace's obliquity here, cf. Ferri (1993) 68–9.   [58] Ferri (1993) 70.

[59] Cf. Préaux (1968) 138. The epistle turns the ode into an envoi by casting a third person instead of the poet's *ego* in the role of the difficult-to-please recipient.

[60] For aesthetic "sweat" see E. 2.1.169 and Ars 241 (poetry composed from everyday materials requires not less but more "sweat" than the loftier genres); for the aesthetic "stumble" cf. E. 1.1.9 (the lyric poet as an aging horse liable to trip) and Ars 265–6 (on the *peccata* of the poet's metrical "feet").

carry, and what they can" (*sumite materiam vestris, qui scribitis, aequam* | *viribus, et versate diu, quid ferre recusent,* | *quid valeant umeri, Ars* 38–40). It does indeed require unusual "strength," a strength Horace elsewhere pretends to lack, to carry off a poem addressed to the emperor.[61]

In fact the messenger's journey merges the paths of poetic and social success. What will "arrive," if Vinnius prevails, is at once the poetry and the poet. The epistle thus contains not only an *ars poetica* but also and simultaneously a script for social advancement. Vinnius' "journey to the court" is in effect an allegory of social ascent. This is why the epistle coincides in so many respects with Horace's letter to the upwardly mobile Scaeva of *Epistles* 1.17. In both poems, Horace exploits a comically disproportionate rhetoric of military heroism, inviting Scaeva to seek glory through clientage (*E.* 1.17.33–5), Vinnius to "conquer" his assigned task (*victor propositi, E.* 1.13.11).[62] Both men will prove their manhood by persevering on their respective ways – Scaeva on his career path, Vinnius on his literal road. Both must shoulder the "burden" (*onus, E.* 1.13.12, *E.* 1.17.39) and "stay the course" (*perferre, E.* 1.13.7; *perfert, E.* 1.17.41) so as to "arrive at the goal" (*perveneris, E.* 1.13.11; *pervenit, E.* 1.17.38). And once arrived, both parvenus will need to watch their tongues and master their behavior – Scaeva in eliciting gifts from his patron (*E.* 1.17.43–51), Vinnius in presenting his gift to the emperor (*E.* 1.13.11–18).

Scaeva's "burden" is strictly metaphorical; it stands for the labor of the social climber and is displaced, after a single reference, by a description of that labor. By contrast, Vinnius' "burden" is itself the product of Horace's labor and itself the means of his social ascent. The thing with which Vinnius is entrusted is named over and over again – as "sealed bookrolls" (*signata volumina, E.* 1.13.2), "little books" (*libellis,* 4), "sack weighted with my papers" (*meae gravis . . . sarcina chartae,* 6), "saddlebags" (*clitellas,* 8), "burden" (*onus,* 12), "bundle of books" (*fasciculum . . . librorum,* 13), and finally (with something of the effect of a punch line) "poems" (*carmina,* 17).[63] This multiplication of descriptions, a kind of comically solicitous

---

[61] Cf. *S.* 2.1.12–13 (*vires* | *deficiunt*), *E.* 2.1.259 (*vires ferre recusent*), in each case regarding an epic on Augustus' *res gestae.*

[62] On the pervasive militarism of the diction in *E.* 1.13, see Préaux (1968) 137–40. This diction may be tailored to the identity of the addressee (possibly a centurion's son; see Nisbet [1959] 75–6); but the addressee may also have been chosen to match the rhetorical requirements of the epistle.

[63] I exclude *mandata* at line 19, which succeeds in meaning both "your commission" (i.e. the present poem) and "the poems I've entrusted to you."

verbal clutching on Horace's part, suggests how precious the object is to its sender. The emphasis on the palpable materiality of Vinnius' burden is also in keeping with this epistle's general tendency to literalize what is elsewhere figurative.

But this materiality takes on a further significance from the juncture of Horace's epistle to Vinnius with the epistle to Iccius that immediately precedes it. That epistle closes with a review of recent imperial victories: Agrippa's in Spain, Tiberius' in Armenia, and, as the climax of a tricolon, Augustus' over Parthia: "Phraates, submitting on his knees, has accepted the law and rule of Caesar" (*ius imperiumque Phraates | Caesaris accepit genibus minor*, E. 1.12.27–8). Augustus' Parthian "victory" is also celebrated at the midpoint of the epistle to Lollius, where Horace refers to Augustus as "the general who is currently unfastening our standards from the temples of Parthia" (*duce qui templis Parthorum signa refigit | nunc*, E. 1.18.56–7). In fact the return of these standards, which had been captured from Crassus in 53 BCE, was both the central accomplishment and the main symbol of Rome's "conquest" of Parthia. Coins struck in honor of the event show a kneeling Parthian with a standard in his outstretched hand, along with the slogan *signis receptis* ("on the occasion of the recapture of the standards"), and Augustus in his *Res gestae* describes the victory in similar terms: "I compelled the Parthians to return the spoils and standards [*spolia et signa reddere*] of three Roman armies and to petition on their knees [*supplices*] for the friendship of the Roman people" (29.2).[64] Although the close of the epistle to Iccius does not mention the standards, they are so closely bound up both with the victory and with the iconography of the kneeling Parthian as to be virtually present in Horace's description of Phraates "submitting on his knees."[65] In this setting, and given Horace's comically reiterated emphasis on the weight and material presence of his bookrolls, we may detect in the phrase *Augusto reddes signata volumina* ("hand over the sealed bookrolls to Augustus," E. 1.13.2) an audio-visual trace of Parthia's surrender of the Roman standards. Horace's privately minted coin shows his "standard-bearer" in a Parthian posture, deferentially bowing before the emperor, and with an oversized bookroll in his outstretched hand.

[64] The reading *reddere* is restored from the Greek ἀποδοῦναι. For an illustration of the coinage, see Zanker (1988) 188. As Zanker (1988) 189–92 points out, the close of E. 1.12 (Parthian victory + Cornucopia) is well illustrated by the cuirass of the Prima Porta Augustus.   [65] Cf. Wickham (1891) 272.

The epistle to Vinnius is thus in effect the poet's own act of "surrender" to Augustus.[66]

But the surrender is not total. Let us note that this epistle, which is an envoi in both the literal and the literary sense (Horace dispatches his messenger and his poetry in the same instant),[67] would not be out of place at the end of the collection. The reference to *carmina* at line 17 has convinced most critics that Vinnius has been entrusted with a special presentation copy of Horace's collected *carmina*, *Odes* 1–3. But if the epistle closed the book, no one would doubt that what weighs Vinnius down is nothing other than *Epistles* 1 itself.[68] As things stand, such an interpretation produces something of a logical paradox (a metapoetic act such as the envoi belongs at the border; either the beginning or the end, of the collection to which it refers). My point is not that Vinnius is "really" carrying *Epistles* 1 but that the epistle to Vinnius can be read as an alternative end-poem, one that Horace chose to displace rather than discard.[69] This alternative ending would discover Horace in the act of offering to Augustus the verses he purported to refuse Maecenas, thereby transferring his poetry, if not himself, from Maecenas' house to Augustus' palace. If *Epistles* 1.13 occupied the place of *Epistles* 1.20, moreover, it would serve to confirm the truth of the accusation leveled against Horace at the end of *Epistles* 1.19: "you're keeping that stuff of yours for Jupiter's ears" (*Iovis auribus ista | servas*, E. 1.19.43–4).[70] This is, of course,

---

[66] The link between the two epistles is reinforced by the chiasmus of proper names (*Phraates, Caesaris, Augusto, Vinni*, in each case with the giver at line end and the imperial recipient at line opening) that bridges the gap between them and by the parallel appearances of *Caesaris* heading their penultimate lines (the name "Caesar" appears only once elsewhere within E. 1, at E. 1.5.9).

[67] Thus Ferri (1993) 70–1 identifies the epistle as a variation on the "address to the book."

[68] For the identification of Vinnius' *carmina* with *Odes* 1–3, see, e.g., Préaux (1968) 137 and (firmly) Mayer (1994) 4, 204; contrast Johnson (1993) 36–7. The plural *volumina* does not rule out an identification with the (single-volume) E. 1; the exaggeration would be in keeping with the epistle's generally hyperbolic tone. Nor does *carmina* necessarily specify lyric; it would be a neat and characteristically Horatian trick thus belatedly to expose the fiction of the first epistle, where Horace swears off verse in verse (*nunc itaque et versus et cetera ludicra pono*, E. 1.1.10). *Carmina* is used of satire at S. 1.10.75 (arguably) and at S. 2.1.63 and 82 – both, significantly, "border" poems.

[69] So it is not surprising that E. 1.13 partially duplicates E. 1.20. Like the personified book, Vinnius takes Horace's poetry on the road; where the book is compared to an ass (*asellum*, E. 1.20.15), Vinnius bears the unpromising cognomen Asina (E. 1.13.8); and both poems recall C. 1.38 as well as, more obviously, the closing *i, puer* of S. 1.10. The poems are treated in tandem (although not compared) by Connor (1982).

[70] While the act of publication undermines the fiction of exclusivity, Horace might still be positing Caesar as his ideal, ultimate reader, as in the punchline of S. 2.1.

just what Horace represents himself as doing when he cautions Vinnius not to tell the world that he is carrying poems fit "for the eyes and ears of Caesar" (*oculos aurisque . . . | Caesaris, E.* 1.13.17–18).

But Horace's epistles are not, any more than are his odes, designed exclusively or even primarily for an imperial audience. The emperor may be a privileged overreader, like Maecenas. But neither man has proprietary rights over Horace's poems. This is why the epistle to Vinnius has to make way for a very different kind of end-poem, one that releases Horace's work to the general public and to posterity. Whereas Vinnius' centripetal journey ends at the palace of Augustus, the bookshop of the Sosii brothers is but a way station for Horace's centrifugal book, which anticipates a career involving a wide range of readers and venues, both at Rome and abroad, in both the immediate and the distant future. In the end, Horace declines to limit his readership by specifying it, even with such a uniquely luminous name as that of the *princeps*. The book is not seeking to exchange its author's patronage for the patronage of Augustus. The book wants to realize the implicit promise of its name. To be a "book," *liber*, is to be "free," *liber*[71] – which means to belong to no one, neither to the author nor to any individual reader.

I will close this chapter with a few remarks on the letter that heads Horace's second epistolary collection, a letter directly addressed to Augustus and composed, so Suetonius informs us, at his express request. "You should know that I'm angry at you," wrote the emperor to the poet, "because in your many writings of this sort you don't talk with me in particular! Or are you afraid that you will be branded by men to come for appearing to be closely associated with me?" (*irasci me tibi scito, quod non in plerisque eiusmodi scriptis mecum potissimum loquaris. an vereris ne apud posteros infame tibi sit, quod videaris familiaris nobis esse?*). Augustus' question identifies Horace's predicament with some precision, and it is not by chance that the epistle Horace produced in response focuses on the making and marring of reputations, both imperial and poetic.

Although the epistle opens with deferential and even reverential praise of Augustus,[72] Horace soon shifts his attention from the arts of empire to the art of poetry. The transition takes the form of a complaint; the poet is,

---

[71] For this pun in Ov. *Tr.* 1.1, cf. Hinds (1985) 13–14.

[72] On Horace's negatively-polite opening, see above, 10–11. As usual, when Horace moves into outright deifying encomium (*E.* 2.1.15–17), he shifts into the communal first person plural.

it emerges, envious of the emperor's anomalous invulnerability to envy. The people of Rome – "that populace of yours" (*tuus hic populus*, E. 2.1.18), as Horace terms them, with a nice blend of flattery and irritation – may show excellent sense in ranking their emperor above all other leaders, but they otherwise display an irrational prejudice against everything contemporary (18–22). It is axiomatic for them that ancient authors are "perfect" (cf. *perfectos veteresque*, 37), the moderns "worthless" (*vilis atque novos*, 38). They are sure, moreover, that this judgment will be shared by posterity; contemporary authors are defined for them as "the sort that both the present and the future age will reject with disdain" (*quos et praesens et postera respuat aetas*, 42). Although Horace doesn't say so directly here (he will come closer later in the epistle),[73] the folly of Augustus' populace consists in its failure to recognize, or even to acknowledge the possibility, that poets such as Horace will be the classics of the future.

That status may depend, however, as Augustus' question *per litteras* implies, on the success with which such poets avoid being absorbed into the contemporary center of power. While authors who fail to please their contemporaries may have little chance of surviving, those who achieve too much favor in the present risk forfeiting it for the future. One of Horace's tasks in this epistle, accordingly, is to keep his poetry out of the imperial sun. This is why, when he writes about the contemporary craze that has turned every Roman into a lyric songbird, he includes himself in the number (*E.* 2.1.111–12) without so much as hinting that he returned to lyric (as Suetonius reports) with the encouragement of Augustus himself. While his defense of the poet's value to the community culminates at the very center of the epistle in what sounds remarkably like a description of his own *Carmen saeculare*,[74] a choral poem commissioned for public performance at Augustus' *Ludi Saeculares* – "Who would teach prayers to chaste boys and unmarried girls if the Muse had not granted us a bard?" (*castis cum pueris ignara puella mariti | disceret unde preces, vatem ni Musa dedisset?*132–3) – it is notably the Muse, not the emperor, who provides a bard for this occasion.

What is at stake here is suggested in the passage that leads up to Horace's praise of the choral poet. Rome may have been stricken with a

[73] "What would now be classic, if the Greeks had hated the contemporary as much as we do?" (*quod si tam Graecis novitas invisa fuisset | quam nobis, quid nunc esset vetus?* 90–1).

[74] Cf. Fraenkel (1957) 391. *E.* 2.1 cannot be securely dated, but the Suetonian *vita* suggests that it was composed after the *Carmen saeculare*; see Brink (1982) 553; Rudd (1989) 1.

plague of mad poets, Horace concedes, but things could be worse; after all, poets are free of many common vices. "The soul of a bard is not readily inclined to avarice" (*vatis avarus | non temere est animus, E. 2.1.119–20*); fixated as he is on his poetry, he can smile at accidents – "losses, runaway slaves, fires" (*detrimenta, fugas servorum, incendia*, 121) – that would move other men to tears; he plots to cheat no man, but "lives on beans and peasant bread" (*vivit siliquis et pane secundo*, 123). This portrait may be a caricature, but it has a familiar defensive function.[75] Was Horace rewarded for composing the kind of choral poem he celebrates a few lines later? If the answer is "yes," does that mean that Horace is a poet for hire, an Augustan hack? So the invidious might maintain. Horace's humorous portrait of the absent-minded poet helps fend off this criticism in advance by drawing the sharpest possible distinction between poetic disinterestedness and economic interest.

Horace's desire to protect his face from the aspersions of both contemporary and future overreaders acquires a particular urgency in the final section of the epistle. Here Horace takes up the question of an "Augustan" poetry, offering the emperor advice on how best "to fill with books your fit offering to Apollo and to spur bards on to seek grassy Helicon with increased enthusiasm" (*munus Apolline dignum | . . . complere libris et vatibus addere calcar, | ut studio maiore petant Helicona virentem, E. 2.1.216–18*). The "fit offering to Apollo" is the library attached to Apollo's new temple, located on the Palatine next to Augustus' imperial residence, and the implication of Horace's virtual equation of Augustus' Palatine library with the Muses' Helicon is that the election and canonization of poets has effectively passed from the Muses' to the emperor's jurisdiction. On the one hand, Horace subjects himself to that jurisdiction by including himself in the number of "us poets" who foil their own ascent – by thrusting their work on the emperor when he is busy or tired (220–1); by shutting their ears to friendly criticism (221–2); by performing unsolicited encores of their own favorite passages (223); by complaining that their artistic labor passes unnoticed (224–5); and by entertaining, at the peak of their arrogance, wild hopes that "the moment you learn we are composing poems, you'll graciously and of your own accord summon us to your presence, forbid us to be in want, and order us to write" (*ut, simul atque | carmina rescieris nos fingere, commodus ultro | arcessas et egere vetes et scribere cogas*, 226–8). On the other hand, Horace's first

---

[75] Cf. especially *S.* 1.1.74, 76–8.

person plural is clearly diplomatic rather than literal, as Horace can trust any well-disposed reader to recognize.[76] Indeed the framing charges concerning the relation of "us poets" to Augustus are refuted in Horace's case by the apologetic opening of this very epistle, which demonstrates that Horace is suitably hesitant to thrust his work upon Augustus and harbors no delusions that the busy emperor will take an active interest in his poetry.[77] And yet, of course, if Horace is not an inept aspirant to Augustus' favor, the reason is that his status as an "Augustan" poet is already assured. The great irony of this passage is that the delusions of grandeur Horace here mocks – to be summoned, supported in suitable style, and ordered to write by the emperor himself – were, in Horace's case, completely realized. By dissociating himself from his group portrait of poetic ambition, Horace represents himself, in relation to Augustus as formerly in relation to Maecenas, as having succeeded without having made any disreputable effort to succeed.

The problem with which Horace is contending, here as elsewhere, is the ease with which the spiritual lapses into the material, value into price, quality into quantity, poem into commodity. Although a poet may receive a gift as a (more or less direct) consequence of writing a poem, that gift is not an adequate measure of the value of the poem, if it is an authentic poem. But in a world where poems are sometimes exchanged for cash, the distinction between market price and poetic value may be hard to see. As Alessandro Barchiesi has pointed out, it is the burden of the next section of the epistle to forge just such a distinction.[78] Having described where poets tend to go wrong, Horace turns to the errors of the patron. Alexander the Great, for example, showered his favor on the inept poet Choerilus, paying for his "bastard verses" (*versibus . . . male natis*, E. 2.1.233) with coins bearing his kingly father's name (*regale nomisma, Philippos*, 234) – certainly a bad transaction from the royal son's point of view. Not only Choerilus' notoriously dreadful poems but Alexander's lapse of judgment mar the royal image for posterity. The right way to go about patronizing poets is exemplified by Augustus, who rewards his poets with decorously unspecified "gifts" in an exchange that does honor alike to the giver and to the recipient (245–7):

[76] See, e.g., S. 1.4.73–4 and S. 1.10.76–90 (Horace's resistance to public performance and respect for the judgment of his friends), *Ars* 240–3 (Horace's seemingly artless art).

[77] See above, 10–11.

[78] Barchiesi (1993) 156 n. 10; on this dynamic in C. 4, see Barchiesi (1996).

> at neque dedecorant tua de se iudicia atque
> munera, quae multa dantis cum laude tulerunt,
> dilecti tibi Vergilius Variusque poetae.

But your beloved poets Virgil and Varius do not disgrace your judgment of them or the gifts that they carried off with much credit to
the giver.

As if to remove any suggestion of a quid pro quo (poetic praise for imperial gifts), Horace represents not the poets but the approving witnesses to
this transaction as lavishing "praise" or "credit" on the emperor, who
manifests the excellence of his judgment by thus rewarding poetic excellence.

Let us note that when he comes down to Roman cases, Horace not
only fails to name himself but takes himself quite out of the running. He
will not win gifts from Augustus, the familiar story goes, because he is
incapable, much to his sorrow, of producing a suitably elevated poem in
Augustus' praise: "I'd rather compose a poem in honor of your great
deeds than these talks of mine that creep along the earth . . . if only my
strength matched my desire!" (*nec sermones ego mallem | repentis per humum
quam res componere gestas . . . si quantum cuperem possem quoque, E.*
2.1.250–1, 257). In the lines I have ellipsed, Horace offers (as is usual in
such poems of refusal) a sample of his purportedly inadequate poetic
wares;[79] and in any case a humble "talk" was, as we happen to know, just
what Augustus wanted from Horace. But what counts for me here is the
way Horace sets his poetry (both past and present) apart not only from
the vile verses of Choerilus but from the remunerated "Augustan" works
of his friends Virgil and Varius – a tendentious distinction, given that
Horace has without a doubt already been remunerated, one way or
another, for his poems. I do not mean to suggest that Horace was paid for
writing either the *Carmen saeculare* or this epistle, any more than Virgil
was directly compensated for writing the *Aeneid*, but that Horace feels
impelled to distance his own poetry, as far as possible, from the whole
sphere of poetic offerings and imperial rewards.

Horace demonstrates his prowess as an escape artist most flamboyantly
at the epistle's close, where he warns Augustus against accepting the
offerings of inept praise-poets by staging an admonitory scene, with the

---

[79] On Horace's demonstration of the dangers of inept panegyric (via the echo of Cicero's
unforgettable *o fortunatam natam me consule Romam*), see Barchiesi (1993) 155–7.

poet himself in the role of the celebrity embarrassed by the disfiguring representations of inept artists.[80] Horace would no more choose to have his character decked out in misshapen verses (*prave factis decorari versibus*, *E.* 2.1.266) than to have his countenance mangled in wax (*ficto | in peius vultu proponi cereus*, 264–5). To be thus commemorated is to risk sharing the unhappy doom of the bad poet – not monumental permanence but dispersal and oblivion (267–70):

> ne rubeam pingui donatus munere, et una
> cum scriptore meo, capsa porrectus operta,
> deferar in vicum vendentem tus et odores
> et piper et quidquid chartis amicitur ineptis.

> . . . for fear I'd turn red at the crass gift and be carried, together with my poet, stretched out in a sealed book-box, down to the street that sells frankincense and perfume and pepper and whatever else gets parceled up in paper devoid of wit.

As Niall Rudd points out, it is to save Augustus from embarrassment that Horace removes him from the encoffining book-box and installs himself in his place.[81] The funeral of the emperor is not to be imagined, not even – or especially not – in these comic colors. Still, Horace might have achieved the same effect by invoking a third person (for example, by reverting once again to the case of Alexander). Horace's use of himself is bold as well as tactful. By putting himself in the emperor's place, Horace locates himself at the other side of the reciprocal structure with which the final movement of the epistle is centrally concerned, casting himself as not the donor but the recipient of a poetic "gift" (*donatus munere*, 267).

And yet this reversal reverts readily enough to a more natural distribution of roles. Horace's anecdote is written over another so as to render it all but illegible: the story not of a poet's deadly gift to a patron, but of a patron's deadly gift to a poet. In another context, the line *ne rubeam pingui donatus munere*, "for fear I'd turn red at the crass gift," might be taken to apply not to Horace as the stand-in for the emperor but quite directly to Horace himself. In that case, we would translate *pingue munus* as not "the crass gift" (the unrefined poem that fails to meet the standards of Callimachean λεπτότης) but "the fat gift" – the gift that enriches a man,

---

[80] The scene is very much in the manner of the adultery skit that closes *S.* 1.2 (127–33), where Horace likewise has the starring role: *nec vereor ne dum futuo vir rure recurrat*, etc.

[81] Rudd (1989) 10–11.

that makes him fat. In one familiar Callimachean topos, these two meanings appear together, for example in *Satires* 2.6, where Horace prays Mercury to "fatten the flock and the rest of the master's property, except his poetic talent" (*pingue pecus domino facias et cetera praeter | ingenium, S.* 2.6.14–15). And beyond the safe preserve of the Callimachean topos, these prayers might be understood as reciprocal and interdependent. The unstated moral, here and elsewhere, is that thin poems merit fat gifts. The problem is that the receipt of such a gift compromises the poet, it makes him blush: *ne rubeam pingui donatus munere*.[82]

I come back finally to Augustus' suggestive question to Horace *per litteras*: "Or are you afraid that you will be branded by men to come for appearing to be closely associated with me?" (*an vereris ne apud posteros infame tibi sit, quod videaris familiaris nobis esse?*). The question is not rhetorical. Like a fat poem, a fat gift may not only embarrass the recipient, it may seal his doom in the eyes of posterity. The works of a poet who is viewed as having "sold out" will end up just where they originated – in the marketplace, the realm of vendors and purchasers, the place of exchanges that are finished when they are transacted, exchanges that leave no saving remainder. The luxury goods Horace imagines such poems as embracing – frankincense, aromatic spices, pepper – may command exceedingly high prices; but these preservatives "immortalize" only dead flesh.[83] And this is not the kind of immortality Horace has in mind, nor the kind he achieved.

---

[82] This is one reason Horace generally downplays the "fatness" of his Sabine farm, emphasizing instead that what the farm "returns" to its owner is not material profit but physical and spiritual health; see, e.g., *E.* 1.16.1–16, where Horace responds to Quinctius' questions about the farm's produce with a description of its unfattening and restorative pastoral pleasures.

[83] On attitudes toward embalming at Rome, see Counts (1996).

5

The art of self-fashioning in the Ars poetica

The author projected by the *Ars poetica* is, more or less by definition, an authority on the poetic art, a master performer who has earned the right to instruct others.[1] What will concern me in this chapter is less the overt aesthetic content of this instruction than the social lessons that are packaged within it. On the one hand, the *Ars* is a profoundly normative textbook that not only describes but helps enforce the rules of the game the Piso brothers are about to enter. This game, like the *ludus* Horace declines to reenter at the start of *Epistles* 1, involves social as well as poetic performance; Horace is teaching the Piso brothers how to fashion their selves as well as their poems. On the other hand, the *Ars* in no way guarantees that these young men will emerge as winners. As Horace recurrently remarks, success depends on a player's ability not merely to follow the rules (by composing a well-formed iambic line, for example) but, more importantly, to improvise a performance within them and sometimes to break them. The sense of decorum that enables such improvisations is something that can be advertised, as it is throughout the *Ars*, but that cannot be taught. What Horace teaches the Piso brothers is finally not what to do or not to do but what he can do and they cannot.

Horace's disquisition on the art which is the source of his authority (social and poetic) is addressed to an audience that boasts conventional social advantages Horace cannot claim, and this conjunction of subject matter and audience produces an extremely volatile blend of authority and deference: a "masterwork" which is also a study in self-defacement,

---

[1] The date of the *Ars* and the identity of Horace's Pisones remain controversial. While certainty on this score is not essential to the argument of this chapter, I follow (e.g.) Rudd (1989) 19–21 and Armstrong (1993) 199–202, who argue for a date of around 10 BCE and identify Horace's senior Piso with Lucius Calpurnius Piso Pontifex (son of the patron of Philodemus). My reading of the *Ars* is much indebted to Armstrong's demonstration of the way the poem is shaped to suit Horace's young, aristocratic, and potentially arrogant Pisonian audience; see Armstrong (1994) 203–16.

an educational essay which is also an exercise in antididaxis. The *Ars poetica* presents a face-off between Horace's poetic authority and his audience's social prestige. And although Horace repeatedly defers to his aristocratic audience, he triumphs over them in the end – triumphs, indeed, by deferring. The monstrously indecorous figures that frame the *Ars* (and that will also frame my discussion) may be ridiculous, but they enjoy the last laugh.

Fashioning men

The social side-effect, as it might be termed, of Horace's poetic instruction is most readily discerned in the famous opening lines of the *Ars poetica*. While this opening can be and generally has been read simply as a statement of poetics, such a reading is maintained only at the cost of ignoring the surprising form this statement takes. The educational content of Horace's negative *exemplum* is in fact highly overdetermined (*Ars* 1–5):

> Humano capiti cervicem pictor equinam
> iungere si velit, et varias inducere plumas
> undique collatis membris, ut turpiter atrum
> desinat in piscem mulier formosa superne,
> spectatum admissi risum teneatis, amici?

> If a painter wished to join a human head to a horse's neck and to plaster all kinds of feathers on limbs gathered from all over, so that a woman beautiful on top ended foully in a black fish – let in for a viewing, could you hold back a laugh, my friends?

To represent the vice of aesthetic incoherence, Horace could have proceeded any number of ways. He might have had his painter depict a body with disproportionate limbs (a tiny head on a thick neck) or with ill-assorted limbs in another arrangement (a fish body on human feet). As it stands, the painting contains the profiles, blurred but unmistakable, of thoroughly familiar monsters, in particular the horse–man Centaur and fish–woman Scylla.[2] Moreover, although Horace's *ut*-clause superimposes one profile upon the other, retroactively specifying the "human head" of line 1 as the head of a beautiful woman (who is "beautiful," it

---

[2] See Brink (1971) 85. As remarked by Frischer (1991) 74–85, Horace's art criticism positively invites a suspicious reading, since this style was favored not only by the imperial circle but also, it seems, by Horace himself (the Sabine villa identified as Horace's was decorated with griffins and sphinxes).

follows, only from the neck up),[3] this syntactical logic is countered by the powerful descriptive coherence of the final figure – a figure reminiscent, as commentators note, of Virgil's biform Scylla, fair maiden above and sea-monster below (*pulchro pectore virgo | pube tenus, postremo immani corpore pistrix*, *Aen.* 3.426–7). Rhetorically if not syntactically, Horace's pictured mermaid displaces the centaur-like figure of the opening lines. And it is at this moment that the description thickens and the tone darkens into disgust: *turpiter atrum*. In the end it is the female who makes manifest the gap between form and deformation, outside and inside, surface and depths, fair beginnings and foul endings.

In this scene of viewing, both roles are sexually specified. The emergence of a figure marked as female precipitates the emergence of an audience marked as male – Horace's masculine "friends" (*amici*, *Ars* 5). The spectacle of the female monster will cause these friends, Horace predicts, to emit an irrepressible laugh. But this involuntary expenditure of masculine energy is figured as a sign of solidarity, not impotence. Horace's long-awaited main clause establishes both syntactical and sexual order by subjecting the female figure to the scrutiny of a group of men. The opening of the *Ars* is thus an episode in the history of the construction of what is now commonly termed the "male gaze." Indeed, if the sexual dynamic of this Horatian scene has passed unremarked, one reason is that it matches the norms of European pictorial representation so precisely as to be invisible.

It is not by chance that the first word of Horace's *Ars* is "human," followed by the complementary noun "head." To be human is, as it were, to keep one's head, which means to maintain the natural and manly superiority of the head in relation to the rest of the body. The best commentary on the hierarchy that supports the opening of the *Ars* is provided by Cicero, not in his rhetorical writings but in his *De officiis*, a treatise on social and moral propriety addressed to his son at school in Athens.[4] Like the monster in Horace's painting, Ciceronian "human nature" is defined by division: "The essential character of the soul is twofold. One part is centered in the appetite (in Greek ὁρμή), which carries a man off this way and that way, the other part in reason, which teaches and makes plain what should be done and what avoided. And so it comes about that reason governs, appetite obeys" (*Off.* 1.101). The

---

[3] So Rudd (1989) 150; Brink (1971) 86.
[4] For a juxtaposition of the *Ars* and the *De officiis* (in the service of a reconstruction of Panaetius), cf. Labowsky (1934).

implicit metaphor is elaborated in the paragraph that follows: appetites are like horses which must be curbed and guided by reason, the prudent charioteer (102). Nature and reason together militate against behavior that is, in Cicero's instructive collocation, "indecorous or effeminate" (*natura ratioque . . . cavet . . . ne quid indecore effeminateve faciat*, 14). To be a man means to maintain control of one's lower "animal" appetites.

Cicero goes on to map this hierarchy directly onto the human body: "Nature herself seems to have had an excellent plan [*rationem*] for our body: she placed our face and the rest of our figure, which has a respectable appearance, in full view, but covered and hid away those parts of the body which, dedicated to nature's needs, would have been misshapen and foul to see" (*Off.* 1.126–7).[5] Human modesty, *verecundia*, is thus but the imitation of nature: "what nature has concealed, all those who are of sound mind keep out of sight" (*quae enim natura occultavit, eadem omnes qui sana mente sunt removent ab oculis*, 127). Cicero's judgment on the "misshapen and foul" parts of the body (*deformem . . . atque turpem*) corresponds to Horace's judgment on the "foul" ending (*turpiter, Ars* 3) that deforms his fair or "shapely" female (*formosa*, 4). What Cicero helps us see is that the guffaw of Horace's male friends is provoked not only by the incoherence of the painting but also by the sight of the genital fishtail it exposes to view.

The body that conceals its ugliness, by contrast, provides Cicero with a model for the decorous or well-composed life (*Off.* 1.98):

ut enim pulchritudo corporis apta compositione membrorum movet oculos et delectat hoc ipso, quod inter se omnes partes cum quodam lepore consentiunt, sic hoc decorum quod elucet in vita movet approbationem eorum quibuscum vivitur ordine et constantia et moderatione dictorum omnium atque factorum.

For as the beauty of a body with well-composed limbs draws the gaze and gives pleasure on just this account, that all the parts harmonize together with a certain charming effect, so this propriety, which shines out in a person's life, draws the approbation of those among whom that life is spent, on account of the good order and consistency and restraint of all [his] words and deeds.

Whereas the indecorously exposed body resembles the Horatian monster, this beautiful body is its very antitype.[6] Neatly composed of harmonious limbs, its indeterminate sex modestly concealed, this body earns the applause of the spectators as the Horatian monster earns their

---

[5] The male genitalia form a notable exception to Cicero's rule of natural concealment. Are these parts then to be imagined as less "misshapen and foul" than their female counterparts?

[6] For the parallel, cf. Grimal (1988) 12.

ridicule. It is almost as if Horace had designed his monster to illustrate the hideous consequences of a lapse of decorum, in the broad Ciceronian sense of a revolt of animal appetite against the dominion of reason. In the Horatian declension, the priority of the human head is undermined by the centrifugal energy of the lower body parts. "Humanity" is restored when the men put their heads together, chasing the animal back into hiding with a volley of communal laughter.

The opening scene of Horace's *Ars* thus summons the Piso boys to join the social and sexual community to which they "naturally" belong. And the summons is forcefully framed. To withhold assent to Horace's rhetorical question is to position oneself outside the community of *amici*, in the company of the derided monster; to assent (the path of least resistance) is to accept the values of that community and to earn a place within it. The scene is part of what the sociologist Norbert Elias has termed the "civilizing process," the process whereby people "seek to suppress in themselves," and thereafter in their children, "every characteristic that they feel to be 'animal.'"[7] The suppression of everything "animal," a category that is always expanding, maintains the distance not only between the child and the adult but also between the lower classes and the social elite. As Pierre Bourdieu remarks in his study of distinction, "the denial of lower, coarse, vulgar, venal, servile – in a word, natural – enjoyment, which constitutes the sacred sphere of culture, implies an affirmation of the superiority of those who can be satisfied with the sublimated, refined, disinterested, gratuitous, distinguished pleasures forever closed to the profane."[8] The correlated oppositions that define the opening scene of Horace's *Ars* – between the head and the tail, top and bottom, human and animal, male and female, reason and appetite, modesty and obscenity, sanity and insanity, beauty and ugliness, closure and disclosure, form and deformity – all serve to create and maintain a distinction between the knowing spectators and the foolish spectacle, the empowered subjects and the disenfranchised, vulgar object. The monster of the *Ars* is set up like a carnival duck for the Pisones to shoot down, as an exemplary exercise in elementary *humanitas*.

Fashioning gentlemen

The laughter of the Pisones targets the inept painter along with his monstrous painting. Every portrait – every work of art – reflects on its maker,

---

[7] Elias (1978) 120 and *passim*. Erasmus' *De civilitate morum puerilium*, extensively discussed by Elias, is an interesting offshoot of Horace's *Ars*.   [8] Bourdieu (1984) 7.

and the aim of art is to direct one's own performance. If Horace, himself no playwright, devotes so much of his *Ars* to dramatic proprieties, one reason is that drama, more directly than epic or lyric, offers embodied models for acting in public.[9] For Horace as for Cicero, life is essentially a theatrical performance. Whether his venue is the forum, the stage, the dinner table, or the bookroll, the performer who wants to succeed must anticipate the spectator's critical eye. The arts of poetic and social "deportment" alike involve rigorous self-scrutiny and ever more subtle refinements, what Horace terms the "work of the file" (*limae labor*, *Ars* 291) and Cicero describes as a kind of fine-tuning. As Cicero advises his son, it is not the obvious breaches of decorum (*quae multum ab humanitate discrepant*, *Off.* 1.145) but the almost imperceptible false notes in our behavior that require our particular vigilance: "Just as an expert generally takes notice when a lyre or flute is even slightly out of tune, so we ought to see to it that nothing in our life is out of tune, all the more because harmony of actions is much more important and more valuable than harmony of tones" (145).[10] The literary critic is likewise distinguished by his capacity to distinguish the slightest *faux pas*. "Not just anyone," Horace reminds his tutees, "has the judicious eye to spot an ill-measured poem" (*non quivis videt immodulata poemata iudex*, *Ars* 263). In Rome's uncivilized infancy, the meters and the witticisms of a Plautus may have won praise; but critics today will judge those judgments harshly, "granting that we know, you and I" – and the poet's conspiratorial plural politely assumes that the Pisones already possess the knowledge that he is in the process of imparting – "the difference between refinement and rusticity, and that we can recognize, with tapping finger and listening ear, the sound of poetry that obeys the laws of prosody" (*si modo ego et vos | scimus inurbanum lepido seponere dicto | legitimumque sonum digitis callemus et aure*, *Ars* 272–4). The art of discrimination is the prerequisite to success on the social stage, for poets as for senators.

Horace's implicit identification of poetic with social performance may

---

[9] The putative interest of the *maior iuvenum* in drama (so, for example, Kilpatrick [1990] 57) is not a sufficient justification; nor do I find convincing in isolation Dupont's suggestion ([1985] 335–41) that Horace is developing a program for a revived Augustan theater. For a mix of explanations see Williams (1968) 349–53.

[10] This Ciceronian passage is reworked by Castiglione (1959) 96–7. Castiglione's courtier also draws social lessons from Horace's aesthetics; compare, e.g., Castiglione (1959) 55 with Hor. *Ars* 240–2 (on the inimitability of seemingly imitable effects), Castiglione (1959) 58 with Hor. *Ars* 60–9 (on the mutability of words). For a stimulating reading of the *De officiis* as a proto-courtly text, see Narducci (1984) 203–29; on the progressive refinement of the standards of urbanity in this period, see Ramage (1973) 64–76.

help explain not only the emphasis on drama but the de-emphasis of comedy within the *Ars*. To write comedies, in this metaphorically charged atmosphere, would be tantamount to acting like a character out of a comedy. And as Cicero reminds his son in the *De officiis*, the dignity of our human character accords best with what might be called a tragic demeanor: "Nature has fashioned us not for play and jesting, but for sobriety and weightier and more important occupations" (*neque enim ita generati a natura sumus ut ad ludum et iocum facti esse videamur, ad severitatem potius et ad quaedam studia graviora atque maiora, Off.* 1.103). Cicero's social distinction between dignity and frivolity finds its literary counterpart in Aristotle's *Poetics*, where tragedy and comedy are associated with two distinct classes not just of characters but of poets, "more elevated" and "more base" respectively.[11] Within the *Ars*, the personified genres are similarly contrasted (*Ars* 89–92):

> versibus exponi tragicis res comica non vult;
> indignatur item privatis ac prope socco
> dignis carminibus narrari cena Thyestae:
> singula quaeque locum teneant sortita decentem.

> A comic theme doesn't want to be set out in tragic verse; so too the dinner of Thyestes feels slighted if it is recounted in poetry that is informal and better suited to the [comic] sock. Let everything keep the proper place allotted to it.

Assisted by the etymological and semantic proximity of "decorum" and "dignity," Horace's personifications assimilate Comedy and Tragedy to the humble and noble characters with which they are respectively peopled (so Comedy expresses herself bluntly, in a single hexameter closed by two monosyllables, while Tragedy's manner, as if combating Horace's comically mundane handling of the "dinner of Thyestes," is more elevated and roundabout). And while this discussion of diction accords the two genres almost equal treatment, comedy is elsewhere largely driven from the field.[12] The "proper place" of the Pisones is in the company of the severe gods and heroes, not the jesting commoners.

As the opening scene of the *Ars* suggests, Horace is engaged in teach-

---

[11] See *Po.* 1448b, on the primitive poetry of praise and blame, from which Aristotle derives tragedy and comedy (1449a). My text of *Ars* 89–92 below follows Klingner (1959).

[12] Characters such as Ixion and Io (124), subjects such as the Trojan war (129) and the vengeance of Atreus (186), conventions such as the *deus ex machina* and the moralizing chorus (191–201): these are the stuff not of comedy but of tragedy.

ing his pupils how to fend off laughter – not how to elicit it. (Imagine Horace teaching the Piso boys to be comedians; imagine their father's reaction to such a course of instruction.) The comic function is absorbed into the discursive framework of the *Ars*, which stages aesthetic vices for the amusement and benefit of Horace's Pisonian audience. Within the *Ars*, accordingly, laughter is regularly the sign not of comic success but of artistic failure.[13] This does not mean, however, that humor is entirely off limits for a "class" poet or for a gentleman. Cicero makes allowances for moderately comic interludes in the sober business of life, deeming some indulgence in "play and jesting" (*ludo . . . et ioco*) permissible, after the demands of "weighty and serious affairs" (*gravibus seriisque rebus*) have been met, so long as the style of jesting is "not extravagant or unrestrained, but gentlemanly and urbane" (*non profusum nec immodestum, sed ingenuum et facetum, Off.* 1.103). Within the *Ars* it is not comedy but the satyr play that provides the theatrical equivalent of Cicero's decorous comic relief. Like Cicero, Horace stipulates that the shift from sobriety to play (*vertere seria ludo, Ars* 226) should be accomplished, as in the earliest satyr plays, with no impairment of *gravitas* (cf. *incolumi gravitate iocum temptavit*, 222). A certain decorum is to be observed when the gods and heroes of tragedy, "conspicuous a moment before in regal gold and purple" (*regali conspectus in auro nuper et ostro*, 228), join the company of the "laughing" satyrs (*risores*, 225 – the one instance of aesthetically sanctioned laughter in the *Ars*). Tragedy will never lose a sense of her own dignity, even when transferred to the satyric stage (231–3):

> effutire levis indigna Tragoedia versus,
> ut festis matrona moveri iussa diebus,
> intererit Satyris paulum pudibunda protervis.

> Ill suited to spouting trivial verses, Tragedy will be a bit bashful, like
> a matron bidden to dance in honor of a holiday, when associating
> with lascivious satyrs.

It is the same individuals, in Cicero and in Horace, who condescend on occasion from (tragic) gravity to (satyric) levity. The relation between

---

[13] The rule is proved by one apparent exception: although Horace claims that poets must have the power to "lead the spirit of the audience wherever they wish" (*quocumque volent animum auditoris agunto, Ars* 100) – to laughter, that is, as well as tears – he proceeds to treat laughter not as a legitimate dramatic goal but as a form of spontaneous criticism aroused by an inept tragedy (*aut dormitabo aut ridebo*, 105). On the didactic function of laughter within the *Ars*, see Kilpatrick (1990) 38, 52–3.

the passages is reinforced by Horace's concluding simile, which aligns tragedy with the work-day, the satyr play with the holiday – despite the fact that tragedy, like all forms of drama in antiquity, was actually performed *festis diebus*. The final simile might be rewritten, with a Ciceronian emphasis, as follows: the Roman matron, like her husband, customarily behaves with the sobriety of a character in a tragedy; it is only on special occasions that she lightens up enough to join the ritual dance – never failing, however, to preserve her dignity and her distance from the commoners and slaves who crowd the city of Rome as well as the comic stage.[14] So the Piso boys must learn to act in a manner that befits their station.

Fashioning poets

To the extent that the *Ars* is a Horatian *De officiis* in aesthetic dress, it is of a piece with the social and moral fashioning of the young in which Horace elsewhere represents the poet as engaged. As Horace implies when he advises the older Piso brother to "carry away and keep in mind" his fatherly instructor's words of wisdom (*hoc tibi dictum | tolle memor, Ars* 367–8), the detachable *dicta* of the *Ars* are designed to travel with Horace's youthful addressees as part of their equipment for living. They are thus akin to the *dicta* with which Horace's father fashioned his young son (*sic me | formabat puerum dictis, S.* 1.4.120–1), to the memorably versified bits of moral wisdom that Horace elsewhere bestows on young friends, and to the "well-known models" with which the model poet of Horace's letter to Augustus "equips the rising generation" (*orientia tempora notis | instruit exemplis, E.* 2.1.130–1). Similarly nourishing and normalizing old chestnuts, seeds of the *mos maiorum*, are contained in the versified prayers memorized by "unmarried girls and chaste boys" (*castis cum pueris ignara puella mariti, E.* 2.1.132) – prayers which, in the manner of Horace's own *Carmen saeculare*, not only solicit the gods' favor for Rome but help insert the choral performers into the legal and moral order of Augustan Rome. As we have seen, the moment of shared laughter at the start of the *Ars* normalizes the Piso boys along broadly similar lines, inviting them to assume their reserved places in society.

But the *Ars* is of course something other and more than a Horatian *De officiis*. In the course of the *Ars*, Horace treats the poetic performance not only as a metaphor for but as a particular species of social performance.

---

[14] Cf. Elias (1978) 16, linking the courtier's "good form" with the forms of classical French tragedy.

As David Armstrong has pointed out, the *Ars* effectively extends the Republican educational practice of "informal tutelage," a practice designed to produce lawyers and politicians and generals, men equipped to rule their own households and the state, to the production of poets.[15] Horace argues for such an extension in his letter to Augustus, where he contrasts Rome's utterly practical past, when a man would open his house at dawn to clients seeking legal advice (*reclusa | mane domo vigilare, clienti promere iura*, E. 2.1.103–4) and would "learn from his elders and teach his juniors how to increase a fortune and decrease expensive desires" (*maiores audire, minori dicere per quae | crescere res posset, minui damnosa libido*, 106–7), with her utterly frivolous present (108–10):

> mutavit mentem populus levis et calet uno
> scribendi studio; pueri patresque severi
> fronde comas vincti cenant et carmina dictant.

> The fickle populace has changed its disposition and burns with enthusiasm for writing and for nothing else; sons and stern fathers at the dinner table put garlands on their heads and recite poem after poem.

Whereas in the old days experience was respected and the young heeded the wisdom of their elders, the present age fails to discriminate between the generations, and "stern fathers" act as foolishly as their sons. Other professions, Horace complains, have their acknowledged, licensed practitioners (114–16); but just crown your head with a garland, and you can call yourself a poet, the match for any other: "everywhere you look, schooled and unschooled alike, we're writing poems" (*scribimus indocti doctique poemata passim*, 117). In the *Ars*, Horace aims to separate sons from fathers and the unschooled from the schooled by instituting a system wherein Romans will "learn from their elders and teach their juniors" not only how to make a tidy fortune but how to compose a proper poem.

What Horace purports to be fashioning in the *Ars* is, after all, not model citizens but model poets; his *dicta* teach not how to live but how to write.[16] Whereas Horace elsewhere insists on the moral value of measure (*modus*), in the *Ars* he writes, and at some length, about literal verse "measures" – the hexameter, the elegiac couplet, the iamb, the spondee

---

[15] See Armstrong (1994) 202.

[16] On Horace's transfer of the rules of "right living" (*recte vivere*) to the sphere of "correct writing" (*recte scribere*), see Becker (1963) 64–112.

(73–82, 251–62). Conversely, the competing claims of candidates for political office, satirized in Horace's first Roman ode (C. 3.1.9–14), make way here for the competing claims of poets vying for "election" before a kind of "centuriate assembly" of readers (*Ars* 341–4).[17] In *Epistles* 1.2 Horace recommends Homer's exemplary Ulysses to the attention of his young friend Lollius (*quid virtus et quid sapientia possit | utile proposuit nobis exemplar Ulixen*, *E.* 1.2.17–18). But in the *Ars* the instruction derived from the arch-poet is of a very different kind: "As for the exploits and grim battles of kings and generals, Homer has shown in what meter they may be described" (*res gestae regumque ducumque et tristia bella | quo scribi possent numero, monstravit Homerus*, *Ars* 73–4). It is no longer Homer's characters but Homer himself who provides a pattern for the Piso brothers to imitate.

Such transformations may suit the didactic project of the *Ars*, but they also draw attention to its fundamental impropriety. Ulysses may offer Lollius a shining example of virtue and wisdom. But is the blind bard of Chios a suitable role model for the Piso boys? Shouldn't these boys be studying not how to represent *res gestae* but – following the example of the tough *puer* celebrated in Horace's second Roman ode – how to perform them? Again, it is all very well to garner every vote (cf. *omne tulit punctum*, *Ars* 343) from a figurative "centuriate assembly" of readers. But is this the kind of glory the Piso boys should be pursuing? Should they really be devoting themselves to the poetic shadow rather than the socio-political substance of a senatorial career?

It is by no means obvious that poetry is a socially acceptable career for well-born boys such as the Piso brothers. A diversion, yes, a form of polish, even an intensely cultivated side-interest, but not a career. The father of the Piso boys may have been a patron of poets, but he also had a very distinguished public record, and one may presume that he expected his sons to follow in his footsteps. Thus he might have had some sympathy for the father whose hilariously philistine rebuke would one day be recollected (in verse, naturally) by his incorrigibly literary son, the poet Ovid: "More than once my father said to me 'why are you exerting yourself in a useless profession? Homer himself left no fortune'" (*saepe pater dixit "studium quid inutile temptas? | Maionides nullas ipse reliquit opes," Tr.* 4.10.21–2). Ovid's wealthy equestrian father voices the materialistic perspective Horace derides within the *Ars* when he contrasts Greece's

---

[17] See Brink (1971) 356–8.

"greed" for glory (*praeter laudem nullius avaris, Ars* 324) with Rome's focus on money management (*cura peculi*, 330), a skill that literally pays off. A loftier version of the same prejudice is expressed by Virgil's Anchises when he famously instructs Rome to leave the arts of sculpture, oratory, and speculative science to others and to concentrate instead on the practical art of empire-building (*tu regere imperio populos, Romane, memento | (hae tibi erunt artes), Aen.* 6.851–2). When Horace holds out the vision of a Rome as renowned in the arts of language as in the arts of war (*nec virtute foret clarisve potentius armis | quam lingua Latium, Ars* 289–90), he is operating on the highly polemical assumption that Rome would value or should value aesthetic mastery as well as, and perhaps even as highly as, her imperial sway.[18]

It is Rome's misvaluation of the art of poetry, Horace argues, that has kept her from achieving preeminence in the field of letters. Rome's poets are "offended" by what Horace calls "the time-consuming labor of the file" (cf. *si non offenderet unum | quemque poetarum limae labor et mora, Ars* 290–1); they will not condescend to labor over their creations, like the lowly artisan who sweats to give his statues the requisite finish. The roots of this prejudice are exposed in *Satires* 2, where Horace, adopting the perspective of his detractors, often figures art as the recourse of those who have been handicapped by fortune.[19] Those who believe that art does nothing more than supplement (and thus signal) a deficiency will shun art as inherently degrading. Instructed by Horace, the Pisones will know better. The poem in a state of nature cries out for cultivation (291–4):

> vos, o
> Pompilius sanguis, carmen reprehendite quod non
> multa dies et multa litura coercuit atque
> praesectum decies non castigavit ad unguem.

> Sons of the blood of King Numa Pompilius, censure a poem that has not been refined and corrected ten times over by many a day's blotting until its finish satisfies a trimmed nail.

Aesthetic labor is not occasionally but always called upon to smooth the rough surface of the newly created poem. The poem that has not been thus corrected by its maker deserves to stand corrected by its readers. In this context, Horace's comically inflated apostrophe to the "sons of the

---

[18] Cf. Brink (1971) 321.   [19] See above, 51–60.

blood of King Numa Pompilius" serves as a friendly warning. No matter how purple their blood, in the field of poetry the Pisones must bow to the claims of lowly *ars*.[20]

This message is amplified by Horace's satiric sketch of the contemporary crush of "mad poets," would-be geniuses who decline to use the file not only on their poems but on themselves (*Ars* 295–301):

> ingenium misera quia fortunatius arte
> credit et excludit sanos Helicone poetas
> Democritus, bona pars non unguis ponere curat,
> non barbam, secreta petit loca, balnea vitat.
> nanciscetur enim pretium nomenque poetae,
> si tribus Anticyris caput insanabile numquam
> tonsori Licino commiserit.

> Because Democritus believes that inborn talent is more of a blessing than miserable art and refuses to admit sane poets to Helicon, a good number of men don't trouble to trim their nails or their beard, they hunt out remote lairs and avoid the baths. For a man will win the name and reputation of a poet, if he never entrusts his head to Licinus the barber – a head that three townfuls of hellebore will never restore to sanity.

Such a poet equates the flamboyant absence of art with the indisputable presence of genius and the condition of his body with the condition of his poetry; he cultivates a shaggy exterior, one uncoerced and uncastigated by the refinements of razor, file, or bath, in the hope of validating his claim to the glory that belongs to the poet of *ingenium*. But the redundancy of the parallel phrases "three townfuls of hellebore" and "Licinus the barber" (*tribus Anticyris . . . tonsori Licino*, phrases linked by alliteration and consonance, and similarly placed within their respective lines) suggests that what ails his "incurable head" is, after all, nothing that a visit to the barber couldn't cure. By severing the conventional semiotic link between scruffiness and brilliance, the absence of surface polish and the presence of deep genius, Horace exposes the long-nailed ranter as a creature meriting not awe but ridicule. The poem that has not been tested against a critically "trimmed nail" will earn its creator the same treatment.

It is altogether to be expected that the author of the *Ars poetica* should champion the art of poetry. What could not perhaps have been predicted

---

[20] So Armstrong (1994) 209.

is the extent to which Horace's arguments are saturated with the discourse of class distinctions. According to the view that Horace is ridiculing, *ingenium* is *fortunatius* – not simply "attended by good fortune" but "of higher status" or perhaps "wealthier" – than "poor, base art" (*misera ... arte, Ars* 295).[21] Elsewhere Horace may pretend to concede the nighequivalence of "census-rating and inborn talent" (*censum ingeniumque, S.* 2.1.75) and to acknowledge that he ranks below the great Lucilius in both respects – as if the one inferiority automatically entailed the other. But within the *Ars* he labors with some consistency to break the connection between these two terms. One of his most effective weapons is a tactfully collusive irony, as when he rallies to the defense of the gentleman who "doesn't know how to compose verses" but "ventures to do so all the same" (*qui nescit versus tamen audet fingere, Ars* 382). And why should he not? "He's a free man – a freeborn gentleman – and, be it noted, with the census-rating of a knight – and clear of all vice" (*liber et ingenuus, praesertim census equestrem | summam nummorum, vitioque remotus ab omni,* 383–4). The man who is *ingenuus*, endowed by birth with the standing of a gentleman, assumes that he is therefore also *ingeniosus*, endowed by birth with the talents of a poet; and if he is himself "clear of all vice" to which the censors might object, surely his poems are "correct" enough to pass, without further ado, the censorious critic. If the Pisones harbor the belief that their social qualifications automatically qualify them to write poetry, Horace politely sets them straight by assuming that they will join him in mocking the absurdity of such a belief.[22]

Within the *Ars*, poetic and social status tend to be not merely divided but opposed. Not only is it not the case that the well-born and well-to-do are automatically guaranteed the status of poets in good standing; it sometimes seems as if the traditional criteria of status at Rome were substantial barriers to the achievement of poetic distinction. The rich poet, so Horace asserts, will have trouble finding an honest critic to comment on his work before he releases it to the world (*Ars* 419–21). Indeed, the richer he is, the more trouble he is likely to have telling a true from a false friend (422–5). Horace develops the point in an admonitory skit, set at the dinner table, with the poet in the role of a patron attended by a well-fed and wildly appreciative parasite (426–30) – the only audience, Horace implies, with which this poet's work is likely to make a hit. Only the poet

---

[21] While *fortunatius* may evoke τύχη (so Brink [1971] 330), the main resonance here is social.
[22] Similarly Armstrong (1994) 213.

who submits his work to a disinterested professional critic (to Horace, for example) can hope to produce authentic poetry. Horace further demotes the rich amateur by likening him to an auctioneer (419–21):

> ut praeco, ad merces turbam qui cogit emendas
> adsentatores iubet ad lucrum ire poeta
> dives agris, dives positis in faenore nummis.

> Like an auctioneer who ropes in a crowd to buy his merchandise, a poet who is rich in land, rich in money loaned out at interest, invites yes-men to come and collect their cash reward.

As Niall Rudd comments, the point of comparison here is that both men tempt their respective audiences with the promise of a bargain – wares at good prices in one case, a dinner purchased with a few compliments in the other.[23] And yet the points of difference are still more striking. It is an impoverished professional, not a wealthy dilettante, who might naturally be imagined as thus hawking his poetic merchandise. The fluent auctioneer has less in common with the gullible host than with his flattering parasites – men who know how to turn words into substantial profit.[24] The role-reversal that is written into the simile suggests that the rich amateur is not only handicapped in his poetic endeavors but potentially degraded by them.

A central claim of the *Ars poetica* is that it is not the wealthy amateur but the master author who truly merits, regardless of his census-rating, the title of patron and benefactor. His gifts are linguistic; he is a word-coiner who confers a wealth of language on the entire community of Latin speakers, "enrich[ing] his inherited stock of speech" (*sermonem patrium ditaverit, Ars* 57). This benefaction is also celebrated in Horace's second letter to Florus, where Horace describes how the model poet "will pour out his wealth and bless Latium with the riches of his tongue" (*fundet opes Latiumque beabit divite lingua, E.* 2.2.121). Such a poet performs the linguistic equivalent of an exalted civic service. In the letter to Florus, he is likened to an "honorable censor" (*censoris . . . honesti,* 110) who expels words that do not deserve their place of distinction (111–14), restores fine old words that have fallen on hard times (115–18), and adopts new words as needed (119). In the *Ars*, his linguistic creations are linked with the achievements of Roman technology: the creation of a harbor, the transformation of marsh into arable land, the rechaneling or

[23] See Rudd (1989) 219.   [24] On the figure of the *praeco*, see further above, 164.

agricultural "education" of a river (*Ars* 63–8). The context is elegiac –
what Horace insists on here is not the permanence but the perishability
of everything man-made – but the implicit equation redounds nonetheless to the poet's credit.[25]

It is not only society at large but the poet who stands to benefit from
his linguistic gifts. As he makes his fortune, the poet also makes himself.
The metaphorical identification of "new words" with "new men" that is
forged in the epistle to Florus, where the censor-poet is described as
"admit[ting] new words" (*adsciscet nova*, *E.* 2.2.119) to his linguistic
Senate, also underlies Horace's discussion of neologisms in the *Ars*. If
your subject matter should require it, Horace remarks, you will be
granted the license to coin new words, so long as you exercise that license
with discretion and derive your words from a Greek source. But as the
indignant question that follows suggests, this license is not universally
conceded (*Ars* 53–9):

> quid autem
> Caecilio Plautoque dabit Romanus ademptum
> Vergilio Varioque? ego cur, acquirere pauca
> si possum, invideor, cum lingua Catonis et Enni
> sermonem patrium ditaverit et nova rerum
> nomina protulerit? licuit semperque licebit
> signatum praesente nota producere nomen.

> But why will Romans grant to Caecilius and Plautus what they
> deny to Virgil and Varius? Why, if I am capable of adding a little to
> the stock of words, am I evilly eyed, when the tongue of Cato and
> Ennius enriched our native language and brought forth new names
> for things? It has been and always will be our right to produce words
> stamped with the mark of the present.

The topic of the neologism opens up the quarrel between the ancients
and the moderns, and the image of the new word as a new coin figures

---

[25] Recalling that Augustus undertook massive public works along these lines, exercised censo-
rial powers to purge the senate of what Suetonius terms the "unseemly and low-born mob"
(*deformi et incondita turba*, *Aug.* 35) that had infiltrated its ranks, lavished gifts on individuals,
and contributed enormous sums directly to the treasury, we may surmise that Horace's
poet-benefactor is ultimately modeled on the emperor himself. See Dio 52.42; Aug. *RG*
8.2, 15–18; Rudd (1989) 161; Millar (1977) 189–93. The absence of such imperial
figurations of the poet's role in Horace's epistle to Augustus may indicate Horace's sense
that even a metaphorical claim of parity could be taken as an affront to the emperor's
dignity.

this quarrel in social terms as a conflict between established families and arrivistes, old money and new money.[26] Long-dead poets constitute a kind of hereditary nobility of poetry, this nobility being "inherited," as it were, not from the past but from the future – from the canonizing passage of time, which has given their names and their neologisms the patina of accepted currency. Contemporary poets, by contrast, have no stock of years to authenticate their claims to poetic authority. They are "new men" on the poetic scene, and as such they and their innovative words encounter the same social prejudice as political newcomers struggling to make their names.

As the prominence of proper names in Horace's discussion of the neologism suggests, the poet's name (*nomen*) depends on the poet's words (*nomina*) – the poet makes his name in part by exercising his right to coin words. As Horace stresses in the simile that follows, moreover, the invention of new words is not only a matter of the new poet's self-promotion but part of a natural cycle. Old words die, and new words arise to take their place (*Ars* 60–2):

> ut silvae foliis pronos mutantur in annos,
> prima cadunt, ita verborum vetus interit aetas,
> et iuvenum ritu florent modo nata vigentque.

As the forests change their leaves from swift year to year, the first of them fall, so the old age of words passes away, and those just born flourish like the young and are strong.

In one respect, the simile seems to be at cross-purposes with Horace's theme. Whereas the preceding lines champion such distinctive and distinguished proper names as Caecilius, Plautus, Virgil, and Varius, the famous Homeric simile that Horace is reworking here ("As the generations of leaves, so the generations of men," etc., *Il.* 6.145–9) eradicates all such distinctions, arguing that names mean nothing since all men are equally doomed to oblivion. The Homeric allusion signals Horace's acknowledgment of the leveling force of death, an acknowledgment fully articulated in the ensuing passage, which opens in the leveling first-person plural (*debemur morti nos nostraque, Ars* 63) and closes by drawing

---

[26] The conservative sentiment is well expressed in a seventeenth-century French work (François de Callières, *Du bon et du mauvais usage*, Paris, 1694), quoted by Elias (1978) 110, which deplores a "bad turn of phrase, which began among the lowest people and made its fortune at the court, like those favorites without merit who got themselves elevated there in the old days."

out the implications for poets of the general mortal law: "things made by mortals will pass away; still less will the honor and influence of speech continue to flourish" (*mortalia facta peribunt,* | *nedum sermonum stet honos et gratia vivax, Ars* 68–9). Horace's deference inheres in the recognition that it is not only speech but Horatian *sermo*, including the *Ars*, that is destined to fade.

Still, deference tempers but does not muffle the self-authorizing ring of Horace's newly reminted Homeric coin. Unlike Homer's, Horace's simile is in effect not elegiac but assertive, moving from death to life and from age (*vetus . . . aetas, Ars* 61) to youth (*iuvenum,* 62). Moreover, the simile does not, as we might have expected, signal the senior poet's recognition that a fresh generation, represented by "youthful" aspirants such as the Piso boys (*iuvenes,* 24), is arising to take his place. It is Horace himself, the senior but also the modern poet, who is aligned here with the young upstarting word. Indeed, if the Pisones appear anywhere in this simile, it is on the other side. Although Horace's simile may seem to flatter his strong young addressees, it effectively pits the newly arisen poet against his establishment audience. Thus it may have been the social reverberations of the Homeric simile that appealed to Horace at this particular juncture in his *Ars*. "Why do you ask me about my lineage, magnanimous son of Tydeus?" asks Homer's Glaucus, meaning that identifying marks such as the patronymic are irrelevant, however glorious and distinguished one's lineage may be, since every generation is destined to fall and to be replaced. That Horace invokes this famous image of the fragility of names just after insisting on the primacy of the poet's name suggests the diminished value of genealogy as a measure of a name's currency. A name as old and distinguished as that sported by Numa's descendants may be supplanted, in the "natural" course of things, by a new name such as Horace's own.

The immortal leech

If the aesthetic and social lessons of the opening of Horace's *Ars* are readily absorbed, Horace's last lesson, incorporated in the figure of the "mad poet," is more difficult to apprehend. Although the oppositions that structure the opening recur, the stakes have been raised, and the pressure increased. Whereas the opening scene contained deviance within the person of the inept painter, it is Horace himself, no other artist intervening, who authors the grotesque composite figure – joining the metaphor of a leech to the simile of a bear – that deforms his poem's end.

And whereas the monstrous painting is framed on one side by the "human head," on the other by Horace's sensible *amici*, nothing supervenes to contain or control the final image of the poem. Horace's *Ars* as a whole thus repeats the trajectory of the monstrous painting, moving from top to bottom, from head to tail-end, from human to animal, from *humano* to *hirudo*, its mocking echo. We are left to make of this monstrous design what we can, without the assistance of the author, who drops off just when we may feel we need him most.

Here is the passage (*Ars* 453–76):

> ut mala quem scabies aut morbus regius urget
> aut fanaticus error et iracunda Diana,
> vesanum tetigisse timent fugiuntque poetam   455
> qui sapiunt; agitant pueri incautique sequuntur.
> hic, dum sublimis versus ructatur et errat,
> si veluti merulis intentus decidit auceps
> in puteum foveamve, licet "succurrite" longum
> clamet "io cives!" non sit qui tollere curet.   460
> si curet quis opem ferre et demittere funem,
> "qui scis an prudens huc se deiecerit atque
> servari nolit?" dicam, Siculique poetae
> narrabo interitum. deus immortalis haberi
> dum cupit Empedocles, ardentem frigidus Aetnam   465
> insiluit. sit ius liceatque perire poetis.
> invitum qui servat idem facit occidenti.
> nec semel hoc fecit, nec si retractus erit iam
> fiet homo et ponet famosae mortis amorem.
> nec satis apparet cur versus factitet, utrum   470
> minxerit in patrios cineres, an triste bidental
> moverit incestus: certe furit, ac velut ursus,
> obiectos caveae valuit si frangere clathros,
> indoctum doctumque fugat recitator acerbus;
> quem vero arripuit, tenet occiditque legendo,   475
> non missura cutem nisi plena cruoris hirudo.

As with a man afflicted by a repulsive rash or jaundice or frantic wandering inflicted by angry Diana, men of sense are afraid to touch a mad poet and flee him; reckless children follow after and harass him. Suppose, as he weaves along with his head in the clouds, belching his poems, he falls down into a pit or a well, like a bird-catcher intent on blackbirds; though he yell loud and long "Ho, fellow-citizens, help, help!" no one will bother to pull him out. If someone should bother to come to his aid and let down a rope, "How do you know he didn't throw himself down there on purpose and doesn't want to be saved?" I'll say; and I'll recount the end of the Sicilian poet. Longing to be thought an immortal god, icy Empedocles jumped into the flames of Etna. Grant poets the right and the license to die. If you save a man against his will, you've as good as killed him. This isn't the first time he's done this; if you pull him out, don't expect him to join the human race and give up his yearning for a celebrity death. It's not quite clear why he keeps turning out poems. Did he piss on his father's grave, or disturb the sanctity of a somber shrine? At any rate, he's certainly mad and, like a bear whose strength has sufficed to break the confining bars of his cage, he puts everyone to flight, schooled and unschooled alike, this merciless reciter; but if he catches a man, he holds him tight and reads him to death, a leech that won't let go until it's full of blood.

The family resemblance between this portrait and the painting that heads the *Ars* is unmistakable. *Nec . . . fiet homo*: like the human-headed monster, fledged but not airborne, the mad poet aspires to rise above the human condition and ends up far below it. Although his head is in the clouds, his belched-out poetry is a product of the belly; although he hopes to be counted among the gods, he is counted, by sensible men at least (*qui sapiunt, Ars* 456), among the beasts. In Ciceronian terms, he is devoid of the distinctively human faculty of *ratio*, hence incapable of self-restraint; his all-too-visible animal appetite is held in check only by the external imposition of a cage. His accelerating devolution reaches its nadir in the last word of the poem, *hirudo*: a blood-sucking leech, a tail that is all mouth, pure appetite. As the description of the painting moves from head to tail and from centaur to mermaid, so the bear (*ursus*, masculine) ends up a leech (*hirudo*, feminine), a cousin of the mermaid's black fishtail and a graphic or pornographic image of the female sex. Following the lead of Shakespeare's King Lear, who identifies women's nether parts with "the sulphurous pit," we can recognize this voracious leech as a transformation of the devouring Etna into which Empedocles leaped.[27]

While the mad poet brings to life the monstrous painting, he also recalls the aspiring genius who shuns the barber and the baths in the hope of gaining entrance to Helicon (*Ars* 295–301). The poet at the end

[27] *King Lear* IV vi.124–9 (as if conflating the opening and close of the *Ars*): "Down from the waist they are Centaurs, | Though women all above; | But to the girdle do the gods inherit, | Beneath is all the fiend's. | There's hell, there's darkness, there is the sulphurous pit; | Burning, scalding, stench, consumption."

of the *Ars* outdoes this ill-groomed confrere not just by letting his hair grow but by transforming himself (with the help of Horace's simile) into a shaggy bear, the very model of poetic unkemptness. But he resembles him in that he is, for all his feigned unsociability, a creature of society to his very core. His erratic behavior is artfully calculated for its effect on an audience to which he only pretends to be indifferent. Horace's Empedocles knew just what he was up to when he took his famous leap: he wanted men to believe he was a god (*deus immortalis haberi*, 464). So too, when the purportedly absent-minded poet "falls" into a well, the accident may be calculated (cf. *prudens*, 462) to advertise his credentials: "Inspired bard available, suitable all occasions, permanent position preferred." The final image of the *Ars* thus encapsulates one of the central arguments of the poem – that beneath his rough exterior, a shaggy bear may be a slick operator, a leech that is as smooth as smooth can be.[28]

The conjunction of bear and leech, bristling *ingenium* and slippery *ars*, describes perfectly a type familiar to us from Horace's satires. Consider, for example, Horace's description of the singer Tigellius in *Satires* 1.3. Deaf to the requests of his patron, the young Caesar, Tigellius would launch into song only when the fancy struck him (*si collibuisset*, *S.* 1.3.6), but then he was irrepressible: "he'd sing out with his 'Hail, hail Bacchus!' from the first course to the last – now in falsetto, and now in the deepest tone the lyre sounds" (*ab ovo | usque ad mala citaret "io Bacche!" modo summa | voce, modo hac resonat quae chordis quattuor ima*, 6–8). Tigellius presumably believes that he proves his *ingenium* by thus flouting the norms of moderation. A true poet, he might argue, cannot sing to order but must await the stirrings of his god (whom Tigellius here summons with the ritual cry of the devotee); and once possessed or "enthused," he is at the god's mercy – not his patron's. This does not mean, of course, that he scorns the fine food and wine his talents have earned.

Another less genial relative of the bear–leech is the unnamed hanger-on of *Satires* 1.9, a man who likewise prides himself on the copious fluency of his versification (*nam quis me scribere pluris | aut citius possit versus? S.* 1.9.23–4). Attaching himself to Horace (*usque tenebo*, 15) in the hope of winning access to Maecenas, he offers Horace a practical demonstration of his verbal stamina (*cum quidlibet ille | garriret*, 12–13). When Horace breaks in to ask if he has any surviving relatives, his

---

[28] Brink (1971) 431 notes that the metaphor of the leech is "established in Roman comedy for financial blood-sucking" and "is probably proverbial" but is careful to dissociate Horace's "poetic *hirudo*" from this unsavory company.

companion replies that he has none: "I've laid them all to rest," *omnis composui* (28) – a phrase that could also mean "I've versified them all." "Finish me off," Horace moans to himself, *confice* (29) – meaning at once "kill me" and "write me." This was, he recollects, the doom foretold by a Sabellian fortune-teller when he was a boy: "a chatterer will some day consume him; if he has sense, let him shun talkative men when he reaches maturity" (*garrulus hunc quando consumet cumque: loquaces, | si sapiat, vitet, simul atque adoleverit aetas*, 33–4). As if anticipating the end of the *Ars*, Horace here represents an endless flow of speech "exhausting" or "eating up," leech-wise, the very substance of the addressee.

But there is another candidate for the role of the murderously exuberant versifier within the *Ars* itself. In the most literal and immediate sense it is Horace – Horace, who clings and clings to his readers for all of 476 lines (more lines by far than any other poem in the Horatian corpus) before dropping off into silence – who is the leech of the *Ars poetica*. The final image, a quintessentially Horatian self-depreciation, holds the place of an ironic closural apology: "but I've kept you too long, I'm really a terrible pest, you must be utterly drained."[29] The blood-filled leech is thus a grotesque variation on the familiar closural figure of "satiety." At the end of his first satire, for example, Horace underscores the self-reflexive closural potential of this figure by comparing life to a meal and correlating the sated dinner-guest (*satur*, *S.*1.1.119) with the fulfilled or completed poem (*satis*, 120).[30] The same set of associations underpins the magnificent close of *Epistles* 2.2 (214–16):

> lusisti satis, edisti satis atque bibisti:
> tempus abire tibi est, ne potum largius aequo
> rideat et pulset lasciva decentius aetas.

> You've played your fill, you've eaten and drunk your fill; it's time for you to leave – or else, when you've drunk more than you should, the younger generation, in whom wildness is more becoming, will laugh at you and kick you out.

The epistle inevitably illustrates its own lesson, rehearsing the Apollonian injunction "nothing too much" by curbing its own excessive tendencies (to extend the poem beyond this point would be to invite the ridicule

---

[29] The end of the *Ars* thus resembles what Fiske (1920) 89 characterizes as the "abrupt and witty endings . . ., sometimes coupled with ironical mockery of the satirist himself," of Horace's satires. On the affinities between the *Ars* and *S.* 2, see Frischer (1991) 87–100.

[30] See Freudenburg (1993) 192–3.

and abuse with which the aging drunkard is threatened). In these poems the poet makes his quest for a proper, measured conclusion emblematic of the broader ethical problem of living within one's mortal limits. But this larger context is sheared away at the finale of the *Ars poetica*. The author and his audience are here not fellow banqueters who share an ethics and aesthetics of satiety; the audience is itself the feast, its blood supplies the poet's liquor.[31] In this perfectly self-reflexive figure, closure coincides with the separation not of poet and poem (a fiction that leaves space for moral reflection) but of sated poet and exhausted audience. If Horace earlier specifies this audience as "the blood of Numa" (*Pompilius sanguis, Ars* 292), one reason for the specification may be that the leech is by nature partial to blue blood. The founding *iunctura* of the *Ars poetica* is perhaps this juncture of lowly Horatian leech and illustrious Pisonian host.[32]

Horace, who repeatedly boasts of his rise from humble origins to a high destiny and of the success with which he attached himself to the most important men of his day,[33] is after all a shining example of the social value of consummate artistry. But it would be falling into the trap set by Horace's irony simply to identify him with his leech. If the poets Horace derides are leeches in bear's clothing, Horace is a powerful bear concealed within a leech's smooth skin. The bold claims of *Epistles* 1.19, where Horace presents himself as a legislator and model (on a par with Homer and Ennius) for the "servile herd" of his imitators, are put into practice in the final passage of the *Ars*, which demonstrates conclusively that while the "mad poet" may appropriate the trappings of *ingenium*, Horace has the real thing.[34] And insofar as Horace addresses his *Ars* not to the freedmen or impoverished gentlemen who might be eager to imitate his social and literary success, but to a prominent Roman family, his *Ars poetica* is less an instruction manual than a warning or a boast. The civil war not only disordered the *ordines* of Roman society, it also

---

[31] The *plena cruoris hirudo* complements the *conviva satur* of S. 1.1, completing the Lucretian doublet *satur ac plenus* (3.960); earlier in the same passage Lucretius favors *plenus* (*cur non ut plenus vitae conviva recedis?* 3.938)

[32] The semantics of *iunctura/iungere* encompass social as well as verbal conjunctions; cf. S. 1.3.54 (*haec res et iungit iunctos et servat amicos*); E. 1.5.25–6 (*ut coeat par | iungaturque pari*).

[33] Most notably in the capsule autobiographies of S. 1.6, C. 2.20, and E. 1.20. The boast is telling whether or not Horace's depiction of his "humble origins" is accurate; on Horace's status see Armstrong (1986); Williams (1995).

[34] Cf. Brink (1971) 516: the final passage "fascinates because it is written from inside the experience which it professes to ridicule."

changed the very rules of the social game. From here on in, the conventional forms of distinction, centered on military and political achievement, will always be shadowed if not obscured by the dominant figure of the *princeps*. In the future, the poet's status may be worth more than the senator's. If Horace dissimulates his power, masquerading as a mere sane critic, a leech, or as Bernard Frischer suggests a lowly *grammaticus*,[35] the disguise may be designed to deflect the invidious accusations of hubris that this message might be expected to attract.

It is not surprising, then, that Horace's *Ars poetica* offers no recipe for either social or literary distinction. Although Horace teaches what can be taught, although he supplies some of the rules, some of the fundamentals, with which a practicing poet must in fact be equipped, it is, in the end, the art that cannot be taught that holds the key to Helicon. It is the very audacity with which Horace breaks his own rules, defies his own prescriptions, for example with the unimaginable figure of the bear–leech with which his poem does not so much finish as break off or break out, that distinguishes Horace from all would-be imitators. In fact the bear–leech is an excellent example of that "metaphysical wit" famously disparaged by Samuel Johnson as "a kind of *discordia concors,* a combination of dissimilar images," in which "the most heterogeneous ideas are yoked by violence together." With this yoking, Horace constructs a metaphor which at once demonstrates and represents his own *ingenium*.

It is well known that Horace does not discuss metaphor within the *Ars poetica*. One reason is that metaphor by its very nature falls outside the scope of his didactic poem – we have it on good authority (that of Aristotle, followed by Cicero) that metaphor, being "a sign of innate talent," "cannot be learned from another" (*Po.* 1459a).[36] Another reason may be that metaphor is inherently inimical to Horace's decorous scheme, which requires that everything remain in its proper, literal place (*singula quaeque locum teneant sortita decentem, Ars* 92). The social implications of metaphorical dislocation are drawn out in Cicero's *De oratore*, where "proper" words, words which are "born almost at the same moment" as the things they name, are contrasted with words "used metaphorically and set in a place that so to speak does not belong to them" (*quae transferuntur et quasi in alieno loco collocantur, De or.* 3.149). These latecomers should not be too bold or brash. Indeed, a metaphor should

---

[35] See Frischer (1991).
[36] Similarly Arist. *Rh.* 1405a; Cic. *De or.* 3.160 (one reason why we delight in metaphor is that it is *ingenii specimen … quoddam*). On the unteachability of *ingenium*, cf. Brink (1963) 258.

be polite, even bashful, "so as to seem to have been escorted into a place that does not belong to it, not to have broken in, and to have entered by permission, not by force" (*ut deducta esse in alienum locum, non irruisse atque ut precario, non vi venisse videatur*, 3.165).

Within the *Ars*, the gap left by metaphor is partly filled by the inherently more decorous figure of *iunctura*, the art of verbal arrangement.[37] *Iunctura*, which Horace discusses in tandem with the neologism, is another way of achieving novelty. It is a means at once of making a familiar word strange and of setting oneself apart from the crowd: "your diction will be distinguished if a clever conjunction makes a known word new" (*dixeris egregie notum si callida verbum | reddiderit iunctura novum*, *Ars* 47–8). Horace returns to the topic when pronouncing on the diction appropriate to the satyr play (240–3):

> ex noto fictum carmen sequar, ut sibi quivis
> speret idem, sudet multum frustraque laboret
> ausus idem: tantum series iuncturaque pollet,
> tantum de medio sumptis accedit honoris.

> The poem I'll aim for will be fashioned out of familiar materials, such that any poet might hope to do as well, but will only sweat and sweat and struggle in vain when he attempts the same feat: such is the power of connection and yoking, so great the distinction accorded that which is drawn from the common stock.

It is surely not an accident that this boast occurs within Horace's discussion of the satyr play, that middling genre which has clear affinities, in style and pitch if not in substance, with Horace's satires.[38] In the fashioning of a poem as of a gentleman, it is easy enough to make a silk purse out of silk, harder to achieve the same result with a sow's ear. What distinguishes the poet is the art by which he transforms the familiar and commonplace (*notum, medium*) into something novel and distinguished. Nor does Horace explain how such effects – effects that others will discover that no amount of labor can reproduce – are to be achieved. The art of "connection and yoking" here inherits the mysterious, unteachable, and inimitable power and distinction typically associated with *ingenium* and its chief exponent, metaphor.

The indecorous combination of leech and bear at the end of the *Ars*

---

[37] For *iunctura* as "the 'refreshment,' which may or may not be metaphorical, of ordinary words in a pointed context," see Brink (1971) 139.

[38] So Perret (1964) 165–6; Innes (1989) 264.

both demonstrates and represents the power – the aggressive meekness, the deferential authority – that forever takes us by surprise. The poet who begins the *Ars* by penning the monster in ends by letting it out of its cage. The anti-closural impulse extends to the closural figure of "satiety," which here expresses not philosophical resignation (the diner's readiness to depart the banquet of life) but a violently antic resistance to the force of time. The finale of the *Ars* is littered with grave sites – the "well or pit" (*Ars* 459), the "flames of Etna" (465), the "father's ashes" (471). But in the end it is not the poet who plunges to his death. It is rather the reader who succumbs to the embrace of the bear, the kiss of the leech. The shocking final image suggests that the leech, like the poet who elsewhere claims that he will "grow forever fresh in the praise of future generations" (*usque ego postera | crescam laude recens, C.* 3.30.7–8), may indeed win a kind of immortality from the blood of its readers. Horace ends not by laughing with his friends but by making a face at them – and by making his face at their expense.

Postscript: Odes 4.3

Quem tu, Melpomene, semel
nascentem placido lumine videris,
   illum non labor Isthmius
clarabit pugilem, non equus impiger
     curru ducet Achaico   5
victorem, neque res bellica Deliis
   ornatum foliis ducem,
quod regum tumidas contuderit minas,
   ostendet Capitolio:
sed quae Tibur aquae fertile praefluunt   10
   et spissae nemorum comae
fingent Aeolio carmine nobilem.
   Romae principis urbium
dignatur suboles inter amabilis
     vatum ponere me choros,   15
et iam dente minus mordeor invido.
   o, testudinis aureae
dulcem quae strepitum, Pieri, temperas,
   o mutis quoque piscibus
donatura cycni, si libeat, sonum,   20
   totum muneris hoc tui est,
quod monstror digito praetereuntium
   Romanae fidicen lyrae:
quod spiro et placeo, si placeo, tuum est.

The newborn upon whom you once turn the placid light of your
gaze, Melpomene – no Isthmian ordeal will give him luster as a
boxer, no lively horse will draw him victorious in a Greek chariot,
nor will martial deeds display him to the Capitol, a general adorned
with Delian leaves for smashing the inflated threats of kings, but the
waters that flow past fertile Tibur and the dense foliage of its groves

will make him renowned for Aeolian song. The offspring of Rome, chief of cities, deign to set me amid the amiable chorus of bards, and already I feel the bite of envy less. O Pierian, you who temper the sweet strum of the golden tortoise-shell lyre, you who can give, if you choose, the swan's note even to silent fish, all this is your gift, that I am pointed out by the finger of passers-by as the musician of the Roman lyre. That I breathe and please, if I do please, is your doing.

Throughout his career Horace has represented himself as engaged in a "Herculean" battle against envious overreaders and onlookers. In the *Epodes*, the upstart poet wilts under the heat of Canidia's evil eye. In *Satires* 1.6, he complains of being "gnawed" by detractors envious of his social successes. In *Odes* 2.20, he imagines flying high above envy's reach. The battle ends in *Odes* 4.3 with Horace's victory – a carefully muted victory, but a victory all the same. In Epode 4, Horace channeled the indignation of passers-by (*ora . . . huc et huc euntium, I.* 4.9) against the upstart freedman. Here, he welcomes the finger-pointing of passers-by (*digito praetereuntium, C.* 4.3.22) awed by his celebrity. These passers-by model their gaze, as future readers are to model theirs, on Melpomene's. Instead of withering the poet with the slant looks of envy, they bathe him in the "placid light" of renown (*placido lumine*, 2).[1]

As the word suggests, *invidia* (a "looking upon") is the inescapable condition of social visibility. For those who are very much in the public eye, gestures of deference can help soften envy's glare. Horace deploys a full array of such gestures in this public and brightly illuminated ode.[2] The self-canonizing boast at the heart of the ode is framed within an homage to Melpomene and is contingent on her favor (cf. *si placeo*, 24). The boast is itself couched as a token of Horace's humility: far from demanding a triumph, Horace lowers himself before the collective "offspring of Rome" who "deign" to recognize his worth. Unlike the garlanded *triumphator*, moreover, the poet is not so much exposed to view as shaded from view by the dense foliage that ennobles him (cf. *nobilem*, 12). Where *Odes* 3.30 advertised his accomplishments, *Odes* 4.3 remains modestly silent; as in the early apology of *Satires* 1.6, so here Horace

---

[1] Horace's Melpomene is modeled on Callimachus' Muses, who look upon their infant favorites "with eye not aslant" (ὄθματι ... μὴ λοξῷ, *Aet.* 1.1.37–8); see Putnam (1986) 72.

[2] The conjunction *nascentem placido lumine* recalls the Ennian and Lucretian *in luminis oras*. The same original light shines in the golden honey that drips from the poet's gifted tongue in the repeated <u>Mel</u>pomene, <u>sem</u>el of the opening line; cf. *testudinis aureae*, 17.

represents himself as meriting but not laboring for social distinction. The poet of this ode is above all a recipient – of the Muses' favor, the landscape's labor, Rome's canonizing approval, the man-in-the-street's admiration. The deferential climax of the ode is the magnificent reversal at its center, where the poet is not a maker but himself an artifact, fashioned by his landscape.[3]

Horace abdicates authority here twice over – by removing himself from the subject-position, and by erasing the individuating features of his authorial persona. This ode includes no mention of Horace's origins, no tribute to his father, nothing equivalent even to the minimal *ex humili potens* of *Odes* 3.30 ("from humble origins risen to power," 12). Where Horace once anchored his fame to the river of his native Apulia (the *violens . . . Aufidus* of *C.* 3.30.10), he now credits the streams of Tibur, a place with fewer ineradicably personal associations. The only suggestion of his lowly beginnings comes near the end of the ode, where he praises Melpomene's power to make "mute fish" sing like swans – an almost ridiculous image, reminiscent of the final composite figure of the *Ars poetica*, that at once obliquely acknowledges and makes light of Horace's ascent from anonymity to renown, from speechlessness to song, from the obliterating ocean to the starry heavens. One episode of Horace's biography that is palpably absent is his composition of the *Carmen saeculare*, the ode that was performed by a chorus of boys and girls at Augustus' *Ludi Saeculares* in 17 BCE. Elsewhere in *Odes* 4 Horace manifests his pride in this accomplishment. It is in this connection that he introduces his name into the final line, an abbreviated epitaph, of *Odes* 4.6, where he imagines a young bride recalling being "taught the measures of the poet Horace" (*docilis modorum | vatis Horati*, *C.* 4.6.44). In *Odes* 4.3, the roles are reversed and the favor is reciprocated. Instead of training boys and girls to sing his choral ode, Horace is himself given a choral identity by the "offspring of Rome," who place him in the bardic chorus.

And yet the unadorned modesty of this self-portrait itself bespeaks Horace's authority. If Horace does not rehearse his autobiography, one reason is that the overreading audience of this late ode is expected to recognize Horace's face, just as the passers-by do. As Philip Hardie has remarked, Horace is casting himself in the image of a "breathing statue" – a self-sculpted monument of his own magnificence.[4] We read the brief

---

[3] On "the surface tone of humility and deference" in this ode, see Putnam (1986) 68–71; for a detailed discussion of Horace's "submersion of the personal," see Estévez (1982).

[4] Hardie (1993) 132–3.

but resonant *titulus* inscribed on the monument: *Romanae fidicen lyrae,* "musician of the Roman lyre."

The ode is, indeed, a triumph of exclusions. As if by magic, it makes earlier troubles disappear. Canidia's stepmotherly look (*quid ut noverca me intueris, I. 5.9*) is canceled by the genial gaze Melpomene directs upon the newborn poet, and the labored breathing of which Horace complained in Epode 17 – "my chest is tight, I can't breathe" (*neque est | levare tenta spiritu praecordia,* 25–6) – is cured by the "inspiring" Muse who lends her poet breath (cf. *quod spiro . . . tuum est,* 24). In his earlier collections, Horace wrestled with the competing demands of his own and his patron's face. Here, there is no patron to contend with. The *princeps* who singled Horace out for the honor of composing the *Carmen saeculare* finds his place preoccupied here by *Roma princeps.*[5] And Maecenas, to whom Horace originally appealed for canonization (*quodsi me lyricis vatibus inseres, C. 1.1.35*), makes way for the "offspring of Rome," of whose favorable judgment Horace now rests assured. In his first epode, Horace thanked Maecenas for his generosity; in *Epistles* 1.7, he tempered gratitude with self-assertion. But there is no Sabine villa to be either celebrated or disowned in *Odes* 4.3. It is Horace's emphatic expression of a different order of "gratitude" that draws our attention to the absence of his mortal benefactor. Here it is Melpomene who is the donor (*donatura,* 20), Melpomene who gives the great gift (*muneris,* 21), Melpomene to whom Horace is forever in debt (*tuum est,* 24).

Horace's apostrophe to Melpomene reflects the poet's power back upon him.[6] But this does not mean that the gesture is an empty one. Horace's expression of gratitude is surely heartfelt. The gift of the Muse is the inalienable gift of *ingenium* – something that it was not within Maecenas' or Augustus' power to bestow. But Horace also has a gift to give, in the shape of his poems. And the generosity of this benefaction demands an answering generosity from the reader. When Horace writes *quod spiro et placeo, si placeo, tuum est,* he is writing not only to Melpomene but to us. The ode that opens with the birth of a poet and imagines his luminous future is a postscript that entrusts Horace to posterity. It is Horace's future readers who will keep him in breath by continuing to read his poetry with pleasure.

---

[5] Horace nowhere acknowledges the "several gifts" with which Suetonius tells us the emperor "enriched" him (*unaque et altera liberalitate locupletavit*). It is interesting, however, that a mention of Tibur (where Augustus may have given Horace some property) is followed by the "corrective" *Romae principis.*   [6] Cf. Culler (1981) 142–3.

WORKS CITED

Ahl, Frederick (1984) "The Rider and the Horse: Politics and Power in Roman Poetry from Horace to Statius," *ANRW* II.32.1:40–124

(1985) *Metaformations: Soundplay and Wordplay in Ovid and Other Classical Poets.* Ithaca

Ancona, Ronnie (1994) *Time and the Erotic in Horace's Odes.* Durham and London

Anderson, W. S. (1982) *Essays on Roman Satire.* Princeton

(1995) "*Horatius Liber*, Child and Freedman's Free Son," *Arethusa* 28:151–64

André, Jean-Marie (1983) "Mécène écrivain (avec, en appendice, les fragments de Mécène)," *ANRW* II.30.3:1765–87

Armstrong, David (1986) "*Horatius Eques et Scriba: Satires* 1.6 and 2.7," *TAPA* 116:255–88

(1989) *Horace.* New Haven

(1993) "The Addressees of the Ars poetica: Herculaneum, the Pisones and Epicurean Protreptic," *MD* 31:185–230

Austin, J. L. (1975) *How to Do Things with Words.* Cambridge, Mass. 2nd ed.

Babcock, Charles L. (1966) "*Si Certus Intrarit Dolor:* A Reconsideration of Horace's Fifteenth Epode," *AJP* 87:400–19

(1974) "*Omne Militabitur Bellum*: The Language of Commitment in Epode 1," *CJ* 70:14–31

Bain, David (1986) "'Waiting for Varus?' (Horace, *Epodes*, 5, 49–72)," *Latomus* 45:125–31

Baker, Robert J. (1988) "Maecenas and Horace *Satires* II.8," *CJ* 83:212–32

Barchiesi, Alessandro (1993) "Insegnare ad Augusto: Orazio, Epistole 2, 1 e Ovidio, Tristia II," *MD* 31:149–84

(1994a) "Alcune difficoltà nella carriera di un poeta giambico. Giambo ed elegia nell'epodo xi," in Rosario Cortes Tovar and Jose Carlos Fernandes Corte (eds.) *Bimilenario de Horacio*, 127–38. Salamanca

(1994b) "Ultime difficoltà nella carriera di un poeta giambico: l'epodo xvii," in *Atti Convegno Oraziano*, 205–20. Venosa

(1996) "Poetry, Praise, and Patronage: Simonides in Book 4 of Horace's *Odes*," *CA* 15:5–47

Barton, Carlin A. (1993) *The Sorrows of the Ancient Romans*. Princeton
  (1994) "All Things Beseem the Victor: Paradoxes of Masculinity in Early
  Imperial Rome," in R. C. Trexler (ed.) *Gender Rhetorics*, 83–92.
  Binghamton

Becker, Carl (1963) *Das Spätwerk des Horaz*. Göttingen

Bernstein, Michael André (1992) *Bitter Carnival: Ressentiment and the Abject Hero*.
  Princeton

Berres, Thomas (1992) "'Erlebnis und Kunstgestalt' im 7. Brief des Horaz,"
  Hermes 120: 216–37

Bing, Peter (1988) *The Well-Read Muse: Present and Past in Callimachus and the
  Hellenistic Poets*. Göttingen

Bond, R. P. (1985) "Dialectic, Eclectic, and Myth (?) in Horace, *Satires* 2.6,"
  Antichthon 19: 68–86

Bourdieu, Pierre (1977) *Outline of a Theory of Practice* (trans. Richard Nice).
  Cambridge. Orig. publ. 1972
  (1984) *Distinction: A Social Critique of the Judgement of Taste* (trans. Richard
  Nice). Cambridge, Mass. Orig. publ. 1979

Bowditch, Lowell (1994) "Horace's Poetics of Political Integrity: Epistle 1.18,"
  AJP 115: 409–26

Bradshaw, Arnold (1989) "Horace *in Sabinis*," *Studies in Latin Literature and
  Roman History* 5: 160–86

Bramble, J. C. (1974) *Persius and the Programmatic Satire: A Study in Form and
  Imagery*. Cambridge

Bremmer, Jan N. (1987) "The Old Women of Ancient Greece," in Josine Blok
  and Peter Mason (eds.) *Sexual Asymmetry: Studies in Ancient Society*,
  191–215. Amsterdam

Brink, C. O. (1963) *Horace on Poetry*, 1: *Prolegomena to the Literary Epistles*.
  Cambridge
  (1971) *Horace on Poetry*, 2: *The "Ars Poetica."* Cambridge
  (1981) *Horace on Poetry*, 3: *Epistles Book II: The Letters to Augustus and Florus*.
  Cambridge

Brisson, Jean-Paul (1988) "Horace: pouvoir poétique et pouvoir politique," in
  R. Chevallier (ed.) *Présence d'Horace*, 51–64. Tours

Brown, Penelope and Levinson, Stephen C. (1987) *Politeness: Some Universals in
  Language Usage*. Cambridge

Brunt, P. A. (1990) "Laus imperii," *Roman Imperial Themes*, 288–323. Oxford

Büchner, K. (1970) "Die Epoden des Horaz," *Studien zur Römischen Literatur:
  Werkanalysen*, 8, 50–96. Wiesbaden

Burrow, Colin (1993) "Horace at Home and Abroad: Wyatt and Sixteenth-
  Century Horatianism," in Charles Martindale and David Hopkins (eds.)
  Horace Made New, 27–49. Cambridge

Bushala, Eugene W. (1968) "Laboriosus Ulixes," *CJ* 64: 7–10

Carrubba, Robert W. (1969) *The Epodes of Horace*. The Hague

Castiglione, Baldesar (1959) *The Book of the Courtier* (trans. Charles S. Singleton). New York. Orig. publ. 1528

Cavarzere, Alberto (1992) ed. *Orazio. Il libro degli epodi*. Turin

(1994) *"Vate me.* L'ambiguo sigillo dell'epodo XVI," *Aevum Antiquum* 7: 171–90

Citroni, Mario (1986) "Le raccomandazioni del poeta: apostrofe al libro e contatto col destinatario," *Maia* 38:111–46

(1995) *Poesia e lettori in Roma antica: forme della comunicazione letteraria*. Rome

Clayman, D. L. (1975) "Horace's *Epodes* VIII and XII: More Than Clever Obscenity?," *CW* 69: 55–61

Collinge, N. E. (1961) *The Structure of Horace's Odes*. London

Commager, Steele (1962) *The Odes of Horace*. New Haven

(1980) "Some Horatian Vagaries," *SO* 55: 59–70

Connor, P. J. (1982) "Book Despatch: Horace *Epistles* 1.20 and 1.13," *Ramus* 11: 145–52

(1987) *Horace's Lyric Poetry: The Force of Humour*. Berwick, Victoria

Corbett, Philip (1986) *The Scurra*. Edinburgh

Counts, Derek B. (1996) *"Regum Externorum Consuetudine*: The Nature and Function of Embalming in Rome," *CA* 15: 189–202

Culler, Jonathan (1981) "Apostrophe," *The Pursuit of Signs: Semiotics, Literature, Deconstruction*, 135–54. Ithaca

D'Arms, John H. (1990) "The Roman *Convivium* and Equality," in Oswyn Murray (ed.) *Sympotica*, 308–20. Oxford

(1991) "Slaves at Roman Convivia," in W. J. Slater (ed.) *Dining in a Classical Context*, 171–83. Ann Arbor

Davis, Gregson (1991) *Polyhymnia: The Rhetoric of Horatian Lyric Discourse*. Berkeley

Desch, W. (1981) "Horazens Beziehung zu Maecenas," *Eranos* 79: 33–45

Detienne, Marcel (1977) *The Gardens of Adonis* (trans. Janet Lloyd). London. Orig. publ. 1972

Dickie, Matthew W. (1981) "The Disavowal of *Invidia* in Roman Iamb and Satire," *Papers of the Liverpool Latin Seminar* 3: 183–208

Doblhofer, Ernst (1966) *Die Augustuspanegyrik des Horaz in formalhistorischer Sicht*. Heidelberg

(1981) "Horaz und Augustus," *ANRW* II.31.3: 1922–86

Drexler, H. (1963) "Zur Epistel 1, 7 des Horaz," *Maia* 15: 26–37

Dunn, Francis M. (1995) "Rhetorical Approaches to Horace's *Odes*," *Arethusa* 28: 165–76

Dupont, Florence (1985) *L'Acteur-Roi, ou, Le théâtre dans la Rome antique*. Paris

DuQuesnay, I. M. Le M. (1984) "Horace and Maecenas: The Propaganda Value of *Sermones* I," in A. J. Woodman and David West (eds.) *Poetry and Politics in the Age of Augustus*, 19–58. Cambridge

(1995) "Horace, *Odes* 4.5: *Pro Reditu Imperatoris Caesaris Divi Filii Augusti*," in Harrison (1995), 128–87

Dyson, M. (1973) "Horace, *Odes* iii. 14," *G&R* 20: 169–79

Eck, Werner (1985) "Senatorial Self-Representation: Developments in the Augustan Period," in Fergus Millar and Erich Segal (eds.) *Caesar Augustus: Seven Aspects*, 129–67. Oxford

Elias, Norbert (1978) *The History of Manners* (trans. Edmund Jephcott). New York. Orig. publ. 1939

Esser, Dieter (1976) *Untersuchungen zu den Odenschlüssen bei Horaz*. Meisenheim am Glan

Estévez, Victor A. (1982) "*Quem tu, Melpomene:* The Poet's Lowered Voice (*C.* IV 3)," *Emerita* 50: 279–300

Fedeli, Paolo (1978) "Il V epodo e i giambi d'Orazio come espressione d'arte alessandrina," *MPhL* 3: 67–138

Feeney, Denis (1993) "Horace and the Greek Lyric Poets," in Rudd (1993), 41–63

Ferri, Rolando (1993) *I dispiaceri di un epicureo: Uno studio sulla poetica oraziana delle Epistole*. Pisa

Fiske, George Converse (1920) *Lucilius and Horace: A Study in the Classical Theory of Imitation*. Madison

Fitzgerald, William (1988) "Power and Impotence in Horace's *Epodes*," *Ramus* 17: 176–91

(1989) "Horace, Pleasure and the Text," *Arethusa* 22: 81–104

Fowler, Don P. (1989) "First Thoughts on Closure: Problems and Prospects," *MD* 22: 75–122

(1995) "Horace and the Aesthetics of Politics," in Harrison (1995), 248–66

Fraenkel, Eduard (1957) *Horace*. Oxford

Freudenburg, Kirk (1993) *The Walking Muse: Horace on the Theory of Satire*. Princeton

(1995) "Canidia at the Feast of Nasidienus (Hor. *S.* 2.8.95)," *TAPA* 125: 207–19

Frischer, Bernard (1991) *Shifting Paradigms: New Approaches to Horace's Ars Poetica*. Atlanta

(1995) "Fu la Villa ercolanese dei Papiri un modello per la Villa Sabina di Orazio?," *Cronache Ercolanesi* 25: 211–29

Girard, René (1977) *Violence and the Sacred* (trans. Patrick Gregory). Baltimore. Orig. publ. 1972

Goffman, Erving (1959) *The Presentation of Self in Everyday Life*. New York

(1967) *Interaction Ritual*. New York

Gold, Barbara K. (1987) *Literary Patronage in Greece and Rome*. Chapel Hill

(1992) "Openings in Horace's *Satires* and *Odes*: Poet, Patron, and Audience," *YCS* 29: 161–85

Gowers, Emily (1993a) *The Loaded Table: Representations of Food in Roman Literature.* Oxford

(1993b) "Horace, *Satires* 1.5: An Inconsequential Journey," *PCPS* 39: 48–66

Grassmann, Victor (1966) *Die erotischen Epoden des Horaz.* Munich

Greenblatt, Stephen (1980) *Renaissance Self-Fashioning.* Chicago

(1990) *Learning to Curse: Essays in Early Modern Culture.* New York

Griffin, Jasper (1984) "Augustus and the Poets: 'Caesar qui cogere posset,'" in Fergus Millar and Erich Segal (eds.) *Caesar Augustus: Seven Aspects,* 189–218. Oxford

(1993) "Horace in the Thirties," in Rudd (1993), 1–22

Grimal, Pierre (1988) "L'éclectisme philosophique dans l' 'Art Poétique' d'Horace," in A. Ceresa-Gastaldo (ed.) *I 2000 anni dell' Ars Poetica,* 9–26. Genoa

Habinek, T. N. (1986) "The Marriageability of Maximus: Horace, *Ode* 4.1.13–20," *AJP* 107: 407–16

Hahn, E. Adelaide (1939) "*Epodes* 5 and 17, *Carmina* 1.16 and 1.17," *TAPA* 70: 213–29

Hallett, Judith P. (1981) "*Pepedi / Diffissa Nate Ficus*: Priapic Revenge in Horace, *Satires* 1.8," *RhM* 124: 341–7

Hardie, Philip (1992) "Augustan Poets and the Mutability of Rome," in Powell (1992), 59–82

(1993) "*Ut pictura poesis?* Horace and the Visual Arts," in Rudd (1993), 120–39

Harrison, S. J. (1986) "Philosophical Imagery in Horace, *Odes* 3.5," *CQ* 36: 502–7

(1988) "Deflating the *Odes*: Horace, *Epistles* 1.20," *CQ* 38: 473–6

(1992) "Fuscus the Stoic: Horace *Odes* 1.22 and *Epistles* 1.10," *CQ* 42: 543–7

(1995) ed. *Homage to Horace: A Bimillenary Celebration.* Oxford

Henderson, John (1987) "Suck It and See (Horace, *Epode* 8)," in Whitby, Hardie, and Whitby (1987), 105–18

(1993) "Be Alert (Your Country Needs Lerts): Horace, *Satires* 1.9," *PCPS* 39: 67–93

(1994) "On Getting Rid of Kings: Horace, *Satire* 1.7," *CQ* 44: 146–70

Hertz, Neil (1985) "Medusa's Head: Male Hysteria under Political Pressure," *The End of the Line: Essays on Psychoanalysis and the Sublime,* 161–93. New York

Hierche, Henri (1974) *Les Epodes d'Horace.* Brussels

Highet, Gilbert. (1973) "*Libertino patre natus*," *AJP* 94: 268–91

Hinds, Stephen (1985) "Booking the Return Trip: Ovid and *Tristia* 1," *PCPS* 31: 13–32

Horsfall, Nicholas (1993) *La villa sabina di Orazio: il galateo della gratitudine.* Venosa

Hudson, Nicola A. (1989) "Food in Roman Satire," in S. H. Braund (ed.) *Satire and Society in Ancient Rome,* 69–87. Exeter

Hunter, R. L. (1985) "Horace on Friendship and Free Speech (Epistles 1.18 and Satires 1.4)," *Hermes* 113:480–90

Ingallina, S. S. (1974) *Orazio e la magia*. Palermo

Innes, Doreen C. (1989) "Augustan Critics," in George A. Kennedy (ed.) *The Cambridge History of Literary Criticism*, 1: *Classical Criticism*, 245–73. Cambridge

Johnson, W. R. (1967). "A Quean, A Great Queen? Cleopatra and the Politics of Misrepresentation," *Arion* 6: 387–402

(1982) *The Idea of Lyric: Lyric Modes in Ancient and Modern Poetry*. Berkeley

(1993) *Horace and the Dialectic of Freedom: Readings in Epistles I*. Ithaca

Jones, C. P. (1991) "Dinner Theater," in W. J. Slater (ed.) *Dining in a Classical Context*, 185–98. Ann Arbor

Kennedy, Duncan F. (1992) "'Augustan' and 'Anti-Augustan': Reflections on Terms of Reference," in Powell (1992), 26–57

Kiessling, Adolf, and Heinze, Richard (1957) eds. *Q. Horatius Flaccus: Satiren*. Berlin. 6th ed.

(1958) eds. *Q. Horatius Flaccus: Oden und Epoden*. Berlin. 9th ed.

(1959) eds. *Q. Horatius Flaccus: Briefe*. Berlin. 6th ed.

Kilpatrick, Ross S. (1986) *The Poetry of Friendship: Horace, Epistles 1*. Edmonton

(1990) *The Poetry of Criticism: Horace, Epistles 2 and Ars Poetica*. Edmonton

King, Helen (1989) "Tithonus and the Tettix," in Thomas M. Falkner and Judith de Luce (eds.) *Old Age in Greek and Latin Literature*, 68–89. Albany

Klingner, Friedrich (1959) ed. *Q. Horati Flacci Opera*. Leipzig

Konstan, David (1995) "Patrons and Friends," *CP* 90: 328–42

Labate, Mario (1981) ed. *Quinto Orazio Flacco: Satire*. Milan

Labowsky, Lotte (1934) *Die Ethik des Panaitios: Untersuchungen zur Geschichte des Decorum bei Cicero und Horaz*. Leipzig

La Penna, Antonio (1963) *Orazio e l'ideologia del principato*. Turin

Leach, Eleanor W. (1971) "Horace's *Pater Optimus* and Terence's Demea: Autobiographical Fiction and Comedy in *Serm.* 1.4," *AJP* 92:616–32

(1993) "Horace's Sabine Topography in Lyric and Hexameter Verse," *AJP* 114:271–302

Lefèvre, Eckard (1993) *Horaz: Dichter im augusteischen Rom*. Munich

Lejay, Paul (1911) ed. *Œuvres d'Horace: Satires*. Paris

Lilja, Saara (1976) *Dogs in Ancient Greek Poetry*. Helsinki

Lowrie, Michèle (1992) "A Sympotic Achilles, Horace, *Epode* 13," *AJP* 113: 413–34

Luce, J. V. (1963) "Cleopatra as *fatale monstrum*," *CQ* 13:251–7

Lyne, R. O. A. M. (1995) *Horace: Behind the Public Poetry*. New Haven

Macleod, Colin (1983) *Collected Essays*. Oxford

Mankin, David (1995) ed. *Horace: Epodes*. Cambridge

Manning, C. E. (1970) "Canidia in the *Epodes* of Horace," *Mnemosyne* 23: 393–401

Martindale, Charles (1993) "Introduction," in Charles Martindale and David Hopkins (eds.) *Horace Made New*, 1–26. Cambridge

Maurizio, Lisa (1989) "Engendering Invective," American Philological Association meeting, Boston, December 1989

Mayer, R. G. (1985) "Horace on Good Manners," *PCPS* 31: 33–46

(1994) ed. *Horace: Epistles Book I*. Cambridge

(1995) "Horace's *Moyen de Parvenir*," in Harrison (1995), 279–95

McGann, M. J. (1969) *Studies in Horace's First Book of Epistles*. Brussels

Millar, Fergus (1977) *The Emperor in the Roman World*. London

Miller, Paul Allen (1994) *Lyric Texts and Lyric Consciousness: The Birth of a Genre from Archaic Greece to Augustan Rome*. London

Minadeo, Richard (1982) *The Golden Plectrum: Sexual Symbolism in Horace's Odes*. Amsterdam

Moles, John (1985) "Cynicism in Horace *Epistles* 1," *Papers of the Liverpool Latin Seminar* 5: 33–60

Muecke, Frances (1993) ed. *Horace: Satires II*. Warminster

(1995) "Law, Rhetoric, and Genre in Horace, *Satires* 2.1," in Harrison (1995), 203–18

Müller, Reimar (1985) "Prinzipatsideologie und Philosophie bei Horaz," *Klio* 67: 158–67

Murray, Oswyn (1993) "Symposium and Genre in the Poetry of Horace," in Rudd (1993), 89–105

Nagy, Gregory (1979) *The Best of the Achaeans: Concepts of the Hero in Archaic Greek Poetry*. Baltimore

Narducci, Emanuele (1984) "Il comportamento in pubblico (Cicerone, *de officiis* I 126–149)," *Maia* 36: 203–29

Nicolet, Claude (1991) *Space, Geography, and Politics in the Early Roman Empire* (trans. H. Leclerc). Ann Arbor. Orig. publ. 1988

Nisbet, R. G. M. (1959) "Notes on Horace, *Epistles* 1," *CQ* 9: 73–6

(1983) "Some Problems of Text and Interpretation in Horace *Odes* 3.14 (*Herculis Ritu*)," *Papers of the Liverpool Latin Seminar* 4: 105–19

(1984) "Horace's *Epodes* and History," in A. J. Woodman and David West (eds.) *Poetry and Politics in the Age of Augustus*, 1–18. Cambridge

Nisbet, R. G. M. and Hubbard, Margaret (1970) *A Commentary on Horace: Odes, Book I*. Oxford

(1978) *A Commentary on Horace: Odes, Book II*. Oxford

O'Connor, Joseph F. (1990) "Horace's *Cena Nasidieni* and Poetry's Feast," *CJ* 86: 23–34

Oliensis, Ellen (1997) "The Erotics of Patronage: Readings in Tibullus, Propertius, and Horace," in Judith P. Hallett and Marilyn B. Skinner (eds.) *Roman Sexualities*, 151–71. Princeton

Onians, R. B. (1951) *The Origins of European Thought*. Cambridge

Owen, Stephen (1989) *Mi-Lou: Poetry and the Labyrinth of Desire*. Cambridge, Mass.

Pearcy, Lee T. (1977) "Horace's Architectural Imagery," *Latomus* 36: 772–81
(1994) "The Personification of the Text and Augustan Poetics in *Epistles* 1.20," *CW* 87: 457–64

Perret, Jacques (1964) *Horace* (trans. Bertha Humez). New York. Orig. publ. 1959

Petrey, Sandy (1990) *Speech Acts and Literary Theory.* New York

Piccaluga, Giulia (1974) *Terminus: I segni di confine nella religione romana.* Rome

Poeschl, Viktor (1991) *Horazische Lyrik: Interpretationen.* Heidelberg

Porter, David H. (1987) *Horace's Poetic Journey: A Reading of Odes 1–3.* Princeton

Powell, Anton (1992) ed. *Roman Poetry and Propaganda in the Age of Augustus.* London

Préaux, Jean (1968) ed. *Horace: Épîtres Livre I.* Paris.

Pucci, Pietro (1975) "Horace's Banquet in *Odes* 1.17," *TAPA* 105: 259–81

Putnam, Michael C. J. (1982) *Essays on Latin Lyric, Elegy, and Epic.* Princeton
(1986) *Artifices of Eternity: Horace's Fourth Book of Odes.* Ithaca
(1990) "Horace *Carm.* 2.9: Augustus and the Ambiguities of Encomium," in Kurt A. Raaflaub and Mark Toher (eds.) *Between Republic and Empire: Interpretations of Augustus and his Principate*, 212–38. Berkeley
(1994) "Structure and Design in Horace *Odes* 1.17," *CW* 87: 357–75
(1995) "From Lyric to Letter: Iccius in Horace *Odes* 1.29 and *Epistles* 1.12," *Arethusa* 28: 193–207

Raaflaub, K. A. and Samons, L. J., II (1990) "Opposition to Augustus," in Kurt A. Raaflaub and Mark Toher (eds.) *Between Republic and Empire: Interpretations of Augustus and his Principate*, 417–54. Berkeley

Ramage, Edwin S. (1973) *Urbanitas: Ancient Sophistication and Refinement.* Norman

Rawson, Elizabeth (1985) *Intellectual Life in the Late Roman Republic.* Baltimore

Reckford, Kenneth J. (1959) "Horace and Maecenas," *TAPA* 90: 195–208
(1969) *Horace.* New York

Richlin, Amy (1984) "Invective Against Women in Roman Satire," *Arethusa* 17: 67–80
(1992) *The Garden of Priapus: Sexuality and Aggression in Roman Humor.* New York. Revised ed.

Rimmon-Kenan, Shlomith (1983) *Narrative Fiction: Contemporary Poetics.* London

Rubino, Carl A. (1985) "Monuments and Pyramids: Death and the Poet in Horace, *Carmina* 3.30," *CML* 5: 99–111

Rudd, Niall (1966) *The Satires of Horace.* Cambridge
(1979) trans. *Horace: Satires and Epistles; Persius: Satires.* Harmondsworth
(1986) *Themes in Roman Satire.* London
(1989) ed. *Horace: Epistles II and "Ars Poetica."* Cambridge
(1993) ed. *Horace 2000: A Celebration.* Ann Arbor

Saller, Richard P. (1982) *Personal Patronage Under the Early Empire*. Cambridge

Santirocco, Matthew S. (1986) *Unity and Design in Horace's Odes*. Chapel Hill
(1995) "Horace and Augustan Ideology," *Arethusa* 28: 225–43

Schenker, David (1993) "Poetic Voices in Horace's Roman Odes," *CJ* 88: 147–66

Schmidt, Ernst A. (1990) "Das Epodenbuch des Horaz," *Notwehrdichtung*, 131–70. Munich

Scholz, Udo W. (1971) "Herculis ritu – Augustus – consule Planco," *WS* 84: 123–37

Schrijvers, P. H. (1973) "Comment terminer une ode?," *Mnemosyne* 26: 140–59
(1993) "*Amicus liber et dulcis*. Horace moraliste," in W. Ludwig (ed.) *Horace* (Entretiens Hardt 39), 41–90. Geneva

Seager, Robin (1993) "Horace and Augustus: Poetry and Policy," in Rudd (1993), 23–40

Seeck, G. A. (1991) "Über das Satirische in Horaz' Satiren oder: Horaz und seine Leser, z.B. Maecenas," *Gymnasium* 98: 534–47

Serres, Michel (1982) *The Parasite* (trans. Lawrence R. Schehr). Baltimore. Orig. publ. 1980

Shackleton Bailey, D. R. (1982) *Profile of Horace*. London

Shoptaw, John (forthcoming) "Lyric Cryptography: A Poetics of Reading," *Poetics Today* 19 (1998)

Stégen, Guillaume (1963) *L'unité et la clarté des épîtres d'Horace*. Namur

Sturrock, John (1993) *The Language of Autobiography*. Cambridge

Syndikus, Hans-Peter (1972) *Die Lyrik des Horaz: Eine Interpretation der Oden, 1*. Darmstadt
(1973) *Die Lyrik des Horaz: Eine Interpretation der Oden, 2*. Darmstadt

Traina, Alfonso (1986) "Semantica del *carpe diem*," *Poeti Latini (e Neolatini)*, 227–51. Bologna. 2nd ed.

Troxler-Keller, Irene (1964) *Die Dichterlandschaft des Horaz*. Heidelberg

van Rooy, C. A. (1972) "Arrangement and Structure of Satires in Horace *Sermones* Book 1: Satires 9 and 10," *AClass* 15: 37–52

Vermeule, Emily (1979) *Aspects of Death in Early Greek Art and Poetry*. Berkeley

Vessey, D. W. T. (1986) "The *Fons Bandusiae* and the Problem of the Text," *Studies in Latin Literature and Roman History* 4: 383–92

Wallace-Hadrill, Andrew (1987) "Time for Augustus: Ovid, Augustus, and the *Fasti*," in Whitby, Hardie, and Whitby (1987), 221–30

Watson, Lindsay C. (1983) "Two Problems in Horace *Epode* 3," *Philologus* 127: 80–6
(1987) "*Epode* 9, or The Art of Falsehood," in Whitby, Hardie, and Whitby (1987), 119–29
(1995) "Horace's *Epodes*: The Impotence of *Iambos*?," in Harrison (1995), 188–202

West, David (1967) *Reading Horace.* Edinburgh

Whitby, Michael, Hardie, Philip and Whitby, Mary (1987) eds. *Homo Viator: Classical Essays for John Bramble.* Bristol

White, Peter (1993) *Promised Verse: Poets in the Society of Augustan Rome.* Cambridge, Mass.

Whittaker, C. R. (1994) *Frontiers of the Roman Empire.* Baltimore

Wickham, E. C. (1877) ed. *The Works of Horace,* 1: *The Odes, Carmen Seculare and Epodes.* Oxford. 2nd ed.

(1891) ed. *The Works of Horace,* 2: *The Satires, Epistles, and De Arte Poetica.* Oxford

Wickham, E. C. and Garrod, H. W. (1912) eds. *Q. Horati Flacci Opera.* Oxford

Wilkinson, L. P. (1963) *Golden Latin Artistry.* Cambridge

Williams, Gordon (1968) *Tradition and Originality in Roman Poetry.* Oxford

(1969) ed. *The Third Book of Horace's Odes.* Oxford

(1994) "Public Policies, Private Affairs, and Strategies of Address in the Poetry of Horace," *CW* 87: 395–408

(1995) "*Libertino Patre Natus:* True or False?," in Harrison (1995), 296–313

Winkler, John J. (1990) *The Constraints of Desire: The Anthropology of Sex and Gender in Ancient Greece.* New York

Witke, Charles (1983) *Horace's Roman Odes: A Critical Examination.* Leiden

Woodman, A. J. (1974) "*Exegi Monumentum*: Horace, *Odes* 3.30," in A. J. Woodman and David West (eds.) *Quality and Pleasure in Latin Poetry,* 115–28. Cambridge

Wyke, Maria (1992) "Augustan Cleopatras: Female Power and Poetic Authority," in Powell (1992), 98–140

Zanker, Paul (1988) *The Power of Images in the Age of Augustus* (trans. Alan Shapiro). Ann Arbor

Zetzel, J. E. G. (1980) "Horace's *Liber Sermonum*: The Structure of Ambiguity," *Arethusa* 13: 59–77

(1982) "The Poetics of Patronage in the Late First Century BC," in Barbara K. Gold (ed.) *Literary and Artistic Patronage in Ancient Rome,* 87–102. Austin

POEMS DISCUSSED

238

GENERAL INDEX